ZEN AND THERAPY

Zen and Therapy brings together aspects of the Buddhist tradition, contemporary western therapy and western philosophy. By combining insightful anecdotes from the Zen tradition with clinical studies, discussions of current psychotherapy theory and forays into art, film, literature and philosophy, Manu Bazzano integrates Zen Buddhist practice with psychotherapy and psychology.

This book successfully expands the existing dialogue on the integration of Buddhism, psychology and philosophy, highlighting areas that have been neglected and bypassed. It explores a *third way* between the two dominant modalities, the religious and the secular, a *positively ambivalent* stance rooted in embodied practice, and the cultivation of compassion and active perplexity. It presents a life-affirming view: the wonder, beauty and complexity of being human.

Intended for both experienced practitioners and beginners in the fields of psychotherapy and philosophy, *Zen and Therapy* provides an enlightening and engaging exploration of a previously underexplored area.

Manu Bazzano is a psychotherapist and supervisor in private practice. He has studied eastern contemplative practices since 1980 and in 2004 was ordained a Zen monk in the Soto and Rinzai traditions. A primary tutor at Metanoia Institute, London, and visiting lecturer at the University of Roehampton, London, and various other schools and colleges, he facilitates workshops and seminars internationally. He is editor of *Person-Centered and Experiential Psychotherapies*, and associate editor for *Self & Society – International Journal for Humanistic Psychology*. www.manubazzano.com.

Also by Manu Bazzano

ZEN POEMS
HAIKU FOR LOVERS
BUDDHA IS DEAD
THE SPEED OF ANGELS
THE PERPETUAL BEGINNER (in Italian)
SPECTRE OF THE STRANGER
AFTER MINDFULNESS (Editor)
THERAPY AND THE COUNTER-TRADITION (Co-editor)

Music albums:
DAEDALO: WALK INSIDE THE PAINTING
NAKED DANCE
SEX, RELIGION AND COSMETICS

ZEN AND THERAPY

Heretical Perspectives

Manu Bazzano

Routledge
Taylor & Francis Group

LONDON AND NEW YORK

First published 2017
by Routledge
2 Park Square, Milton Park, Abingdon, Oxon OX14 4RN

and by Routledge
711 Third Avenue, New York, NY 10017

Routledge is an imprint of the Taylor & Francis Group, an Informa business

British Library Cataloguing in Publication Data
A catalogue record for this book is available from the British Library

Library of Congress Cataloging in Publication Data
A catalog record for this book has been requested

ISBN: 978-1-138-64630-8 (hbk)
ISBN: 978-1-138-64631-5 (pbk)
ISBN: 978-1-315-62338-2 (ebk)

Typeset in Bembo
by Keystroke, Neville Lodge, Tettenhall, Wolverhampton

To Nigel, wayward pilgrim,
and Sarita, sunbeam on the path.

CONTENTS

Acknowledgements   *ix*

Introduction   1

1   Self, no-self and doing the next thing   19

2   All's well that ends: on living-and-dying   31

3   Zen and therapy: two expressions of unconditional hospitality   43

4   Presence, mindfulness and Buddha-nature   59

5   Why Zen is not transpersonal   80

6   This body, this Earth: incarnate practice and ecopsychology   95

7   On differentialism   115

8   Imperceptible mutual aid: Zen, therapy and the unconscious   136

Index   *159*

ACKNOWLEDGEMENTS

I have gained much from conversations with friends and colleagues that helped shape some of the ideas presented in this book. My thanks to Sarita Doveton, Dennis Genpo Merzel, John Davis, Dagmar Edwards, Claudio Rud, Virginia Moreira, Devang Vaidya, Anna Leung, Stephen Batchelor, Ernesto Spinelli, Beatrice Millar, Diana Voller, Dheeresh Turnbull, Subhaga Gaetano Failla, Zoe Shobbrook-Fisher, Mo Mandic, Toby Bull, Hugh Knopf, Jocelyn Chaplin, Jeff Harrison, Sarah Nettleton, Hank Earl, Bob Chisholm, Marcia Gamsu, Richard House, David Kalisch and Ron Purser.

I am especially indebted to Julie Webb, Nigel Armistead and John Mackessy who read drafts of the book and made priceless suggestions.

I extend my thanks to my clients and supervisees; to psychotherapy trainees and colleagues in the various schools where I work, including Roehampton University and the Metanoia Institute; to the Zen friends who regularly join our London meditation group.

For their encouragement and assistance in getting this project off the ground, my heartfelt thanks to Joanne Forshaw and Sam Birchall at Routledge, and Kelly Winter and the team at Keystroke.

All client names have been changed and clinical examples are all fictionalized.

INTRODUCTION

Prince Charles, questioning a monk in Kyoto about the road to enlightenment, was asked in reply if he could ever forget that he was a prince. 'Of course not,' Charles replied, 'One's always aware of it. One's always aware one's a prince.' In that case, said the monk, he would never know the road to enlightenment.

Hare, 2016

Postcards from the edge

I write at the cusp of Zen and therapy, from a borderline between these two realms where no checkpoint has yet been erected and no passport is required. For the time being, I luxuriate in the relative freedom of an existence lived in this transient plane. Many fellow travellers decided to abandon this uncertain terrain in order to occupy more substantial dwellings. Some of them have decided that Zen (and Dharma practice in general) belongs to 'spirituality' and can be confidently categorized within the broad church of transpersonal psychotherapy. Others have added mindfulness techniques to their bag of therapeutic tools, and others still are happy to call themselves Buddhist therapists. Being a chronically slow learner, sceptical of systems and of expedient formulas, I am still waiting for these two important strands to organically coalesce in my life and practice. Until that happens, I carry on dwelling more or less happily in this borderland. I hope these dispatches will be of some use to others.

Relative and absolute

There are different ways to travel. An airplane will get to our destination quicker than a train or a car, but we will miss the terrain and the landscape. Similarly, regular Zen practice may give us a fleeting glimpse of what is generally called the ultimate nature of reality. For a brief moment, we may see into the seemingly insubstantial, fluid nature of the world and perceive the impermanence of our own self within it – only to realize that it will now take months, or years, to bring that insight into everyday life.

I turned to therapy after years of practising meditation and studying Buddhism and Zen. I did so with the expectation that it would help me see the terrain at close range and get in touch with those fractions of experience that Zen practice alone could not access. I soon realized how simplistic my expectation was. It is true that Zen and therapy are widely different ways of responding to our being in the world, yet the notion that Zen addresses the *absolute* (the ultimate, the sublime, the relation of the finite self with the infinite and so forth) while therapy addresses the *relative* (love and work, feelings and emotions) is a little too naive. Perhaps it is more accurate to say that each can inform the other and together they may allow us greater agility and supple movement between the absolute and the relative dimensions. This is when 'working on oneself', that stern imperative of self-improvement culture, becomes more akin to playing or dancing.

To be stuck with God (the absolute) is as undesirable as to be stuck with the world (the relative). One's predilection for peak experiences may conceal incompetence in dealing with paying the bills, as well as immaturity in relating to others. Or, despite one's impeccable conduct and emotional maturity, one may lack the imagination and the wisdom that a concrete encounter with the infinite can bring forth. What matters is to develop the ability to move back and forth at will between the relative and the absolute, according to what is required of us in each situation. This point may be further clarified by the following three stories.

Arjuna

Excited by the publication of a formidable new version that brings it to vivid life (Satyamurti, 2015), I recently went back to reading passages from the monumental *Mahabharata*, a 2,000-year-old epic masterpiece, its importance comparable to great works of antiquity such as Homer's *Iliad* and Virgil's *Aeneid*. Relatively unknown to western readers, the Mahabharata is both a tale and a religious text. A chapter in Book VI, 'The Song of the Lord', features a passage recounting a dialogue taking place in the battlefield between the warrior Arjuna and his spiritual friend and advisor, the god Krishna. This same dialogue also constitutes the *Bhagavad Gita* and presents us with insights that are useful to this discussion. A *Kshatriya,* a member of the high military cast, Arjuna is a skilled warrior as well as a devoted seeker of the truth. At this point in the story, on the very morning of a mighty battle, with every soldier eager and prepared to act upon his orders, this great fighter and winner of countless victories stops his chariot, visibly distressed, tears running down his cheeks. Observing the enemy's ranks (as it happens, they are his own cousins) he finds them strikingly human, just like himself. The hovering presence of death, moments before the clashing of weapons and shields, sharpens his perceptions and he feels deeply moved. Whatever the outcome of the battle, he knows it will result in tremendous suffering and anguish for both parties. He turns to Krishna and loudly declares that he refuses to fight: to engage in battle under the circumstances is wrong; it goes against the Dharma. Krishna smiles in response, as one would to an immature person. His refusal to kill seems principled, he tells Arjuna, even admirable, but he is deeply mistaken. A classic defence of the absolute position follows, which will eventually persuade Arjuna to perform his duty as a warrior and dispel his hesitation, now seen as momentary confusion. At the heart of Krishna's argument is the notion that compared to the eternal life of the soul, this life of flesh and blood is illusory and fleeting – illusory *because* it's fleeting. We travel from one incarnation to the next, he tells Arjuna; we inhabit one body after another in the same way as we change the clothes we wear. Moreover, the task of a human being is to be active in the world. Similarly, the task of the warrior is to go to war, rather than meditate in the solitude of a forest or a monastery. Although there is great value in deliberately choosing not to play an active role in the world, in espousing renunciation and contemplation, liberation can be equally attained by pursuing the right action – by acting without thoughts of selfish gain, and by dedicating one's deeds to the deity. One by one, all of Arjuna's doubts and objections are dispelled, and at one point he experiences a breakthrough – his body shivering, his heart and mind stooping at the sheer radiance of his divine friend and teacher. The ambiguity now dissolved, Arjuna is filled with light and clarity and is ready and eager to enter the battlefield.

There is much to learn from the above dialogue and from Krishna's argumentation. No one in his right mind would dare argue with a deity. He speaks convincingly against the facile division between the spiritual and the mundane, a stance held by Arjuna and by a great number of people to this day. He also affirms with great poetic flair what is a common refrain in spiritual literature: this impermanent, fleeting life of ours is unreal compared to that of everlasting reality. Our existence, ruled by desire and aversion, is not as real as the true life of the soul. Implicit in this affirmation, however, is an essential denigration of life before death as well as the metaphysical belief that there is a transcendent dimension *outside* the world as we know it. Krishna is effectively telling Arjuna that only God exists; that individual beings are but empty shells, vessels of the life force. In the great theatre of living-and-dying, this singular existence is insignificant, an ephemeral episode devoid of intrinsic existence or substantiality. The absolute view Krishna expounds has truth and grandeur. But its appeal can blind us to its undeniably problematic aspects, especially when it leads to neglect of the body, self-avoidance, the belittling of our individual creativity and resources and to a general misapprehension of the concrete situation we find ourselves in as humans. It suspends the ethical in the name of spirit; it sidesteps the relative dimension – the concrete domain of ethics – which is where the next tale takes us.

The sick mother

This story is apocryphal, set in an unspecified time, and it too involves Krishna. A devotee performs spiritual practices for years: he chants, prays and meditates at the crack of dawn; he observes fasting on appointed days and often prostrates in front of his home shrine. A humble man of simple means, he is looking after his old, frail mother and is consumed by a great yearning: to be granted an apparition, to see Krishna in the flesh. One winter night, he is woken up by the sound of his mother's moaning. She is in pain. He promptly gets up, goes to her and says some soothing words to her. Then, as he starts massaging her feet in the hope of giving her some relief, Krishna appears. The man says to Krishna, 'I'm delighted and honoured to see you. But I'm rather busy at the moment: as you can see, my mother is unwell, and I do need to take care of her. Would you mind coming back some other time?'

The above is an example of suspending the spiritual in the name of the ethical – the very opposite of the previous position. The devotee sets aside the transcendent dimension in order to attend to the task at hand and respond as adequately as he can to the situation. Broadly speaking, one may tentatively identify spirituality with the absolute, and psychotherapy with the relative dimension. Within the latter, we are inclined to pay greater attention to ethics, here understood as the self's genuine attempt to respond adequately to the presence of the other (Bazzano, 2012b). But ethics is also *Sittlichkeit*, obedience to customs, rules and regulations. This can be a good thing; but to genuinely think that all there is to ethics is playing by the rules would be a mistake. I may abide by this or that professional ethical code, yet be unethical. Or, I may break the rules and be ethical in a deeper sense. I may be able and willing to conform to the dictates of my clan, tribe and society only in order to please them, to be accepted and respected and be comfortably aligned to the common knowledge of conscience (from *con-scire,* to know with).

As with the absolute stance, settling with the relative position is also problematic. Attempting to build durable foundations on either terrain may result in us becoming trapped. This is where Zen is helpful: it hints at a third, dynamic position, illustrated by the following story.

'I haven't sat down yet!'

The haiku and Zen scholar R. H. Blyth (1978) recounts this short dialogue between a monk and a Zen teacher called Isan. The monk went to visit Isan to receive instructions. Entering the room, and noticing that Isan was about to get up, he said, 'Sir, please, there is no need to get up', to which Isan replied, 'I haven't sat down yet'. The monk said, 'But I haven't bowed yet', and Isan shouted back, 'You insolent fool!'

Isan's 'spiritual instructions' are impressively agile: he has set things up in such a way that the monk finds him in an indistinct bodily posture, between sitting and standing. The monk's first response comes from the (relative) level of courtesy towards the older man and teacher. This is the learned response of good behaviour. You and I would probably say the same if, in entering a room as guests, we saw the older host getting up to greet us. 'Don't bother getting up' we'll say. But Isan turns the tables on his guest. This is no ordinary polite conversation, but one more opportunity for spiritual teaching. 'I haven't sat down yet' can mean a number of things. Isan may be asking: 'How do you know I'm not on my way down (about to sit) rather than on my way up (about to stand)?' (Magliola, 1984, p. 102). Besides, Isan may be saying, 'Why do you interpret my action so literally, i.e. at the *relative* level? My action may come from the absolute and symbolic level where "I haven't sat down yet" can mean "I haven't given you guidance yet"'. Here the monk gets a hint of what Isan is driving at and replies with a clever answer from the 'absolute' level: 'I haven't bowed yet'. I am assuming with Blyth that the monk had already bowed just before entering the room and that with his response he is signalling, even showing off his metaphysical sophistication. But Isan pulls the rug from under him yet again ('you insolent fool!') by going back to the relative level where ordinary courtesy is expected.

The above exchange may sound strange to readers who have not studied Zen formally. As it happens, I do recognize the poor monk's plight here and cannot but sympathize with his awkwardness and his all-too-earnest, self-conscious effort. He's trying so hard to do the right thing, but the teacher goes on dragging him out of his complacency. The strangeness of these Zen dialogues may bring a smile to one's face. I can assure you that finding yourself at the receiving end of one of these exchanges is no laughing matter but genuinely unsettling. And yet what is hinted at here is invaluable. Genuine Zen practice does not allow the practitioner to settle in the relative *or* the absolute dimension. Even the distinction between absolute and relative is itself relativistic, a paradox pointing to the limits of language and knowledge (John Mackessy, 2016, personal communication). Rather than building a home somewhere, perhaps the task is to carry on the infinite journey of discovery.

The practice of the perpetual beginner

A beginner frequently approaches the practice he/she embarks on with genuine thirst and an aspiration to learn. They will find themselves at a threshold and may experience the 'threshold level', i.e. a degree of intensity that must be exceeded in order for a particular event or process to occur. This event or process is usually called *transformation*. The moment of stepping onto the threshold is rare and exhilarating, even though what brought one there might have been a crisis. Once we step onto the threshold, we may find that the possibilities seem endless; we may then rise to the occasion by leaving our preconceptions aside, by being willing to be more open to experience than we usually would allow.

At the heart of Zen practice is the counterintuitive and painstaking cultivation of this fundamental openness, what Suzuki Roshi memorably called *beginner's mind* (Suzuki, 1983). The implication is that the beginner does not 'graduate' into becoming an expert or a specialist. Even though practice deepens and a certain amount of knowledge is acquired, one aims to maintain the beginner's stance throughout one's life and practice.

We may approach Zen with a desire to alleviate our personal distress. Similarly, we may come to therapy in order to resolve an impasse, deal with a crisis and gain a better understanding. In that particular moment, if we are in touch with beginner's mind, we are open to try something, experiment and maybe learn anew. We feel more open. All too often however, this precious quality of openness is lost. After a while, we start to believe that now we *know*; the field of possibility shrinks and what could have been a transformation turns into the acquisition of a new set of skills, techniques and items of knowledge. We do ourselves no favours when, as counselling trainees, we go to therapy solely in order to fulfil the requirements of our course, for in this instance the outcome will be very different compared to when the aspiration to become a therapist arises out of genuine want.

From merely wounded to wounded healer

The fundamental question here appears to be: what are the motives for engaging in training in the first place? When emerging naturally out of a desire for self-discovery, perhaps brought about by a crisis, the transition from merely wounded to wounded healer becomes part of a natural process. The advantage here is that therapy is learned as a *craft* and characterized by a period of apprenticeship where the foundations are learned in the crucible of experience. What is then acquired is not knowledge but what Lama Yeshe used to call *knowledge-wisdom* (Sarita Doveton, personal communication, 1992). Knowledge alone – *episteme* – is arguably born out of fear: the hope is that by acquiring data and techniques we may be able to shield ourselves from the uncertainty that is inherent in our existence and our being-in-the-world. We are then lulled into the fantasy world of *false assurances*. Conversely, knowledge-wisdom (known in Buddhism as *prajna*) recognizes uncertainty as a manifestation of impermanence. As a result of this recognition, the possibility arises of gaining *certitude in the midst of uncertainty*: a sense of poise that emerges from one's willingness to respond to the new and the unforeseen – the very opposite of our apprehensive need to control experience.

Heretical perspectives

Let us go back to the three stories related above. Each of them presents us with a different perspective. The dialogue between Krishna and Arjuna exemplified the conventional religious stance of predilection for the absolute and the eternal over the relative and the ephemeral. The second story alerted us to the importance of the relative and ethical dimensions which are normally bypassed when we give excessive importance to the absolute. The third one walked an ambiguous path, one that does not allow us to settle with either the relative or the absolute position. There are many instances of this third perspective within the vast corpus of Zen literature but, because of its subtlety, it is either misconstrued or aligned with the first or the second perspective. The common tendency is to think of Zen in terms of the absolute, that is as a discipline aiming at the attainment of an unperturbed state of mind that allows one to float above the tears of things – the view of what I call the 'cosmic consciousness brigade'. Alternatively, we find a view of Zen that emphasizes compassion, loving-kindness (or *Metta*, the Pali term for friendliness), and varying degrees of involvement with the world – this is the view of the '*Metta* brigade'. If there is more than a hint of sarcasm in my words, this is mainly directed at myself, as I have identified at one time or other with each perspective: hunting for *satori*, the great spiritual breakthrough one day; striving to be a *bodhisattva*, and put others first the next. The third view (alluded to by the third story) invites practitioners to greater flexibility: we give ourselves permission to remain undecided in relation to what is ultimately true while being open to the fluidity of experience. An example of what this could mean in psychotherapy is the cultivation on our part, alongside commitment in learning and practising various psychological theories, of engaged ambivalence, particularly when formulations are earnestly imparted as Gospel and/ or constitute shibboleths of tribal belonging.

It would be fair to say that the views on Zen and therapy expressed here are 'heretical' in the literal sense of the word, i.e. they imply a *choice*. The term *heresy*, from the ancient Greek *aíresis*, means *choice*, in this case the choice made by individuals to abstain from accepting a particular dogma or received wisdom and opt instead for a different view that is more in agreement with how they perceive the world and their place in it.

My particular form of heresy is partly influenced by *differentialism*, a compelling, counter-traditional perspective that has been brought to vivid life in the nineteenth century by Nietzsche and in the second half of the twentieth century by Jacques Derrida and more generally by thinkers, Deleuze and Blanchot among them, who came to be known as 'post-structuralists'. In essence, something similar to differentialism was present already in strands of ancient Buddhist thought, particularly in Nāgārjuna and in aspects of Chan and Zen teachings. Some of these developments will be discussed in more detail in Chapters 4 and 7. What I wish to underline here are the three vital and interdependent aspects championed by differentialism as I understand it.

a)   A *reversal* of Platonism: giving greater importance to *appearance* (to what is perceived by our embodied experience) than to *essence*. This is at the heart of existential phenomenology, at least of those strands of phenomenology that steer clear of theological and Platonist influences – especially the work of Merleau-Ponty that was to influence Gestalt, body psychotherapy and large sections of humanistic and psychoanalytic psychotherapy.

b)   A system of thought, or set of religious beliefs or therapeutic theory, however coherent and comprehensive, has inbuilt within it the seeds of its own *undoing*. This is because no system can claim to apprehend the entirety of life and/or of human experience without displaying totalitarian claims to truth. Reality is *inexhaustible* and the notion that it can one day be exhausted, i.e. that we can make complete rational sense of it, is a delusion.

c)   What follows from (a) and (b) is that a differentialist practice is keen to doubt, revise and update the theoretical tenets and ethos guiding and orienting us. This is as true in the field of therapy and spirituality as it is in the world of science and in the arts. An open, unembarrassed attitude of perplexity at the magnitude of the world, and of human life within it, is not inimical to science but conducive to its progress because it is less disposed to be dazzled by its dominant tenets and capable of suspending or bracketing them. We find this attitude of open enquiry in Zen and in the best phenomenological tradition, as well as in a psychotherapy practice that sincerely applies the latter without concession to Platonist notions of 'Being'.

Culture and indoctrination

At best, the differentialist approach advocated here brings freshness, renewed passion and genuine curiosity to our work – all things I believe most of therapists and meditation practitioners would welcome. But this entails reformulating our understanding and not settling into cosily accepted modes of thinking and being. A vibrant example of this stance is found in the work of one of the jazz greats, Miles Davis. As a way to bring about the best in a musician, he once told guitarist John McLaughlin to 'play guitar like you don't know how to play guitar' (Shatz, 2016, p. 62). Davis famously discarded styles he himself had helped create:

> Easily bored by what he called 'old shit', Davis shed styles as soon as they risked settling into formula. When 'cool' lost its edge in the hands of white West Coast musicians, he pioneered hard bop, a simplified, funkier style of bop that reasserted jazz's roots. When hard bop hardened into its own set of sweaty clichés, he gravitated to 'modal' jazz, which used scales rather than chord changes as a harmonic frame.
>
> *Shatz, 2016, p. 62*

The above stance, with its overtones of unsettled, edgy creativity is not for everyone. Not everyone can be Miles Davis. Many among us will settle with rehashed therapeutic principles that we then go on imparting year in, year out to trainees and that we are more than ready to swear by in our own clinical work. Reliable and solid, they provide us with a sense of ease and comfort. However, they also help create, instead of a *culture* of innovation and inspiration a stale design of *acculturation* or even indoctrination.

A philosophy of difference

If invited to forego for a moment, categories such as *identity, unity, being*, and entertain a line of enquiry unburdened by overt metaphysical crutches, many of us may come to experience a sense of unease. This is because, whatever our learning or line of work, our fundamental way of thinking and being is steeped in western metaphysical thinking. With globalization exporting 'our way of life' all over the world, this increasingly applies to other cultures as well. Two engrained precepts of western metaphysics are the Cartesian *cogito* (from which our cherished notion of a 'self' derives) and Aristotelian logic, the very fabric of how we build our conceptualizations about the world. Zen thought challenges both, inviting us to consider, for instance, that a being is not a unitary entity but already a product of *co-arising*, of 'simultaneous happening of different elements that together construct what we call a self' (Park, 2006a, p. xii). A being is at all times *already* 'in the web of movement without a moment's possibility of creating a "presence" of "entity"' (Park, ibid, p. xiii). This is an example of what Nāgārjuna, the Mahayana teacher and philosopher, acknowledged as the fourteenth great ancestor in the Zen tradition, called *śūnyatā*, often translated as 'emptiness' and, interestingly as 'the void'. To a conventional way of thinking, steeped in western metaphysics, the above description sounds like annihilation – hence the rather ominous term 'void'. This was largely Hegel's view in his lectures on religion of 1831 (Hegel, 2008).

Similarly the notion of identity of non-identity (*anattā*), namely that all things in the world are devoid of self will be understood as a 'violation of the Aristotelian logic' (Park, ibid, p. xiv). When faced with the sheer otherness of Zen teachings, the customary response is twofold: a) rejection of this philosophical and religious practice because deemed to be 'nihilistic'; b) assimilation of its otherness within customary metaphysical categories.

For Zen perspectives and ideas to be experienced directly and appraised fairly, we need to turn to the intensive somatic practice of *zazen* (silent sitting meditation) and to familiarize ourselves with counter-traditional aspects of philosophy (Bazzano & Webb, 2016). Often at the margins of canonical thought, the counter-tradition has provided valid and altogether different views of the world and of our place in it. We find this very early on with Heraclitus (575–435 BC), the philosopher who privileged *becoming* over *being* and saw reality as dynamic flux. We need to look no further than Hume (1711–1776) to find a valid critique of our cherished notion of personal identity. In the nineteenth century, Nietzsche regales us with a capacious bag of sophisticated tools, party tricks and vivid clues for the undoing of western metaphysics. But it was with post-structuralism, deconstruction and strands of the 'Frankfurt School' in the twentieth century that the counter-tradition found concerted scope and breadth. They gave us, albeit indirectly, new tools for approaching the otherness of Zen thought and practice. They created a significant break in philosophy by capitalizing on developments that had advanced in Europe over a long time. They did so by emphasizing, among other things, and each in their own unique way, the importance of *difference*. They did more than that: they declared that our era is the *era of difference*. Difference is crucial when applied to metaphysics, religion and to any transformative practice such as psychotherapy. This is because a thought that recognizes difference will not be reducible to ontotheology, to the reduction of phenomena to 'Being'. It will also go beyond the limitations of negative theology which is but 'another reflection of our determination to identify Being or essence as existing beyond the confinement of our language' (Park, 2006b, p. 17). A philosophy of difference will perceive identity not as substance but as a mere construct, intimately linked to the notion of non-identity.

Contemporary and modern

There is an important difference, I believe, between the 'modern' and the 'contemporary'. Let us consider modernity first. The first thing to say, rather brusquely perhaps, is that modernity is a genteel word for capitalism and its manifold effects on society and culture. In this sense, post-modernity can be defined as a cluster of cultural reverberations of late, globalized capitalism. The way in which Zen is being adapted to our contemporary world is directly related to how each different practitioner relates to modernity. There appear to be many stances, including subversion and resistance. Here I would like to highlight only three of them which I hope will be useful to this discussion: a) *refusal*; b) *unengaged acceptance*; and c) *engaged recognition*.

Refusal of modernity often goes together with nostalgia for a (supposedly) more authentic past. Unengaged acceptance cannot envision a different order of things and sees modernity (and post-modernity) as the 'end of history' – a very fashionable notion only a few years back. A stance of engaged recognition identifies the reality of the present, its ambivalence and diversity which in turn allow for the possibility of creative innovation. Let's have a closer look.

a) *Refusal*. An approach to Buddhism and psychotherapy steeped in a refusal of modernity will invariably be 'religious' (in the narrow sense of the term) as well as traditional. It will refer to canonical texts preserved in the aspic of ritual and doctrine, considering them to be more genuinely attuned to the allegedly transcendent, ahistorical message of the Buddha. This approach will find ways to articulate a 'Buddhist psychology' rather than a psychology that creatively and effectively reinterprets the Dharma.

b) *Unengaged acceptance* of modernity (and post-modernity) will emphasize a secular approach to Buddhism. In my experience, this can be both exhilarating and problematic. It is liberating to be able to cast aside some of the liturgical paraphernalia and hierarchical trappings – particularly if one is too strongly attached to them. The difficulty arises when self-confessed secularist stances do not 'work through' the implications of secularism. For one thing, secularism *depends* on religiosity, transcendence and the cloistered life against which it sets itself. Most of all, secularism *embraces* religious morality: it refrains from extending the critique of religion to religious morality itself. It shies away from reframing the ethical domain from bourgeois ideology. Secular Buddhism risks becoming one with its religious version in condemning the problematic facets of human experience ('the passions') and focusing on ideals of moral perfection. In other words, with secularism the pursuit of enlightenment often gives way to an equally idealistic aspiration for moral perfection.

c) A stance of *engaged recognition* would be confidently ambivalent in straddling the religious *and* the secular, recognizing the rich legacy of mythical, symbolic and poetic elements present in the former as well as the vigorous refusal of transcendent metaphysics in the latter. This particular position – what I call 'contemporary' – is still in the making. This book aims to instigate, contribute to and deepen this very same stance.

User-friendly

Modernity is closely associated with modernism, a cultural phenomenon that yielded exciting experiments in art and literature. Here, a tangible source of encouragement is found in what the term *modern* meant for literature – from the 1850s onwards, and particularly with *Madame Bovary*, originally published in 1856 (Flaubert, 2003) where, among other things, we find a further shift, already present in the realist novel, from the domain of narrative to that of *affect* (Jameson, 2014). The innovations and experimentations of modernist literature, its overall fondness for meaning and high-mindedness, its questioning of self-consciousness and identity are as stimulating and radical today as they were more than 150 years ago. Yet all of the above is largely considered with suspicion. This is partly due to our predominant fondness for cynical realism and an unhealthy suspicion of more demanding standards usually deemed 'elitist' and not 'user-friendly' enough. Particularly in North America and Europe, this manifests, in the words of Susan Sontag (2007) as 'a bullying reaction against the high modernist achievement', which is considered as 'difficult, too demanding of audiences, not accessible' (p. 218).

An equivalent is found in the ways in which Zen is currently being (supposedly) *decoded*: its ambivalence and subtlety are jostled away in favour of easy-to-use coping strategies for dealing with the stress of hypermodern living. In psychotherapeutic training, this is apparent in the widespread and shameless reduction of richly ambivalent psychological notions to a list of bullet points. Rather than levers to be used in order to foster the luxuriant uncertainty of (heartful) thought – the core of education and culture – these quickly are assumed as fetishes and portents of certainty.

The overall dumbing down I'm aiming to describe here is also, paradoxically, a by-product of modernism, for modernism also gave us logical positivism, the ground for the type of scientism that is influential today. By 'scientism' I mean unwarranted faith in the power of scientific knowledge and methodologies. Bolstered by the optimism that followed the construction of heavy industry, modernism in science engendered scientism, and the natural step after that was postmodernism – healthy scepticism in relation to grand theorizing at first, but increasingly a display of cool cynicism and the flaunting of 'ephemeral language-games' (Jameson, 2015, p. 103) which ended up beautifying instead of challenging the status quo. One influential offshoot of postmodernism is *presentism*, which brings together the woolly mysticism of the 'here and now' (to which mindfulness-oriented, Buddhist-tinged psychologies gullibly subscribe) and the rapacious exploits of late capitalism whose 'vision' is blind to history and cannot see beyond the chance of turning a quick buck.

Psychotherapy: the fourth treasure?

Despite their inevitable limitations, secular adaptations of Zen and Buddhism popular at present have injected new life into the living stream of the practice. A truly contemporary interpretation of the Dharma is still very much work in progress; we will need to take into account multiple dimensions and perspectives presently excluded from current secularist and religious Buddhism. Among these, the role of psychotherapy is crucial because it contends with everyday life and the life of *psyche*. In the golden days of Chan and Zen, attention to everyday life meant applying one's awareness to 'chopping wood, carrying water'. Our contemporary equivalent is perhaps something like 'paying the bills, dealing with relationships, driving kids to school'. My own sense is that psyche may well be beyond the grasp of secularism *and* spiritualism. This is because it encompasses an area of experience that is deeply ambivalent and it is either dismissed as irrational or literalized as numinous. Could it be that psychotherapy is the Dharma's *fourth treasure*? Allow me to explain.

A Zen practitioner takes refuge in, and is inspired by, the *three treasures* (Buddha, Dharma and Sangha). They afford invaluable support on the path. The first treasure is the vivid example of the historical Buddha. The second treasure, the Dharma, is the corpus of his teachings, and Sangha, the third treasure, is the encouraging presence of a community of practitioners united by a common intent. One interpretation, attributed to Taizan Maezumi (1931–1995), sees the three treasures manifesting in different times in history. The age of the Buddha would then be the time of Siddhartha Gautama, known as the awakened one or Buddha, who lived in Nepal during the sixth to fourth century BC and characterized by his direct influence as a living spiritual teacher. The second is the age of the Dharma, a time of consolidation (also perhaps institutionalization) of Buddhism as a doctrine and set of practices (Bazzano, 2016). The third would be the present era, a time where the emphasis is on Sangha or community, understood not only in the narrower sense of fellow practitioners but as the larger human (as well as non-human) society. The emphasis here is on ethics, on the social dimension and on the actualization of the teachings in the crucible of our everyday interaction with others. The present era may then be the time when psychotherapy adds something valuable to the point where it may be considered as the Dharma's fourth treasure (Bazzano, 2016). The treasure in this case is a deeper level of understanding *psyche* as well as 'unconscious emotional communication in the relational field' (Bobrow, 2010, p. xxxi), something that could effectively 'complement, enrich and challenge Buddhist practice and teaching' (ibid, p. xxxi).

White pebbles, black pebbles

Two decades before taking up Zen training, I went to a Tibetan institute to do a *Lam Rim* ('stages of the path') course in Tuscany. I was 21 years old, fresh from the enthusiasms and disillusionments of the students' movement. I remember asking one of the resident teachers whether this thing he kept referring to as 'enlightenment' was the same as poetic intuition. The answer was gentle but peremptory: enlightenment was a momentous event that would happen only after countless lives of conscious and dedicated striving and the accumulation of merit through selfless practice and virtuous deeds. No chance for me then, I thought.

To complicate things further, I had also received a letter from a friend inviting me to go to a Lou Reed concert at the nearby stadium in Florence. At that evening talk, the monk talked of white pebbles and black pebbles, of virtuous and not so virtuous actions, and how accumulating the former and shedding the latter would bring good karma. Lou Reed's songs meant the earth to me (they still do): the poetry in the lyrics, the gritty guitars, the alternatively sly and pounding rhythms, the distinctively unholy associations: being high, having sex, laughing away the pain in a hazy, sovereign disdain 'beyond good and evil'. Enlightenment would have to wait. I postponed my spiritual quest and hitched a ride to Florence.

Days later, resurfacing in my university campus bedsit from marijuana-induced visions of Dionysian rapture and the rehearsals of a life of poetry and polyamorous experimentation, I soberly reflected on my question to the Tibetan teacher. I went over his answer, and felt embarrassed and ashamedly naive for even suggesting that link. Reflecting on it now though, I feel some tenderness towards that 21-year-old. I even think, probably not without self-indulgence, that he may have been on to something, despite lacking the confidence to articulate his obscure thoughts. For it now appears to me that what my younger self called 'poetic intuition' can be several things. It may describe an ability to perceive the impermanence of things and their inherent beauty – all the more precious and worthy of appreciation because fleeting. Moreover, being an intuition (a hunch, an insight), the 'truth' it gestures towards is not fixed, pre-existing or separate from experience. Being poetic (rather than say 'scientific' or 'religious'), it does not preach, elucidate or lecture. Instead, it hints; it speaks indirectly. It does strive to convey the mystery of things but it does not attempt to indecorously unveil it. Poetry, in short, may provide us with a third way beyond science and religion (Bazzano, 2012a). By poetry, I do not mean only rhyme and verse, but a sensibility closely allied to philosophy: a way of perceiving and appreciating the world that is non-utilitarian and capable of singing the world; one that is not oblivious to the incarnate, situated nature of human experience and to the ultimate unknowability of living-and-dying.

The resident teacher in the Tibetan monastery had directed me towards a religious system. He did so out of compassion; I was grateful to him even though his reply may have been clunky or doctrinaire and a long way from the serene wisdom of the wonderfully mischievous Lama Yeshe, whom I was to meet a few months later. Whether Buddhist, Platonist or Christian; whether Muslim, Darwinian or atheist, a system provides us with metaphysical explanations. Science, too, when elevated (or rather downgraded) to the level of scientism, becomes as metaphysical as any religious or philosophical system. Our penchant for manufacturing explanations is akin to an instinct – at times a compulsion. It is part of being human and as such unavoidable. What *can* be avoided though is the fossilization of our temporary explanations into dogmas. With our thirst for the essence (or the ideal, or the origin of things) momentarily quenched by a poetic image or the creation of a new philosophical concept, the journey continues instead of halting at the superstore of second-hand metaphysics. The term 'metaphysics' from the Greek *ta meta ta phusika*, the things beyond nature, is conventionally the domain of religion and abstract thought, dealing with notions such as being (ontology), and providing us with a rational account of the world (cosmology). Today, metaphysics also refers to any explanation of the world articulated in a system that precedes and/or is placed outside the world. Conventional, old-fashioned metaphysics presupposes the existence of 'Spirit' placed more or less outside 'matter'. Modern metaphysics may be materialistic in outlook, i.e. empirical and/or phenomenological, but will still provide us with an equally expedient explanation of the world. Both types of metaphysics also grant us the consolation that the wide world 'out there' is not a chaos but a cosmos.

To know that metaphysics are unavoidable is humbling. We realize that in the process of making sense of the world we are bound to lean towards the first building blocks of a grand theory or, at any rate, subscribe/add a footnote to an existing grand narrative. The opposite stance – thinking we can avoid metaphysics by going back to the pre-Socratics, or the wisdom of the East, or by choosing paganism, mystical Christianity, Judaism or an empirical pragmatism that believes itself free of metaphysics – is at best naive, at worst conceited.

An alternative to neo-positivism

What to do? Faced with an unknowable world, we could remain silent. But is silence better than words? My utterances skip the world's surface with sounds, concepts and commentaries, or onomatopoeically replicate the sounds of the world I inhabit – sounds among sounds. The problem arises when I believe too sternly in the sounds I emit, the words I speak – when I begin to take for granted that my temporary constructions, which in turn echo and are verified by a dominant system of thought, are representations of reality. Could this be a definition of neo-positivism? In a general sense, this view now encompasses most orientations, whether within spiritual or psychotherapeutic traditions. The neo-positivist stance is by far the dominant discourse of our age. Roughly put, it sees the world as an orderly cosmos. It believes that humans can navigate, deal with and master it to their advantage, and that knowledge (particularly scientific knowledge) can curb the anxiety and uncertainty of living-and-dying.

Experience taught me that to openly disagree, deviate from, or even question the dominant neo-positivist view would elicit charges of cynicism, post-modern relativism, or even of holding unreconstructed superstitious beliefs. A suspension of the neo-positivist stance is unthinkable for writers or practitioners unable to sustain being ousted. Nonetheless, active foreswearing of neo-positivist discourse is essential, for it is a good way to verify its claims. The inspiration here is the phenomenology of Merleau-Ponty (1964; 1969): rather than rejecting science outright, he invited us to temporarily suspend and re-examine its claims and reminded us that science is, after all, a human endeavour hence not superior to human experience (Bazzano, 2014).

A straightforward but simplistic view commonly ascribes a solitary 'meditative' domain to Zen practice and a relational dimension to therapy. According to this view, *zazen* is the place where one enquiries into the nature of the self, whereas therapy is the designated area of intersubjectivity. In other words: we meditate alone; we do therapy with another. This pervasive view does not take into account several important factors. First, Zen practice is at heart *collective*: the whole tradition is steeped into communal practice; sitting meditation, mostly practiced with others, is only one of its components and, some would say, not the most important. It is only through its adaptation to life in late capitalism that the practice has become a more private affair, something one does at the margins of a working day. Second, psychology itself (and psychotherapy) has changed *almost* in the opposite direction, from 'one-person field to a two-person (relational) psychology' (Miller, 2002, p. 86). Incidentally, this change has been, in my view, sensationalized: we are led to believe that psychology miraculously moved from the alleged isolated Cartesianism of Freudian psychoanalysis to the 'discovery' of intersubjectivity (Stolorow et al., 1994) when, for instance, already in the work of Karen Horney we find a gradual move away from subjectivism. She clearly saw the potential transformation that can take place in us when we are 'held within the context of a neutral yet caring relationship' (Miller, 2002, p. 86). Interestingly, Horney met the well-known Zen scholar D. T. Suzuki in 1950, two years before her death. She learned from the encounter, adapting some ideas from Zen in her *Final Lectures* (Horney, 1987).

A similarly sensationalized narrative runs through humanistic therapy and now constitutes the staple of much contemporary person-centred therapy training. It goes something like this. Although a psychologist of great insight, Carl Rogers was still a man of his time, with a worldview steeped in the individualism of the 1950s and 1960s. Then along came a host of modernizers who rectified this arguably individualistic streak into a more palatable relational framework. It may be that each generation of practitioners needs to prove itself and take a dramatic stance against the previous one. But the narratives it creates are often caricatures. Even *before* Rogers, at the cusp of psychoanalysis and humanistic therapy the alleged shift from individual to a two-person psychology had already taken place, for example, with the work of Otto Rank (1996) and Jessie Taft (1933).

I previously mentioned that psychology (and psychotherapy) *almost* moved in the opposite direction, in this case from subjectivity to intersubjectivity: this is because I believe that as it is understood by the current consensus, the relational domain is still largely steeped in subjectivity. The dominant notion is that in psychology progress is linear and it moves *ad meliora*, always towards better things. But I am not convinced. We have, for instance, *regressed* from Freud's fertile notion of *evenly suspended attention* (Freud, 1958) which he saw, at least for a time, as the fundamental psychoanalytic technique, the recommendation that the therapist 'must turn his own unconscious like a receptive organ towards the transmitting unconscious of the patient', adjusting themselves to the client 'as a telephone receiver is adjusted to the transmitting microphone' (ibid, p. 115). This stance can be described as neutral, or in Zen terms, as a stance of equanimity. Casting aside personal investment and expectations is supremely useful both in meditation and in dyadic therapeutic encounter. This stance is at least indirectly linked to Margaret Mahler's notion of constancy (Mahler, 1968) and Carl Rogers's notion of unconditional positive regard (Rogers, 1951), both of them suggesting a quality of love that has no strings attached.

A comparative study

The Dharma is a multilayered set of teachings and practices with ethical, religious and mythical connotations, and with applications in philosophy and the arts. How it will continue to influence other branches of human knowledge and practice, including science and psychology, is unpredictable. We already know how the Dharma has been influenced by the modern world. The impact of modernity has been twofold. On the one hand, it has dispelled some of the mystifications and trappings inexorably associated with an ancient religious tradition. At the same time, it has promoted too cosy an adaptation to the essentially Protestant ethos of private spiritual cultivation and personal salvation. This latter trend has effectively pared it down to a handful of mindfulness techniques aimed at reducing stress, anxiety and depression.

In their otherwise commendable aspiration to make the Dharma accessible to more people, a few contemporary Dharma teachers and practitioners are keen to combine some of its more basic components – mostly the practice of mindfulness – with equally basic notions taken from psychotherapy and the self-help industry. Aspects of the Dharma are now as a result more readily accessible, but at the price of becoming assimilated to a market that arbitrarily blends the technologization of meditation and the obscurantism of the new age. In this perplexing dance, *zazen* is confused with trance, trance blends with mindfulness, and mindfulness does a polite stand-in for ethics – all in the service of productivity and of what a different, more searching era would have justifiably referred to as 'alienated work'.

This book can be described as a comparative study not only because it draws comparisons between two very different disciplines and practices, but also because this writer does his best to acknowledge and even cultivate that sense of strangeness and absence that is the prerequisite of good comparisons (Anderson, 2016). The ever-present danger I see, and rather obsessively skirt around, is the parochialism of assumed 'psychotherapeutic' and 'Buddhist' stances. A lot of what I write here will inevitably be housed in the pigeonhole of this or that orientation. But my intention is to drift, be estranged and observe from the vantage point of being lost. This is not new to me: as a boy on an excursion with the school, visiting some nearby town, I always made a point of getting lost. I enjoyed this immensely, even though it frightened me.

A guide to getting lost

> It's hard to get lost – it's so hard that I'll probably quickly figure out some way to find myself, even if finding myself is once again my vital lie.
>
> *Lispector, 2014, p. 4*

Therapy can find inspiration in Zen, a practice rooted in the cultivation of perplexity and wonder. This can provide a welcome antidote to a counterproductive compulsion to know and control human experience. Zen can find inspiration in therapy, at its best a craft that helps one explore the human condition compassionately and unflinchingly.

The pages that follow tackle different subjects – the self, living-and-dying, mindfulness, the transpersonal and the unconscious and more – and bring together aspects of the Buddhist tradition, contemporary western therapy and western thought. My objective is to expand the existing dialogue on the integration of Buddhism, therapy and philosophy by highlighting areas that have been neglected or insufficiently articulated.

One of the perils of being a therapist today is becoming a guide, trying to fulfil our culture's demands for goals, quick-fixes and ready-made answers. It is possible to play, more or less happily, the role of moral guide or evidence-based researcher and often help others to find what they are looking for. However, there is another way to respond to the need to be assisted in 'fulfilling one's goals': to encourage exploration and facilitate disorientation, so that what is found comes as genuine surprise and learning. This means partly to be willing to explore a third way that leaves behind the dominant modalities of the spiritual/religious on the one hand and the secular on the other, opting instead for a positively ambivalent stance rooted in somatic practice, the cultivation of compassion and active perplexity.

References

Anderson, B. (2016). *A Life Beyond the Boundaries*. London: Verso.

Bazzano, M. (2012a). *Spectre of the Stranger: Towards a Phenomenology of Hospitality*. Eastbourne: Sussex University Press.

Bazzano, M. (2012b). Immanent vitality: Reflections on the actualizing tendency. *Person-Centered and Experiential Psychotherapies*, 11(2): 137–151. doi:10.1080/14779757.2012.672930.

Bazzano, M. (2014). The poetry of the world: A tribute to the phenomenology of Merleau-Ponty. *Self & Society*, 41(3): 7–12.

Bazzano, M. (2016). The fourth treasure: Psychotherapy's contribution to the Dharma. In R. E. Purser, D. Forbes & A. Burke (Eds), *Handbook of mindfulness: Culture, context and social engagement* (pp. 293–304). New York: Springer.

Bazzano, M. & Webb, J. (2016). *Therapy and the Counter-tradition: The Edge of Philosophy*. Abingdon: Routledge.

Blyth, R. H. (1978). *Games Zen Masters Play*. New York: New American Library.

Bobrow, J. (2010). *Zen and Psychotherapy: Partners in Liberation*. London: W.W. Norton & Co.

Flaubert, G. (2003). *Madame Bovary*. London: Penguin.

Freud, S. (1958). *Recommendations to Physicians Practicing Psychoanalysis*. London: Hogarth Press.

Hare, D. (2016). *Why the Tory project is bust*. The Guardian, 8 March, http://theguardian.com/politics/2016/mar/08/david-hare-why-the-tory-project-is-bust Retrieved 8 March 2016.

Hegel, G. W. F. (2008). *Lectures on the Philosophy of Religion*. Oxford: Oxford University Press.

Horney, K. (1987). *Final Lectures*. New York: W.W. Norton & Co.

Jameson, F. (2014). *The Antinomies of Realism*. London: Verso.

Jameson, F. (2015). The aesthetics of singularity. *New Left Review*, (92) March–April, pp. 101–132.

Lispector, C. (2014). *The Passion According to G.H.* London: Penguin.

Magliola, R. (1984). *Derrida on the Mend.* West Lafayette, IN: Purdue University Press.

Mahler, M. (1968). *On Human Symbiosis and the Vicissitudes of Individuation.* New York: International Universities Press.

Merleau-Ponty, M. (1964). *Sense and Non-sense.* Evanston, IL: Northwestern University Press.

Merleau-Ponty, M. (1969). *The Visible and the Invisible.* Evanston, IL: Northwestern University Press.

Miller, M. (2002). Zen and psychotherapy: From neutrality, through relationship, to the emptying place. In P. Young-Eisendrath & S. Muramoto (Eds), *Awakening and insight: Zen Buddhism and psychotherapy* (pp. 81–92). New York: Brunner-Routledge.

Park, J. Y. (2006a). General introduction. In J. Y. Park (Ed.), *Buddhisms and deconstructions* (pp. xi–xxii). Lanham, MD: Rowman & Littlefield.

Park, J. Y. (2006b). Naming the unnameable: dependent co-arising and différance. In J. Y. Park (Ed.), *Buddhisms and deconstructions* (pp. 7–20). Lanham, MD: Rowman & Littlefield.

Rank, O. (1996). *A Psychology of Difference: The American Lectures.* Princeton, NJ: Princeton University Press.

Rogers, C. R. (1951). *Client-centered Therapy.* London: Constable.

Satyamurti, C. (2015). *Mahabharata: A Modern Retelling.* New York and London: W.W. Norton & Co.

Shatz, A. (2016). The Sorcerer of Jazz. *New York Review of Books*, LXIII(14): pp. 62–64.

Sontag, S. (2007). *At the Same Time.* London: Penguin.

Stolorow, R. D., Atwood, R. D. & Brandchaft, B. (1994). *The Intersubjective Perspective.* Lanham, MD: Jason Aronson.

Suzuki, S. (1983). *Zen Mind, Beginner's Mind.* New York and Tokyo: Weatherhill.

Taft, J. (1933). *The Dynamics of Therapy in a Controlled Relationship.* New York: Macmillan.

1

SELF, NO-SELF AND DOING THE NEXT THING

Kanzeon and the samurai

I heard a story once, set in medieval Japan. It takes place in a small village not far from the mountains and renowned for the healing powers of its hot springs. One autumn night a man dreams of a stranger who tells him: 'Tomorrow, at two in the afternoon, Kanzeon Bodhisattva, the deity of compassion, "she who hears the cries of the world", will visit your village. She will appear in the guise of a man, a samurai in his forties, on horseback. Be prepared. And tell the villagers to be ready.'

The man wakes up in the dead of night, euphoric and also a bit worried. A thought reassures him: he will ask for instructions from the monk who is stopping by the village on his way to the mountain monastery. He can barely wait for daybreak. In the morning, the news spreads quickly. Instructed by the monk, the residents are soon busy scrubbing the village clean, adorning it with flowers, lighting incense and placing water offerings in small bowls. Then at the appointed hour they all gather silently around the hot spring to welcome the Bodhisattva. The village clock strikes two. Nothing happens; no one appears. Another long, silent hour goes by uneventfully, then two. A few minutes after four, with the sun already setting behind nearby Mount Hiei, a samurai on horseback appears. Everyone prostrates before him. He seems exhausted, maybe wounded – and visibly perplexed at the spectacle before him. 'What is going on?' he asks. A monk tells him about the oracle. Baffled, the samurai explains that he is injured and that is why he has come to the spring. But the villagers keep praying and prostrating. At this point the samurai gives in. 'OK – he says, in that case I must be Kanzeon.' The monk ordains him and the next day, having medicated his wounds, the samurai decides to travel with the monk to Mount Hiei, to become a disciple of the Zen master Kakucho.

Two things strike me about this story. First, the samurai's readiness, past his moment of perplexity, to respond to the situation and be what is required of him.

This may be linked to a *situational* understanding of ethics: summoned by you, I respond. In attempting to respond to your request in the best way I can, I satisfy not only an ethical requirement, I also manifest myself more fully – true nature arises in endeavouring to meet your silent ethical request. This may also be linked to the hazy, dormant feeling that the heart of this ordinary and imperfect person contains the seed of Buddhahood.

Second, it seems to me that the samurai's decision to be ordained is truly remarkable. He wants to be instructed in the Buddha Way; his readiness to respond to the villagers' need becomes grounded beyond his initial, spontaneous response. By deciding to undergo Zen training, the samurai is willing to turn a fleeting glimpse of his true nature into embodied reality. In this way, he will carry out more fully the villagers' request. Without the latter part of the story, his response 'I then must be Kanzeon' could represent all sorts of things: a shrug of resignation, a form of wish-fulfilling, even plain opportunism. Instead, he is willing to train and rise to the occasion. He is not behaving like a politician but is ready to fulfil the pledge he made to others, i.e. to be Kanzeon.

There is a parallel here with the practice of therapy. I remember when a co-tutor and I were interviewing applicants to a counselling course in a university psychology department. We were on the top floor of a very tall building in a glass-panelled room that afforded dazzling views of the sprawling edge of London, which is maybe why I remember those endless, gruelling hours of work rather fondly, even wistfully. The interviews took place over several days, yet after a few hours we both figured out that although their circumstances and backgrounds were different, applicants could broadly be divided into two 'types'. There were those who, assuming they already knew a thing or two about counselling and psychology, were animated by a craving to help others; and there were those whose motivation to undergo the training was grounded in the desire to learn more about themselves. By and large, the former came to counselling stirred by a desire for a career change; the latter were motivated by a personal crisis, or because some recent shift in their life had made them question the world and their place in it. Needless to say, our preference almost invariably went to the latter group. We felt that their keen interest in what is commonly known as 'self-development' provided more fertile ground for the making of a good therapist.

As with the samurai story, the aspiration to play a different role has to be matched by a genuine desire to undergo a form of training, a rite of passage or a period of learning that allows one to rise to the occasion and respond more readily to the task.

Reincarnation and the Devil

'Don't look in the mirror at night, or you'll see the Devil.' My mother said this to me once when I was seven or eight. It was bedtime and she had probably noticed my fascination with a large mirror in the corridor, whose baroque-looking frame looked unusual to me in the dim light. I don't know for certain whether she was warning me against self-absorption or passing on a piece of superstition, but I took her counsel literally and for years didn't dare to look in the mirror. Then in my mid-twenties, after university, I travelled to India and lived there for a few years. There with many others I played around with what were deemed to be techniques of spiritual liberation. One of these consisted of staring into the mirror at night by the light of a candle. This was both unsettling and exhilarating as I could see my face changing and, bizarrely, other faces emerging who stared back at me. I hasten to say, I did not imbibe anything before or during these exercises. Rather than the devil, this time around I was told that appearing before me were semblances of who I had been in past lives. I am now sceptical about this sort of thing and a little more than resistant to metaphysical explanations: as with the notion of an afterlife in Christianity, I now find, rightly or wrongly, that belief in reincarnation is an imaginative attempt to dodge the finality and existential edge of death, although back then it spoke to my youthful mystical leanings. These were severely put to the test when, working once as a translator in a large group on 'experiencing past lives', I was surprised to notice that many of the participants had a proclivity for drama: most men found they had been pirates, glamorous conspirators or artists and most women witches, shamanic squaws or amazons. You could not find a single Victorian cleaner or run-of-the-mill medieval butcher.

Multiplicity

Despite everything mentioned above, there is one thing that the mirror-gazing exercise vividly evokes. Putting on one side religious accounts of various kinds, as well as, I imagine, all plausible scientific explanations of the phenomenon, what lingers with the experimenter is the sense of vertigo resulting from exposure to the *multiplicity of the self*, an experience in regard to which the psychotherapeutic tradition has shown ambivalence even when seemingly accepting it. In my own clinical experience, awareness of organismic multiplicity often dawns on clients as inconsistence, inner conflict, and *dilemma* (a '*twofold* proposition') between, for instance, organism and self-concept, or instinct and civility. What I suggest here is that this either/or battle, so typical of the western mindset, is only the threshold of the larger province of multiplicity. Dormant and ignored in sections of psychotherapy that steer away from psychoanalysis and analytical psychology, this notion has now begun to resurface under many different guises, including that of 'configurations of self' (Mearns & Thorne, 2007) as an attempt to understand the psyche's multiplicity. The difficulty here consists in not being able to conceive multiplicity *outside* the confines of the self (configurations *of self*), in harking back to a Freudian as well as Kleinian notion of *parts* and introjected *objects*, and in reducing 'the infinite multiplicity of unconscious affects to the logical unity of a signifier' (Deleuze & Guattari, 1987, p. 27). Despite these inevitable difficulties, to allow greater space for the exploration of multiplicity in therapeutic and meditative settings expands the horizon of our enquiry and is to be warmly welcome.

Ash and firewood

At times I wonder whether despite advances in psychology and the greater popularity of mindfulness and meditation, it is more troubling to our contemporary sensibilities than it was in other epochs to envisage the self as split, multiple or even insubstantial i.e. anything other than the solid unit conceived by the western philosophical, religious and scientific traditions. The unconscious and the *double* were common features of nineteenth-century/early twentieth-century literature and psychology, whereas contemporary science and psychology seemingly favours narratives dominated by notions of *resilience* and *managerialism*. Positive psychology (Seligman, 2006) increasingly portrays resilience as something divorced from a healthy notion of strength that embraces inescapable human fragility and associates it instead with the outdated injunction to 'toughen up' heard from their fathers by sons of my generation – almost as if all the progress earned by 70 years of psychotherapy has been regressed to a single reductive formula (Bazzano, 2016a). As for managerialism, now ubiquitous in the humanities, this manifests as the consistent move away from freer explorations of human experience and psyche towards a 'stultifying . . . culture of surveillance, audit and bureaucratic control' (House, 2016, p. 151).

At heart, both notions are steeped in the bourgeois view of the human being that universalizes its imagined solidity, self-sameness and psychological consistency. As such, the person (and the world he/she lives in) has to be *defended* and *managed*. The first notion, resilience, was influential in bringing about the controversial application of psychological and psychotherapeutic expertise and knowledge (as well as mindfulness techniques) in the military. One example may suffice here to illustrate this point: a psychologist recently came up with the notion of 'adaptive killing': a set of cognitive and behavioural techniques 'focus[ed] on eliminating irrational thoughts and beliefs . . . on changing a soldier's belief structure regarding killing'. As he sees it, 'these interventions could be integrated into immersive simulations to promote the conviction that adaptive killing is permissible' (Matthews, 2014, p. 187).

In turn, managerialism (the second notion) seeks to administer and control human nature. This is because it sees human nature as essentially unruly and unpredictable. This view is problematic: not only is it devoid of 'soul', it is also divorced from an organismic view of the human dimension and as such is no longer interested in describing the fluctuations of an organism in search of actualization, meaning and freedom, but it focuses instead on the *factual,* relying on the quasi-scientific collection of quantifiable data. This is known as the McNamara fallacy. For Robert McNamara, US Secretary of Defense during the Vietnam War, decisions must be based exclusively on quantitative observations: 1) measure what can be measured; 2) ignore what can't be measured; 3) assume that what can't be measured is not important; and 4) assume that what can't be measured doesn't exist. Social scientist Daniel Yankelovich famously commented that the first point is OK as far as it goes; the second is misleading; the third is pure blindness and the fourth suicidal (Friedman, 2013).

Both Zen and most of the therapeutic counter-traditions work *outside* the parameters discussed above, i.e. they are less interested in substantiating the self and more keen to explore and deconstruct it. It may be partly for this reason that their natural allies are to be found in the arts.

Broken statue and shadow

It is not surprising that we need to turn to art in order to find examples that fearlessly explore different possibilities, namely, that the self may be fluid, multiple and/or insubstantial. The work of Francis Bacon is one example, and what comes immediately to my mind is his triptych *Three Studies for Self-Portrait*. When gazing at it, 'as the eye moves from left to right', Colm Tóibín, writes:

> the face in the first section appears like a mask. It is fully visible in the center panel, gazing outward. In the right-hand section, the face is already in another realm, some of it having merged with the blackness. What little of it remains has an aura of enormous suffering. It is not nothing . . . Instead of nothing, there is 'all' or the irony surrounding all.
>
> *Tóibín, 2015, Internet file*

An obvious response would be to suggest that Bacon's unsettling triptych, part of his late work, is foreshadowing death. But this feels like a cliché: it's what interpreters of writers or artists' late work tend to do. At close scrutiny, there is no autonomous 'me', a solid entity moving towards death in a straight line. Instead, living beings constantly expand beyond their edges. Life is neither reconcilable nor understandable: this is what is truly unsettling (more unsettling than death itself perhaps) – and exhilarating. The problem with saying that life itself (let alone *late* life) is 'being for death' (*Sein zum Tod*) as Heidegger (1962) and scores of existential psychotherapists are fond of saying after him, turns death into something that can be reconciled and even apprehended by human subjectivity (Levinas, 2001).

It is thrilling to find artists and writers in their twilight years refusing to go gently, to meekly ponder their demise and instead striving to create a new form and a new language (Adorno, 1998; Said, 2008). What is expressed at times by these new forms and new languages disrupts our neatly teleological representations of life and death (including our understanding of life as moving towards death), which are all-too often the hallmark of the anti-aesthetic mind (Schwartz, 1997; Bazzano, 2012). Roused by their provocations, we suddenly notice that things are no longer what they seemed. Even philosophers, notorious for their meek obeisance to the status quo, are capable of doing this at times: in a passage in Dōgen's *Genjōkōan*, written when he was 33, he confronts several metaphysical and existential assumptions at once. Firewood becomes ash, he says; it doesn't revert to firewood. Likewise, we shouldn't presume that ash is future and firewood past. Firewood does not become firewood again once it is ash, and in the same way we do *not* go back to birth after death. The challenge he poses in the next sentence is even more telling: birth does not turn into death but has to be understood as *no-birth*. Birth is a complete expression in itself – as it is death. They are akin to winter and spring; we do not speak of winter as the beginning of spring, nor do we call summer the end of spring (Dōgen, 1233). There is no straight line between life and death.

There is no linearity either within the self which at all times is found cohabiting with its shadow-self, as one can see in some of Francis Bacon's late paintings: in his 1984's *Still Life: Broken Statue and Shadow* the grey-black wrecked sculpture emits a shadow whose shape is different from the statue and whose texture suggests a new kind of flesh. Tóibín (2015) likens Bacon's work to that of Samuel Beckett, as he sees both as presenting the idea of the figure 'as fluid rather than . . . single or inert', an idea that has its origins 'in necessity as much as in philosophy'.

Reflection and reflected

Whether or not attached to a particular belief system, intense mirror-gazing can be unsettling. But the mirror also presents us with a useful turning point in this discussion on self and identity. Normally, we assume a clear-cut distinction between representation and what is being represented, between the reflection and the reflected. As a rule, one is a by-product of the other. There is an origin, i.e. 'me', and then there is a secondary factor, i.e. my reflection in the mirror. In this case, I am the source and my reflection is derivative. Here too, as with previous examples, we find a conveniently linear narrative. But what if, as Derrida says (Derrida, 1976, p. 36), 'representation mingles with what it represents'? What if there is 'a dangerous promiscuity and a nefarious complicity between the reflection and the reflected'? What if 'in this play of representation, the point of origin becomes ungraspable'? It is curious and heartening to find once more a philosopher (what are the chances of a psychologist doing that today?) disrupting our snug teleological ways, and scandalously suggesting the elusiveness and insubstantiality of the origin, the source, the spring – the solid 'me', the origin of the reflection I see in the mirror:

> There are things like reflecting pools, and images, an infinite reference from one to the other, but no longer a source, a spring. There is no longer a single origin. For what is reflected is split in *itself* and not only as an addition to itself of its image. The reflection, the image, the double, splits what it doubles.
>
> *Derrida, 1976, p. 36*

What if the reflection in the mirror, traditionally seen as secondary, 'doubles back . . . and *alters*' (Magliola, 1984, p. 9) the reflected? What if my image reflected in the mirror equally reflects me? In that case, one could say that 'the signified equally mirrors the so-called signifier' (Magliola, ibid, p. 10). For Derrida, studying the tradition and working through its principles meant that 'all so-called signs can only be *pure signifiers*, that is, *only* signifiers, through and through' (Magliola, ibid, p. 11).

Humanistic detours

If we apply the above to the notion of personal self-identity, the implication is that the person who says 'I' *mirrors* what is reflected rather than *being mirrored*. Within the best humanistic psychology tradition some have similarly said, in a refreshingly anti-humanist style, that the *organism* (Goldstein, 1995; Rogers, 1951) with its biological, genetic properties and its neurological impulses *precedes* the self-concept or the moment of self-identity. In the case of Rogers in particular, one sometimes wonders whether the implications of what he was saying were fully clear to him. Perhaps no writer or practitioner can ever claim to discern fully the implications of what he or she says. This is perhaps a task best left to history, to the development of a particular line of enquiry which the writer/practitioner participates in, and open to what Walter Benjamin, writing about Proust (Benjamin, 1999), called the *now of know-ability* (*Jetzt der Erkennbarkeit*) or moment of readability: a moment in time when a particular notion, text or work of art suddenly becomes not only crystal clear but indicates an array of possibilities hitherto unknown and untouched. I would not go so far as to say, for instance, that the Dharma is simply not readable in our time. Some Buddhist scholars, however, have presented a convincing argument in this vein (i.e. Lopez, 2012), effectively saying that our era has the Buddha it can understand or deserves, a 'scientific' Buddha, and nothing more. More simply perhaps Benjamin's *now of knowability* provides us with a sober reminder of our limitations in 'truly' apprehending the Dharma's multifaceted practices and texts across many centuries. It is fair to say, however, that the Dharma's inherently subversive element has been neutered in order to accommodate vested interests. If at all true, Benjamin's notion is one more case in favour of a non-teleological understanding that is more than linear sequence (*chronos*), one that stands for mysterious and fortuitous opportunity, for occurrences full of pregnant possibilities – what the Greeks called *kairos*.

If it is true, for instance, that psychotherapy is 'a process whereby man becomes his organism' (Rogers, 1961, p. 111), then the notion of *person* (embedded as it is in the principle of self-identity) begins to lose its grip and leaves room for a therapeutic exploration of a wider phenomenological field. I believe this was left uncharted in Rogers's later writings (and consequently for much of person-centred therapy). He tended to align himself with more transcendent notions such as the formative tendency (Rogers, 1980, p. 124), which instead of deconstructing the identity principle made it into a holistic universal structure.

Unlike humanistic psychology, often compromised to an anthropocentric fondness for the human self, Zen nimbly eludes the trap of self-identity thanks to the scrupulous notion of *śūnyatā* ('emptiness') that registers the flux of experience, the relativity as well as impermanence of 'the ten thousand things'. Crucially, it recognizes two things: a) myriad reality is not a holistic formation; and b) nor does it imply an eternal, immutable entity or final truth.

Doing the next thing

A notion in Chan Buddhism that finds intriguing parallels in western philosophy (particularly in Nietzsche and Hegel) is that the person is 'not a sort of being, but first and foremost a doing and making' (Ames, 1991, p. 150). *Xing* (nature) and *renxing* (human nature) cannot be so easily adapted or reduced to our western notion of a priori, innate beings that exist separately from their actions in the world. For Nietzsche (1996), there is no doer behind the deed, no substratum: '"the doer" is invented as an afterthought – the doing is everything' (Nietzsche, 1996, pp. 25–26). The 'I' is in this sense a useful reference point in grammar. Similarly for Taizan Maezumi one of the key aspects of Zen practice is 'doing the next thing' (Genpo Merzel, personal communication, 1998), which I understand to mean responding without preconceptions to experience as it presents itself. Hegel (1977) likewise presents a relation between doer and deed that is based *not on intentionality but on expression* (Bazzano, 2016b), a view admirably articulated by Robert Pippin (2006) and one that, if seriously taken into account, will bring about a considerable reframing of existential phenomenological therapy as we know it.

The deed is 'inherently social and historical . . . I see myself in the deed' (Bazzano, 2016b, p. 20) whereas my intentions, supposedly located within a self-existing 'I' are simply 'provisional starting points, formulated with incomplete knowledge of circumstances and consequences' (Pippin, 2006, p. 382). Because there is no entity that exists independently from my deeds, it is from the latter that I learn who I am. Or, 'Ethical self-consciousness now learns from its deed the developed nature of what it actually did' (Hegel, 1977, p. 283).

Nirvana and ataraxía

Two parallel notions run at around the same time in both Greek and Indian thought. The ancient Greeks, across their different philosophical 'schools', whether Stoics, Cynics, Epicureans or Sceptics – spoke of *ataraxía* or imperturbability; the Buddha and subsequent thinkers in his tradition spoke of *nirvana*. Both terms point towards the lived, incarnate experience of serenity and the cessation of affliction. Both states of mind have been conventionally understood as permanent and static, as pointing towards a goal that, once reached, ends the spiritual and philosophical path. They have also been described as accomplished detachment and often inscribed within a Judaeo-Christian ethos of disdain for human entanglements with the sweat and tears of history and the everyday. This has been by and large the predominant view, but I wonder whether both nirvana and ataraxía point instead towards a threshold (or Dharma gate in Buddhist parlance). If so, one could move the hypothesis forward and suggest the following; moments of incarnate knowing of nirvana and/or ataraxía make a person capable of sustaining the magnitude and unpredictability of becoming with greater equanimity. What this will look like and what sort of person will achieve this we cannot know. If we did or pretended, the whole enterprise would turn into a kind of facile humanism. It would call forth a 'type' of human being, the model and prototype for a new humanity. Instead, it is much more likely, if anything, that the threshold or Dharma gate will usher the subject towards a point of rupture, a moment of seeming crisis where the very existence of the self is rattled to the core. This is not, however, an affirmation of 'no-self' for that would entail a lapse into the absolute perspective, effectively a form of spiritual bypass and abdication to a transcendent position. An effective pointer here is Nietzsche's notion of the overman. Despite giant efforts to turn it into a new humanism (let alone the gross misinterpretations of Nazi propaganda) this notion points towards the rupture and dissolution of the self and the emergence of the *dividual* (Vattimo, 2005; Bazzano, 2016b). That this vision was more fully realized in modernist art and literature, rather than in philosophical practice or psychotherapy, testifies to its baffling and fluid nature and the difficulty with bending it to a systematic project. But then again Nietzsche did have human exemplars who for him fully represented openness of the subject to rapture/rupture – his most vivid example being Goethe. The Zen tradition has the example of the Buddha. Psychotherapy traditions also have their own exemplars and role models, as well as pointers such as a fully functioning person (Rogers, 1961) or the ambivalent notion of self-actualization (Maslow, 1962). What is relevant here is not to let a pointer fossilize and instead allow for a fluid perspective emphasizing the point of crisis, of risk and rupture – what opens the self to experiencing the wider phenomenal world. The latter is by definition transcendental though not transcendent, i.e. forever in excess and unreachable, yet immanent, within the dimension we all inhabit.

Beyond mortification and exaltation

In practising Zen, I experienced two pitfalls of my own making, though fairly common: one is *mortification*, the other *exaltation*. Mortification, from the Latin *mors* (death) and *facere* (to make), is to 'make dead', to deaden, to become as dead. The Dharma has been conventionally aligned to life-denigrating ideologies that essentially see life as sinful, imperfect and polluted – our stopover in this world as mere groundwork for the real life that will unfold after death. Attempting to turn one's living, breathing body into a stone Buddha is of course an impossible challenge. Curbing craving and desire, attempting to 'manage' strong feelings and emotions – all those unruly passions chastised by philosophers and religious people since ancient times – becoming, in short, a mindful Buddhist '24/7' is a mighty task indeed. Born and raised a Catholic, I often associated contemplation with atonement and repentance. With hindsight, I can now see that the first couple of years of my Zen training were done in a spirit of purging 'bad behaviour'. I harboured the secret hope that by doing this difficult spiritual thing as often and intensely as I could – essentially intensive Zen retreats and regular meditation – the scales of my personal karma would tip towards the good. I may have not thought these exact thoughts, but this was the gist. This is not to say that repentance only applies to Catholics. Other religious and secular systems of thought have their own particular angle on this and find their own way to articulate the very same denigration of life.

The other pitfall is exaltation. It is often preceded by the expectation that something special will happen through concentrated practice: enlightenment, *satori*, the 'great death' or at the very least some interesting insight. Inevitably, this is followed by the recognition that something *did* happen, despite the fact that in my case the world failed to take notice. The sun rose the next day as it always does. The rain and the snow kept falling accordingly. No one stopped on their way to work during rush hour to gaze in wonder at the formidably meditative aura emanating from my person. In those early days, exaltation often took a romantic turn. I would invariably get enamoured of some silent retreatant. Something in the shape of her nose, perhaps, or the poise, or her meditative gait, the way she might place her meditation cushion before settling for *zazen* would make me think that she had all the attributes I sought in a woman. I can't think of those days without a mixture of wistfulness and amusement. I was also prone to intellectual exaltation, believing that I had found novel ways to articulate the beauty and complexity of the Dharma. Perhaps I still am prone to this particular type of rapture and even wonder if some of that is spurring me on to write this book.

What is common to both mortification and exaltation is narcissism, broadly understood here as a deep concern about 'me'. That there may be narcissistic traits to exaltation is not, I believe, too far-fetched an idea. But that this should apply to mortification may sound strange. How could the desire for repentance and atonement deserve the charge of narcissism? This is because the notion that I am bad substantiates what in essence does not inherently exist. By looking more closely, one may find that often there is an over-riding preoccupation for the unique nature of my wickedness. This is as vain (both futile and vainglorious) as an exaggerated sense of one's own goodness. At a more immediate, sensorial level, what one may try to escape from in this case is a neutral feeling tone, which becomes unpleasant if not accurately perceived and apprehended: *drama*. Even the drama of wickedness is more entertaining and more desirable than the neutral feeling tone that is often perceived as boring, empty, or at times threatening. If understood, the neutral feeling tone may be perceived as restfulness (Martine Batchelor, 2012, personal communication).

At the opposite pole of narcissism is humility. It is important, however, to rescue the term from moral and religious pieties and the unspoken saintly will-to-power that effectively states, when one reads in between the lines: 'I'm a *most* humble person'. Perhaps a better word, a Zen word, is ordinariness. As in the Zen saying *ordinary mind is the Way*, i.e. not putting another head over the one we already have; not attempting to become someone we are not: not attempting a nobler, more spiritual version of me but becoming unapologetically who I already happen to be. At closer scrutiny, this may bring about the realization that I don't really know who I am. I'll have to find out by taking action and then, retrospectively, recognizing my own imprint in a particular deed. This brings to mind the work of David Bowie. Cliché dictated that the various 'personas' this great artist embodied throughout his life were *chameleonic* re-inventions, ways to mimic an imagined, dramatic backdrop with which he would supposedly market his next move. My own impression is that his was an exquisite example of an aesthetic of inauthenticity that also hinted at concrete, earthly reality – an art that is a 'radically contrived and reflexively aware confection of illusion whose fakery is not false, but at the service of felt, corporeal truth' (Critchley, 2014, p. 54). At a time when global politics and culture are dominated by personalities and a facile rhetoric of genuineness, Bowie's deep ambivalence intimated the fluid, insubstantial nature of what we call 'self'.

References

Adorno, T. (1998). *Beethoven: the Philosophy of Music*. Cambridge: Polity Press.

Ames, R. (1991). The Mencian conception of Ren Xing: Does it mean human nature? In H. Rosemont (Ed.), *Chinese Texts and Philosophical Contexts* (pp. 72–90). La Salle, IL: Open Court.

Bazzano, M. (2012). *Spectre of the Stranger: Towards a Phenomenology of Hospitality*. Eastbourne: Sussex Academic Press.

Bazzano, M. (2016a). Vulnerability and resilience. *Therapy Today*, 27(10): pp. 18–21.

Bazzano, M. (2016b). Changelings: the self in Nietzsche's psychology. In M. Bazzano & J. Webb (Eds), *Therapy and the Counter-tradition: The Edge of Philosophy* (pp. 9–22). Abingdon: Routledge.

Benjamin, W. (1999). *The Arcades Project*. London: Belknap Press.

Critchley, S. (2014). *Bowie*. New York and London: OR Books.

Deleuze, G. & Guattari, F. (1987). *A Thousand Plateaus*. Minneapolis: University of Minneapolis Press.

Derrida, J. (1976). *Of Grammatology*. Baltimore: John Hopkins.

Dōgen, E. (1233). Actualizing the fundamental point (Genjōkōan). The zen site, http://thezensite.com/ZenTeachings/Dogen_Teachings/GenjoKoan_Aitken.htm Retrieved 18 August 2016.

Friedman, W. (2013). Dan Yankelovich honoured for excellence in public opinion research. www.publicagenda.org/blogs/dan-yankelovich-honored-for-excellence-in-public-opinion-research Accessed 17 June 2016.

Goldstein, K. (1995). *The Organism*. New York: Urzone.

Hegel, G. F. W. (1977). *Phenomenology of Spirit*. Oxford: Oxford University Press.

Heidegger, M. (1962). *Being and Time*. New York: Harper & Row.

House, R. (2016). Beyond the measureable. Alternatives to managed care in research and practice. In J. Lees (Ed.), *The Future of Psychological Therapy* (pp. 146–164). Abingdon: Routledge.

Levinas, E. (2001). *Existence and Existents*. Pittsburgh, PA: Duquesne University Press.

Lopez, D. S. Jr. (2012). *The Scientific Buddha: His Short and Happy Life*. New Haven and London: Yale University Press.

Magliola, R. (1984). *Derrida on the Mend*. West Lafayette, IN: Purdue University Press.

Maslow, A. (1962). *Toward a Psychology of Being*. Princeton, NJ: Princeton University Press.

Matthews, M. D. (2014). *Head Strong: How Psychology is Revolutionizing War*. New York: Oxford University Press.

Mearns, D. & Thorne, B. (2007). *Person-centred Counselling in Action*. London: Sage.

Pippin, R. B. (2006). Agent and deed in the genealogy of morals. In K. Ansell Pearson (Ed.), *A Companion to Nietzsche* (pp. 371–386). Oxford: Blackwell.

Nietzsche, F. (1996). *On the Genealogy of Morality*. New York: Cambridge University Press.

Rogers, C. R. (1951). *Client-centered Therapy: Its Current Practice, Implications and Theory*. London: Constable.

Rogers, C. R. (1961). *On Becoming a Person*. London: Constable.

Rogers, C. R. (1980). *A Way of Being*. New York: Houghton Mifflin.

Said, E. (2008). *On Late Style*. London: Bloomsbury.

Schwartz, R. (1997). *The Curse of Cain: The Violent Legacy of Monotheism*. Chicago, IL: University of Chicago Press.

Seligman, M. (2006). *Learned Optimism: How to Change your Mind and your Life*. London: Vintage.

Tóibín, C. (2015). Late Francis Bacon: Spirit and substance. *New York Review of Books*, http://nybooks.com/articles/2015/11/19/late-francis-bacon-spirit-and-substance Retrieved 16 August 2016.

Vattimo, G. (2005). *Dialogue with Nietzsche*. New York: Columbia University Press.

2

ALL'S WELL THAT ENDS

On living-and-dying

Alive or dead?

A Zen practitioner called Yuan and his teacher Wu went to a house to pay their respects to an acquaintance who had died. Once there, Yuan knocked on the coffin and asked his teacher: 'Alive or dead?' to which Wu replied: 'I won't say'. He can't simply say: it is death. There is more than death here. You can't say: it is life. There is more than life here. It's *deathlife* or *lifedeath*. Yuan asked again but Wu gave the same answer. Later, on their way back, Yuan asked his teacher again. 'If you don't tell me – he added – I'll hit you'. 'Hit me if you want, but I won't say' was Wu's reply. Yuan hit him. Sometime later, after Wu had passed away, Yuan went to see another teacher called Shih Shuang, and brought up the story, repeating his question. 'I won't say' Shuang replied. 'Why?' Yuan asked. 'I won't say' Shuang repeated. In hearing these words, Yuan experienced a breakthrough (Cleary & Cleary, 1992).

Mortal immortality

When I was about 12 years old, my parents thought I was a strange boy. In the summer my cousin would come to visit from Northern Italy and I'd take him to see the town. Mostly though, I was keen to show him my favourite place – the cemetery. I knew the long walk by heart, past the outskirts of my home town, trudging a small empty road and then the steep path up the hill. On the way, we'd pick blackberries and stain our lips and fingers with their red juice before reaching the sombre gates. Italian cemeteries are grim, all stone and marble and putrid flowers, with the hard-up dead stacked up in mini tower blocks and the prosperous tidily trapped for perpetuity amid their relatives in the black marble of brash family chapels. There is none of the leafy, understated serenity of the Presbyterian graveyard. As a boy I was awestruck all the same and I still can't say why. Probably a mixture of things: the comforting silence, the sense of mystery, the treat of being left all alone with my own thoughts.

Last summer I stopped to watch a long cortege of big black cars going by in New York City's Chinatown. They all followed the hearse and a car with its open boot bursting with flowers. They drove through the red traffic lights with dignity and the sovereign disregard of rules that is or should be afforded by the dead. I took off my hat as I always do when I see a funeral. This is an old habit of mine, almost mechanical but also a swift reminder to myself, a sign of respect too for the unknown life that was. That in some places in the world the dead should be buried outside the town is only one of the manifold signs of our very real denial of death. Confining the dead has grown parallel to detaining madness, waywardness and criminality, and could be seen as a defining feature of modern civilization. Even the more pragmatic secularist approach, however, as for instance keeping the deceased's ashes on a mantelpiece as well as their expedient scattering, may be seen as a case of death hiding in plain sight. This is perhaps due to the fact that no matter what strategy one adopts death remains unreal to the living. But its denial cannot be denied; it is alive and well and in recent years has reached new heights. We now live in times of unprecedentedly acute geriatric care, a scenario not out of place in *Gulliver's Travels* (Swift, 1992). In Jonathan Swift's eighteenth-century sardonic tour de force, the protagonist tells us of Luggnagg, an island where humankind's seemingly universal desire for lasting life was granted. The island was populated by the Struldbruggs, people who lived forever while growing older and older: they would lose their hair and teeth at 90, have no sense of taste or appetite, their illnesses would go on without getting better or worse. When talking, they forgot names of things, places and people – even those near to them. They couldn't enjoy reading because memory fails them from one sentence to the next.

> The language of this country being always upon the flux, the Struldbruggs of one age do not understand those of another, neither are they able after two hundred years, to hold any conversation . . . with their neighbours the mortal; and thus they live under the disadvantage of living like foreigners in their own country.
>
> *Swift, 1992, p. 161*

The above was such a mortifying sight that, as a result, the natural appetite for life was greatly diminished among the rest of the island inhabitants. Our desire to live at any cost is only half of the story when we also consider that everlasting life may well be a veritable nightmare. The other half of the truth is that we also want to die and that our ability to appreciate life's beauty is parallel to our awareness of its ephemeral nature.

A more appealing example of 'mortal immortality' is found in Greek myth. Tithonus 'was granted immortal age but not immortal youth . . . by his love Aurora, the goddess of dawn' (Burrow, 2016, p. 15). Similar stories of longing for eternal repetition are found in the Danaides, fated to carry water in sifters, and in the well-known tale of Sisyphus, condemned for eternity to roll a boulder uphill only to watch it roll back down again. Becoming forever older, Tithonus waits for dawn, for his love Aurora, for eternity. The poetic beauty and power of these various images do not conceal the perpetual dismay of the conditions each of these characters is locked in.

The freedom to choose death

Our notion of freedom would be incomplete without our freedom to choose death. For Primo Levi, 'suicide is an act of will, a free decision' (in Lieberg & Parks, 2015, p. 100). This is a thorny subject, however, as a recent discussion on the circumstances of the death of Levi confirms. A reader objected to the writer Tim Parks's description of Levi's death in 1987 as '[throwing] himself down the stairwell [as] grossly unfair to the man and his work' and in contradiction to the 'whirl of activities' (Lieberg & Parks, 2015, p. 100) he was absorbed in until the fateful day. In his reply, Parks wrote:

> Given that Levi's instinct was always to encourage the reader to confront the hardest facts and not take refuge in any comfort zone, we owe it to him to acknowledge the overwhelming evidence of the way he died. His suicide does not diminish his work or his dignity. He was not obliged to his readers to behave in a reassuring way or protect the illusions they had built around his person
>
> *Lieberg & Parks, 2015, p. 100*

The wish to die, whether or not explicitly articulated and acted out, is as important as our wish to live. Failing to uphold one or the other is a classic blunder in psychotherapy. Fortunately, I learned this particular lesson early on in my work when, still a trainee, I found myself working for several months with a client who often presented, as the rather abstract formulation in the trade has it, 'suicidal ideation'. Overwhelmed by ethical codes and concerns and the tangible sense of risk, during one session I heard myself saying to the client: 'Please don't do it'. He was very disappointed. These were the words everyone around him would say. His hope was that to a counsellor at least he could speak freely about wanting to die without being judged. The very difficult challenge here is to effectively suspend the Hippocratic Oath and redress the ethical notion of benevolence to include respect for the client's autonomy. With hindsight, I reluctantly had to agree with Pasolini who understood freedom as the freedom to choose death (Pasolini, 2005). He also wrote, with a characteristic film-maker twist, that death operates a fundamental *montage* (cutting, editing) to the 'untranslatable . . . chaos of possibilities' of our existence:

> *Death* . . . chooses the truly meaningful moments . . . puts them in a sequence, transforming an infinite, unstable and uncertain . . . present into

a clear, stable, certain, and therefore easily describable past . . . *It is only thanks to death that our life serves us to express ourselves.*

Ibid, pp. 236–237, italics in the original

If one agrees on the notion that fundamentally death is a taboo, then an imaginative, 'right brain' type of response may include investigating it and attempting to incorporate its ramifications into the everyday. The cliché that contemplation of death may be enlivening bears some truth after all. On the other hand, a unilateral 'left brain' response will attempt to grasp death consciously and perhaps even sanitize or bend the potent taboo it represents for the ultimate benefit of society, which is why suicide is a crime for the law and a sin for religion (Hillman, 1978). As a society, we instinctively avert our collective gaze from the sight of the grim reaper, particularly when it materializes in the abrupt semblance of suicide. The law orders us to live, unless of course we can be put to good use as cannon fodder. Religion sees suicide as self-homicide, an act of conceit against God's plans for us. But (some) philosophers beg to differ. Here is David Hume:

If Suicide be supposed a crime, it is only cowardice can impel us to it. If it be no crime, both prudence and courage should engage us to rid ourselves at once of existence, when it becomes a burthen. It is the only way that we can then be useful to society, by setting an example, which, if imitated, would preserve to every one his chance for happiness in life, and would effectually free him from all danger of misery.

Hume, 2005, p. 10

The stance of a Zen practitioner who is willing to contemplate death and that of the therapist who is open to converse about suicide with a potentially suicidal client go against collective moral opinion, for in both cases the customs and social mores of the ethical dimension are suspended in the name of ethics. Their stance also challenges the medical, *quantitative* understanding of what constitutes the 'good life', usually measured in terms of growth and longer life rather than in terms of *meaning*. For Hillman (1978), suicide is at heart a demand for a fuller life through death, and our repudiation of empathizing with the experience of those who are driven towards it makes the power of death all the more daunting: 'organic death has absolute power over life when death has not been allowed in life's midst' (ibid, p. 62). But the outcome of our repudiation of death is effectively a duller existence, a life half-lived, for unless 'we can say no to life, we have not really said yes to it' (ibid, pp. 63–64). It may be that unless we come near the threshold and the 'threshold experience' (Bazzano & Webb, 2016, p. 7) – as discussed in the Introduction – we cannot experience life fully. In Zen we speak of living-and-dying (*shōji*) as one and the same, rather than pitting them as *Eros* and *Thanatos* in endless scuffle (the latter is a misleading interpretation: for the Greeks, Eros and Thanatos were joined at the hip; worshipping one always meant remembering the other).

Dāna or generosity

If for a moment we compare the will to live to our desire for self-preservation, could the will to die be likened to the will to give, to give oneself, and, in a manner of speaking, give oneself up? Far from being gruesome, this stance may be understood, in Zen terms, as *dāna* or generosity – the first of the six Buddhist *paramitas* or 'virtues'. Thus apprehended, this particular virtue would then entail freedom from self-boundedness, greater power of thought and action outside the narrow confines of *me* and *mine*. This would mean that beyond the conventional reading of *dāna* as charity and the giving of alms to monastics lies a deeper meaning, one that is at the opposite end of self-preservation, and may be close to the notion of *grace* (Bazzano, 2006), understood as 'giving more than one owes and receiving more than one deserves' (Wills, 2015, p. 13).

Could it be then that what we call the spiritual or religious life begins with glimpses of a way of being that is not entirely dominated by survival? And if so, what would the implications and consequences of this insight be in relation to the dominant survivalist narratives of evolution?

Of thanatologists

Loosely inspired by Epicurus, one of Irvin Yalom's books is boldly titled *Staring at the Sun* (Yalom, 2008). The title reverses La Rochefoucauld's celebrated maxim according to which we cannot stare directly into the face of the sun, or death. By overturning the aphorism and inviting us to confront our own eventual demise squarely by taking 'a full unwavering look at death' (p. 275), Yalom neglects the subtlety of the aphorism. His stance is common among thanatologists (death specialists, from *Thanatos*, death) of all ages and persuasions. The zeal to confront death is such that they overlook two essential things indicated in La Rochefoucauld: a) staring at death is an act of arrogance; and b) like the sun, death is benevolent, 'a counterpart to the great source of life, the sun' (Ricks, 1993, p. 20): we will benefit from both *as long as* we don't eyeball them with our insensitive stare.

Of course thanatologists are well-intentioned. They want to inject a little depth in the ailing body of humanistic psychology, an orientation all too keen to be out with the transpersonal fairies. They redirect the focus from the apparent narcissism of self-actualization to the more nuanced narcissism of being-towards-death, a notion borrowed from Heidegger. In both cases the preponderance of the ego in the psychic landscape remains intact as starry-eyed stabs at manifesting one's potential give way to graver but equally self-mesmerized exercises in confronting death. Coming out of these with a sense of having attained heroic self-transfiguration, the new adept is eager to spread the Gospel of Authenticity. Having indelicately scrutinized death, he now subjects his own existence to the self-punishing enterprise of filtering the authentic from the inauthentic, the real from the false self. So far, so inconsequential; trouble is, emboldened by the newly found truths and brandishing a set of peculiar new words, he then goes off labelling his unsuspecting clients, their bearings and beliefs, making damn sure, now that their more traditional, medical labels start to wear off, that they are comfortably re-pathologized as 'inauthentic' or 'incongruent'.

The above trajectory is the price we pay as therapists if we decide to bypass Freud rather than assimilate him. Needless to say, the tag under the price bears Heidegger's name and logo. Some of us resorted to Heidegger because we dismissed Freud in haste and without understanding him. The rejection of the death principle came back to haunt us as being-towards-death. But in early psychoanalysis at least the death instinct and pleasure principle are intertwined and linked to a dimension deemed from the start ungraspable to the naked eye of consciousness – this is not quite so with Freud, but certainly with Otto Rank, especially from the time of his American lectures, when he began distancing himself from the former (Rank, 1996).

Another rationalist response to death is the naturalist view. This differs somewhat from ontotheology and draws, among others, from Darwin and Freud. This particular perspective refreshingly lacks the transfigurative overtones of 'being-towards-death'. It aims instead at accepting death as an organizing principle, understanding the sadness death gives rise to as a kind of old habit that takes place as a result of our refusal to accept the reality of life. As Adam Phillips notes in a memorable turn of phrase, apart from humans 'nothing else in nature seems so grief-stricken or impressed by its own dismay' (Phillips, 2001, p. 15). The old rationalist assumption is that we could somehow be cured of the consternation death provokes in us and work through our discomfort towards a more liberated, neo-Epicurean and neo-Stoic mode of being.

The assumption on both ends of the rationalist stance is that the implacable presence of death can be 'mediated, comprehended, and hence taken over by human subjectivity in ontological terms' (Rapaport, 2003, p. 110).

Not staring at death or the sun is not a symptom of denial but a sign of common-sense wisdom. Staring at the sun will blind us. Staring at death will obliterate our judgement. And here lies the wide gulf between Zen and latter-day thanatologists.

Staring is an act of hubris – the arrogant stance of a finite being in the face of infinity, the tragicomic, Promethean gesture of wanting to steal what is freely available. It shows, as Thomas Merton would say, the inability to comprehend 'the liberality of God' (Merton, 2003, p. 24). The word 'staring' comes from old English *starian*, of Germanic origin, whose root meaning is rigidity. Hurried arrogance, implicit in the act of staring, wrongly assumes that death is the enemy, a necessary evil, an opponent who invites us to a confrontation that will either annihilate or fortify us. It assumes that the over-riding will in humans is self-preservation. It wilfully ignores that alongside it there lives in us an equally potent urge: the desire for oblivion.

Contemplation of death makes us more aware of its benign effects. But this contemplation is *indirect* and subtle. It can be pursued in meditation, approached through the mirror of art and literature, and addressed through therapy. All of these are art forms, given that they help us contemplate the dark sun of death without being annihilated in the process. 'Indirect' is the key word here; it indicates ambiguity; it is the reflection of the moon on the lake rather than the moon itself. Seen through art, our situation appears both tragic and comic. Pathos and irony may not walk hand-in-hand in great literature and great art, but one is often backstage and ready to come in anytime the other gets the limelight. Staring at life and death without the mediating effect of art, however, we become more easily prone to the generalities of literalism. The closer a meditative practice or therapeutic approach is to art, the better its chances of circumventing the narrow path of reductivism.

Those who incite us to stare at the burning star of death assume that it is possible to become intimate with the mystery of living-and-dying and acquire knowledge of 'the things themselves' by an act of will. This is the standard error of rationalism, both in its materialist version (as with Yalom), and in the spiritualist (as with most believers in the afterlife). When I wrote to Yalom explaining some of my objections, he kindly suggested I take a close look at the writings of Epicurus. I did, and in reading (or rather re-reading) him, I found much that is remarkable. First of all, his genuine imperturbability in the face of death: where death is, I am not, he would say, so why make so much fuss? Then, his endorsement of what he considered the highest values: serene joy, sober conviviality and, above all, warm, inspired conversation and sincere friendship (*philia*). The latter, when untainted by the demon of profit and gain, he saw as the bedrock for philosophy, a discipline that is born in living and breathing conversation. Epicurus and his circle of philosophizing friends exude twilight quietude, all human passions becalmed by the practice of *ataraxía* (imperturbability), which was the very aim of philosophy for many of its practitioners, including Socrates and the Stoics, during the four and a half centuries before the advent of Christianity.

I believe, however, that the gap dividing us from Epicurus is nearly unbridgeable – 2,300 years have elapsed. Christianity instigated a sea change in worldview. In the small pond of humanistic/existential therapy in which Yalom swims, the tackling of the death problem is coloured by Heidegger and his notion of 'being-towards-death'. Here is to be found the true source of the staring.

Staring is the opposite of avoidance. When I deny the reality of death I do so forcibly, averting my gaze with an act of will from a truth that terrifies me, or directing it instead towards trivial distractions. The decision to stare wrenches me from my self-imposed aloofness and aversion. I hold my breath, psyching myself up in my titanic confrontation with the grim reaper. The person who contemplates death is, on the other hand, prepared to play chess with her and in the pauses of the drawn-out game enjoys a strawberry or two.

By averting my gaze, I hide. I entomb myself in the vain hope that death will miss my whereabouts and will walk on. Then, in a burst of overconfidence, I leap out of my enclosure and call out to death: *I'm here! I'm ready. Come back! I want to look at you straight in the eye!* Death retraces her steps and comes closer to this neo-stoic, neo-existentialist fellah. She takes one abstracted look at me and dismisses me with a wry smile and a wave of her left hand. As she walks on, I hear her whisper to herself, *not now. Not yet.* I tremble with fear, but regain my composure after a while. Then I begin to feel strangely animated, even a little manic perhaps. I tell myself I have stared at death in the face – without blinking. The 'being-towards-death' I recall reading about in a handout at my existential counselling training has now been duly experienced. I passed the test. Now I will tell clients, supervisees and colleagues right from wrong, authentic from inauthentic. My own sense of self has been strengthened and with it the chance of gaining real insight has been lost. If you could hear me think, it would be the same conceited, literalist claim that since Socrates and the Stoics echoes through the history of our overrated species: 'I made it. I have won the mighty battle with death'.

Famous last words

Influenced by ancient Chinese poetry, the writing of a short death poem or 'farewell poem to life' (*jisei*) is a centuries-old practice both in Japan and within the Zen tradition, but if you expect religious pieties, you'll be disappointed. Tendo-Nyojo (1163–1228) declared that he had lived 66 years piling up sins and was now ready to leap into hell. In some of these poems, life is described as dew on the grass, appearing briefly and then disappearing. We don't know life, we don't know death either. Hakuin recommends for the young to die now (by which he means to see through the insubstantiality of the self), so that they won't have to die again when death knocks at the door. Another Zen teacher, Deshimaru (2016), describes meditation itself as a kind of death: 'you should practice *zazen* as though you were entering your coffin' (p. 10).

Once a few disciples gathered at the deathbed of a Zen teacher to hear the last nuggets of wisdom from the great man. The teacher, hearing a creaking sound on the ceiling cried out, 'What is that?' and then expired. The question can of course be construed as a profound teaching on not knowing. Some would read it that way given the current penchant for PhDs in Unknowing and Professorships of Uncertainty. My guess is that 'What is that?' means just that, i.e. 'What is that sound I'm hearing?' There has also been a case of a renowned Zen teacher on his deathbed uttering the very unspiritual words 'I don't want to die' to his disciples hungry for spiritual mementos. But the poignancy and truthfulness of the statement (especially considering that the impending death was in this case premature) feels far more meaningful than any high-minded cliché on 'acceptance'.

I also find the two accounts below touching, regardless of the tidiness of reports of this kind that inevitably overlook the gritty reality. I mention them here partly as a little tribute to these two great writers but most of all because, despite the fact neither of them had been associated with Zen or Buddhism, they nevertheless found in their last days an immediate connection to the Dharma.

Days before James Hillman's death in the autumn of 2011, on a little table by his bedside, in the living room of his home with a large window overlooking a glorious New England autumn, there was an anthology of *haiku* poetry by Zen monks, one of which, written by Fukyu, rejoiced in the brightness of the autumn day, a most auspicious day for death's journey.

The poet Wallace Stevens, on his deathbed, complained to his daughter of visits he received by a priest but added that he felt far too weak to protest. Then he requested to his daughter that she bring to the hospital a small jade Buddha from the home. During his last week of life, he turned it over and over in his hands.

'Gotta move on'

The segment in psychotherapy training that deals with death and bereavement is often shaped by the influential writings of psychiatrist Elizabeth Kübler-Ross (2005; 2014). It has been said, tongue-in-cheek, that before her work came along 'people used to die; now they have end-of-life issues' (Mars-Jones, 2015, p. 3). Working as a psychiatrist in 1960s America, she was struck by the stark cultural differences between the way people died in her native Switzerland, usually surrounded by family and friends, and how things were in the US where, despite high-tech medicine (Newman, 2004), they were frequently left isolated. Crucially, Kübler-Ross' initial focus was on the dying person and on better communication between doctors and patients. Based on her interviews with dying patients at the University of Chicago Billings Hospital, she hypothesized, as many readers will know, the existence of five stages of emotions experienced by terminally ill patients, namely: *denial, anger, bargaining, depression* and *acceptance* (Kübler-Ross, 2014). To understand how essential her work was at the time, one must remember that death was not really thought of as an event in the lives of doctors and nurses but rather a condemnation of their abilities (Mars-Jones, 2015).

The five-stages model was quickly applied first to the bereaved and then, in a fascinating cultural twist, to *any* experience of loss such as relocating, retirement, separation and divorce. Both Kübler-Ross and the co-author of her last two books, David Kessler, are keen to emphasize that the stages are neither linear nor prescriptive. Yet, as often happens with ideas of this kind that seep into the wider culture, this is exactly what has taken place. An assumption begins to take root that says that there is something wrong if one does not go through the stages.

I remember a facilitator asking some ten years ago in a group setting whether a protracted feeling of bereavement could be legitimately considered as a kind of pathology. The question, provocatively posed, had the desired effect to spark a lively discussion. I did wonder though whether it uncannily reflected what I perceive as the incessant and widespread incitement of an efficiency-oriented culture to 'move on' – so that we can go back to working and shopping. In some cases, the question is whether 'closure', that shibboleth of therapy culture, is really ever possible. As with being-towards-death, the notion of linearity in matters of living-and-dying may be expedient in a didactic sort of way but it does not particularly reflect reality: Adam Mars-Jones (2015) writes:

> We seem to have a need to imagine dying as a plenary session of consciousness, and to forget that the boundary between life and death is porous, full of intermediate states and no-man's-lands.
>
> *p. 8*

The expectation in some spiritual and therapy circles is that a person who has meditated and/or 'worked on herself' will be a model of serenity. For people who idolized Kübler-Ross, there was an expectation of her dying an exemplary 'good death' in the manner of the sages of old. Instead, she died an ordinary death. Not only that, but some were shocked to find that in the last years of her life she had become very angry and did not fit into the fantasy of the benevolent and serene old woman (Todd, 2004). Her anger was directed at God for depriving her of mobility and of the only few joys left in life. But I find this preferable and more real than the inane 'Zen' serenity people expected of her.

Endings and meditation on death

If it is true that, as I believe, the psychology of loss and bereavement has been applied a little too indiscriminately to all instances of change and separation, it is also true that there is an important link between loss and endings in therapy. This is the place where, for Otto Rank (1996), the essential part of therapeutic work takes place. Endings here also represent new beginnings. There is joy as well as pain in separation, and an ending here also means birth, venturing out into the world after the separation from the therapist-midwife. This re-enactment of birth is the final aim of therapy. There is an ending in sight, the final stage in the journey where Theseus finds his way out of the labyrinth and is born into ordinary unhappiness, leaving behind the 'neurotic' or 'incongruent' part of suffering. Lingering on would be fatal; it would mean, as Kramer says, inspired by Otto Rank:

> remaining chained to the mother . . . or its surrogate, the therapist, is the equivalent of refusing to separate from outworn parts of the I – clinging painfully to fears and desires like a child to a discarded toy.
>
> *Kramer, 1995, p. 9*

When therapy is protracted for too long, both therapist and client risk being doomed to 'a watery death, entombed forever in the labyrinthine womb' (Kramer, 1995, ibid) of the counselling room. The ending can be a reminder, as well as a deliberate affirmation of our strange existence of transient beings, a strangeness that therapy addresses in the first place. It does so when it does not let us get away with our astounding talent for forgetting that we are born to die, and that we are now alive.

Zen does the same in its own way. Rather than staring at death, at the moment of his own demise the Buddha warmly exhorts us to contemplate impermanence:

> Then the Blessed One addressed the brethren, and said, 'behold now, brethren, I exhort you, saying, Decay is inherent in all component things. Work out your salvation with diligence'. This was the last word of the Tathāgata.
>
> *Davids, 1985, p. 114*

I end this chapter with a brief outline of the canonical Buddhist reflection on death, which invites us to consider the following three questions. Whether we find ourselves sitting on a meditation cushion, driving, cooking or doing whatever, we ask ourselves: a) is death unavoidable?; b) when will it happen?; and c) what will be meaningful at the moment of dying? The answer to the first question is pretty obvious: it is a resounding 'yes'. And yet we manage to forget it all the time. The answer to the second question is: anytime. But we manage to put aside this obvious answer and live our lives thinking that at the earliest we'll die is 'only when we reach the statistical life expectancy for our gender or ethnicity' (Higgins, 2016, p. 41). As for the third question, the idea is to pose it right now rather than wait until death comes. We then break it down into further direct questions: What is most meaningful to me right now? What do I value and cherish most? If I am not doing that at present, what would then be the first step in that direction?

References

Bazzano, M. (2006). *Buddha is Dead: Nietzsche and the Dawn of European Zen*. Eastbourne, Sussex and Portland, OR: Sussex Academic Press.

Bazzano, M. & Webb, J. (Eds). (2016). *Therapy and the Counter-tradition: The Edge of Philosophy*. London: Routledge.

Burrow, C. (2016). On Alice Oswald. *London Review of Books*, 38(18): 22 September, p. 15.

Cleary, T. & Cleary, J. C. (1992). *The Blue Cliff Record*. Boston and London: Shambala.

Davids, R. (Trans.). (1985). *Buddhist Suttas*. The Sacred Books of the East, Vol. XI. Oxford: The Clarendon Press.

Deshimaru, T. (2016). A list of question and answers, http://abuddhistlibrary.com/Buddhism/C%20-%20Zen/Modern%20Teachers/Deshimaru%20Roshi/Questions%20and%20Answers/Questions%20and%20Answers.pdf Retrieved 14 February 2016.

Higgins, W. (2016). Treading the path with care. *Tricycle: the Buddhist Review*, Winter: 38–41.

Hillman, J. (1978). *Suicide and the Soul*. Washington, DC: Spring Publications.

Hume, D. (2005). *Of Suicide*. London: Penguin.

Kramer, R. (1995). Insight and blindness: Visions of rank. In O. Rank (Ed.) *A psychology of difference: The American lectures* (pp. 3–50). Princeton, NJ: Princeton University Press.

Kübler-Ross, E. (2005). *On Grief and Grieving: Finding the Meaning of Grief through the Five Stages of Loss*. New York: Simon & Schuster.

Kübler-Ross, E. (2014). *On Death and Dying: What The Dying Have to Teach Doctors, Nurses, Clergy and Their Own Families*. New York: Simon & Schuster.

Lieberg, C. & Parks, T. (2015). How did he die? An exchange. *The New York Review of Books*, 17 December, p. 100.

Mars-Jones, A. (2015). Chop, chop, chop. *London Review of Books*, 38(2): 21 January, pp. 3–8.

Merton, T. (2003). *The New Man*. London: Continuum.

Newman, L. (2004). Elizabeth Kübler-Ross. *British Medical Journal*, 329: 11 September, p. 627.

Pasolini, P. P. (2005). *Heretical Empiricism*. Translated by B. Lawton & L. K. Barnett. Washington, DC: New Academia Publishing.

Phillips, A. (2001). *Darwin's Worms: On Life Stories and Death Stories*. New York: Basic Books.

Rank, O. (1996). *A Psychology of Difference: The American Lectures*. Selected, edited and introduced by R. Kramer. Princeton, NJ: Princeton University Press.

Rapaport, H. (2003). *Later Derrida: Reading the Recent Work*. London: Routledge.

Ricks, C. (1993). *Beckett's Dying Words*. Oxford and New York: Oxford University Press.

Swift, J. (1992). *Gulliver's Travels*. London: Wordsworth Classics.

Todd, P. (2004). *A Quiet Courage: Inspiring Stories from All of Us*. Toronto, ON: Thomas Allen.

Wills, G. (2015). The mind as a beautiful miracle. *The New York Review of Books*, 17 December, pp. 13–14.

Yalom, I. D. (2008). *Staring at the Sun: Overcoming the Terror of Death*. San Francisco, CA: Jossey-Bass.

3

ZEN AND THERAPY

Two expressions of unconditional hospitality

Blue angel

In Takeshi Kitano's bittersweet, quirky road movie *Kikujiro* (Kitano, 1999), the director plays the eponymous hero, a small-time crook who is convinced by his wife to accompany Masao, a 9-year-old boy on his long journey to Toyohashi, where his long-lost mother is living. The two unlikely companions hitch-hike across Japan meeting all sorts of people, from a molester to a juggler to bikers and a travelling poet who takes them on the last leg of their journey to Toyohashi. In the course of their adventure Masao and Kikujiro live by their wits and the generosity of strangers. The happy reunion between the boy and his mother never materializes. The boy's mother lives a different life – she has forgotten him, Kikujiro discovers. He decides to tell Masao that she does not live there anymore and then tries to console the boy with a toy, a tiny blue angel he has taken from two bikers. On their journey back, Kikujiro cheers the boy up with one hilarious and bizarre trick after another. The two become close; both of them, we discover, have effectively lost their mother. The people they meet on their journey back to Tokyo are drifters blessed with an innocent heart, similar to characters from a Fellinian circus or Pasolini's dispossessed who have nothing, but in a sense belong to the whole wide world. I may be reading too much into this warm, quietly formidable film, but the story and the way it is filmed conveyed to me our metaphysical homelessness in the world – a place in which we find ourselves thrown and one that remains, if not wholly foreign, at the very least unknowable.

Homeless vows

To romanticize the lives of drifters, travellers and people at the margins would mean conveniently glossing over the very real suffering and difficulties these lives entail.

Yet at the heart of Zen teachings, as I understand them, we find an emphasis on homelessness (*tokudo*). The person becoming ordained is said to embrace his/her metaphysical, symbolic and, at times, factual refusal of a permanent dwelling. This does not mean we cannot, or should not, make our home on earth. Nor is it an advocacy of uprootedness and of the spindrift gaze towards the heavens. It is important, however, to relativize somewhat the exaggerated importance our culture gives to territory, dwelling and identity and, in parallel, to notions of ownership, all tied to our Promethean attempts at gaining mastery over a world that is by definition excessive and out of our reach. The other important lesson one could learn from the poignant celebration of homelessness in *Kikujiro* is that it points beyond the *familial*, a domain within which all psychotherapies and psychologies have arguably become trapped. One way this could be translated and understood is that the work of therapy and the work of Zen deal with our desires and hatreds, our sorrows and fears in relation to the wide expanses of history and the world – hence not entirely apprehended and settled within the narrow province of family.

'Toska'

In Zen, a *bodhisattva* is a person capable of achieving personal liberation (nirvana) but who delays doing so through his/her compassion for suffering beings everywhere. A bodhisattva is a good host, a quality shared by a Zen practitioner as well as a therapist. Both aspire to offer *unconditional hospitality* – first of all to oneself through acceptance and self-compassion – as well as to others. Unconditional hospitality is a central idea in contemporary ethical philosophy and it has important implications for psychology (Bazzano, 2015). *Conditional* hospitality (in practice, the only hospitality we know) has not really worked. Born in the Greek *polis* and the Roman *forum,* developed further via the Judaeo-Christian tradition and Kantian/Hegelian philosophy, this type of hospitality is *juridical*: it is handled by codes, norms and regulations, and it is inscribed within the metaphysics of violence and coercion. We need a notion of unconditional hospitality because ethics without hospitality is, ultimately, no ethics at all. With this rather absolute-sounding statement I am not forgetting that ethics is always expressed contingently and imperfectly. But to be reminded of the impossibly unconditional nature of hospitality is a useful antidote, I believe, to moral self-congratulation.

We become good hosts by remembering that we are guests on earth, by temporarily interrupting the self and our habitual concerns about 'me' and 'mine' and also by reframing our notion of identity, including national identity. We become good hosts by remembering our condition of *existential homelessness*.

Once in a while I surprise myself, brooding over my seeming lack of patriotic feelings and earnestly wondering whether this is due to some congenital deficiency in my psychological make-up. I am not worried for the absence of nationalistic palpitations when I inadvertently hear the national anthem or glimpse the tricolored flag on a travel guide. I consider inflated attachments to motherlands and fatherlands to be a form of lunacy of the uncreative or 'normotic' kind: either proverbial last refuge of the scoundrel or frantic attempt to sing along and sing away one's fear of loneliness. But I do wonder whether having lived for over 30 years away from it made me scornful of any feelings towards my homeland. I know now that in the early years of living abroad an effective split had taken place: Italy had come to represent everything I loathed or was unable to love about my own identity: in humanistic psychology's lingo, a patchwork of conditions of worth and external loci of evaluation. 'Abroad' had conversely come to mean everything interesting, stimulating and new: the ever-shifting horizon, the future, a rich array of potentialities open to a 28-year-old man. It was only later that a strange new feeling began to emerge. I remember feeling overwhelmed a few years ago over the summer months by the pangs of the 'path not taken', namely by what my life would have become had I not left Italy for good in my late twenties. The trigger was a visit to Tuscany where I participated in a conference on Buddhism and Counselling, hosted by the institute where in 1978 I first encountered the Dharma in the person of Lama Yeshe (1935–1984), an outstanding Tibetan Lama with boundless wisdom, a heart of gold and founder of the Foundation for the Preservation of the Mahayana Tradition (FPMT). No doubt, the beauty of the area played a part. The scent and flavours of my early years, the sound of the wind in the pines, the exuberance and kindness of the people there, all conjured up a strange mix of nostalgia (from the Greek *nostos*, homecoming and *álgos*, pain) and mysterious longing, akin perhaps to what Russians call *toska*, an unspecified longing that finds no resting place in this or that object of desire. The fact that I did not resist this surge of feeling meant that for a few months over that summer I felt conflicted and split between my life in London and this vague call of the homeland. Somewhere within me I also mistrusted this very longing, and it wasn't until I had a conversation with a friend on a morning walk on Hampstead Heath in September that I began to gain some clarity. He too had felt this longing on certain spring and summer days whenever he came to Devon to facilitate retreats. The call of his native land was strong and real. The familiar gentleness of the hills at dusk lured him back to childhood days and at times it felt irresistible. For many years now, when not travelling the world because of work, he has happily lived in France. He had learned to resist the call of the past, and told me of a saying in Tibetan (a language he had learned when training as a Buddhist monk): *Payul pangwa jangsem lag-len yin*: 'to abandon one's land is the practice of the bodhisattva'. Appreciation of home-leaving and existential exile is at the heart of Zen. Counter-intuitive at first to our sensibilities and cultural conditioning, it soon begins to make sense once we allow ourselves to see the bigger picture. Putting aside our atavistic attachment to the *soil* (to which historically we have been willing to sacrifice life itself through countless wars), opens our sense of belonging to the *Earth*.

Red kites

Walking in the woods yesterday in the Chiltern Hills, an hour and a half journey from London, was a rare treat, a chink of time stolen from various chores. Autumn in its faded glory, nearly invisible in the city: we fell silent after a few minutes, the joy of walking rising like sap in the midday dappled glow. Out of the wood and under the open sky we spotted two red kites effortlessly gliding on powerful gusts of wind and circling above us, elegant and rapacious. I have never seen such birds before and I was mesmerized. They can be spotted here in the Chilterns; we kept seeing them on the motorway on the way back for a while and then no more. Do they belong to that area alone? I asked my partner if the quiet joy she felt was linked to a sense of place, to her memories and reverberations of a childhood and youth spent in England. Not particularly, she said, and did I remember our walk in the hills above Salt Lake City years ago at the time of our Zen training? There she felt the same joy despite the lack of past connections to the place. So maybe it was nature herself, we mused; coming near to living, silent things, feeling our own being merge and dissolve within the great family.

Each place if imbued with its distinctive neutral affect; it communicates to us if we pause, listen and feel; we are part of it – beating hearts, translucent flesh against the light, intermittent shadows on the ground as we struggle up and up the steep hill path. But I don't feel this is anything more than the wanderer's heartfelt temporary communion.

Indigenousness and nationalism

As a passer-by, my obligations are towards the place I happen to walk through. But the place does not belong to me. I am nowhere indigenous; nowhere can I make that claim because to make that claim is an act of arrogance: this I have learned from the teachings of the Buddha; this is also what contemporary ethical phenomenology taught me. I am supportive of the sacrosanct rights of indigenous people every-where whose land has been occupied and plundered: this is the infamous history of colonialism down to the occupation of Palestine in 1948, a history of abuse and prevarication. It is an act of violence and aggression to rob a people of their place. But I simply cannot join the present philistine chorus that in privileged parts of the globe erects fences, builds walls glorifying indigenousness and humiliates foreignness even when foreigners are indigent, desperate refugees running for their life. Traditionally, indigenousness has always been closely associated to racism, with the latter being the driving force of oppression and the irrational hatred of the other onto whom we project all that is disowned, undesirable and unacknowledged within us. Globalization later contributed to a fundamental shift towards forms of nationalism that 'officially . . . reject biological racism but by placing great emphasis on geographical origin and citizenship . . . are both exceptionalist and exclusive' (Bull, 2016, p. 10).

The fear of being uprooted has gone hand-in-hand in history with hatred for those who in one's eyes represent and embody uprootedness: Gypsies, Jews, Travellers, refugees and migrants. The common assumption held by the privileged citizen of a nation state is that he or she is on solid ground, a stance that does not take into account the momentous shift that has happened for some time now, namely, 'the destruction of the centuries-old horizon of meaning and ontological stability' (Viriasova, 2016, p. 225), what Nietzsche referred to as the death of God. In other words, *exile* – factual, ontological or symbolic – is our existential condition today. The resurgence of nationalism and xenophobia from the Little Englandism of *Brexit* to the guttural cries of making America 'great again' can be seen in this context, with their appeal to the most ungenerous parts of ourselves, as kneejerk, ultimately pointless reactions to the ineluctability of our situation. Others embraced this state of affairs, opting for *existential migration* (Madison, 2009), the choice to express a preference for the unfamiliar over the familiarity of the homeworld. Having come to the world of humanistic therapy partly via existentialism, I have always assumed that acceptance of otherness and of our ontological condition of exile is a given. The 'philosophy of existence' seemingly embraced our ontological condition of exile announced by Nietzsche. The very word existentialism, beginning with the prefix *ex* ('out' or 'out of') aligns it with *existence exile, exodus, exit, exteriority*; these words 'bear a meaning that is not negative' (Blanchot, 1993, p. 127), a meaning that challenges the sedentary predilection of the philosophical tradition for home, identity and self-sameness. It questions the centrality of the established *polis* in favour of a cosmopolitan community; it challenges a paradigm of homesickness that places the refugee and the exile in the 'inferior position of the supplicant' (Viriasova, 2016, p. 222).

Existentialism resisted the Platonism of the philosophical tradition and confronted its false hopes – self-identity, denial of the body, enclosure within the borders of the city and the state – in order to account for difference, displacement, nomadism and social and political solidarity. These values are, in my view, crucial to my work as a therapist. Does contemporary psychotherapy stand for any of them? As we shall see, this question is crucial in terms of how we understand the role of therapy in contemporary society.

Ethics and morality

It is now a duty in the UK for all public bodies, including the NHS, to educate their staff in recognizing and classifying people who are 'deemed "at risk" of extremism or radicalisation' with the aim to 'report them to the Government's anti-terrorism programme, *Channel*' (Rizq, 2016, p. 6). It is obligatory for psychotherapists working in the NHS to attend 'Prevent', a training session devised by the home office that 'aims to safeguard vulnerable people from being radicalized to supporting terrorism or becoming terrorists themselves' (Home Office, 2016, Internet file). Therapists are asked to work within what is called 'pre-criminal space', a notion which intriguingly first appeared in Philip K. Dick's 1956 *Minority Report*, a science fiction masterpiece depicting 'a dystopian future where a predictive policing system apprehends and detains people before they have the opportunity to commit a given crime'. (Rizq, 2016, p. 6). But this 'pre-criminal space' dangerously conflates words and deeds, closes down the space of association, fantasy and exploration that is integral to the therapeutic space and turns the clinician into an informer who is duty-bound to report words and ideas that go against 'British values'. As Rosemary Rizq (ibid) writes:

> As a clinician, I can't help thinking these are defensive measures speaking to an unconscious, omnipotent fantasy in which the Government believes – and perhaps we too would like to believe – that total security can be achieved if only therapists can be persuaded to monitor and report what is now deemed by the state to be unacceptable.

What's more, at the time of writing, the government has called for 'age-verifying dental tests' to be carried out on child refugees entering the UK from the camp known as 'the jungle' in Calais, France (Onuzo, 2016), another instance reflecting an overriding political agenda that is certainly not geared towards openness and compassion. Given this context, a discussion on the role of psychotherapy becomes urgent. I have drawn elsewhere a distinction between a practice inspired by *morality* and one inspired by *ethics* (Bazzano, 2012; 2015; 2016a). Morality is adherence to the introjected norms of social life, a notion linked to Hegel's *Sittlichkeit* (usually rendered as 'ethical order' from *sittlich*, customary, from the stem *Sitte*, 'custom' or 'convention'). Ultimately, this is adherence to the dictates not of the real community but the state. In this sense, obeisance to the prescriptions of the aforementioned 'Prevent' training would constitute a moral therapeutic practice, but could such practice be deemed 'ethical'? I understand ethics as a person's genuine attempt to respond to the real presence of another; this may or may not coincide with contingent norms. Apprehended thus, the practice of a therapist who uncritically accepts the rules laid out by the 'Prevent' program cannot be called ethical. Some may see this differentiation as didactic and artificial, even preposterous; in practice, the two dimensions – obeisance to custom and existential response – tend to overlap and are not antithetical. However, I have found the demarcation useful in understanding how one conceptualizes the practice of psychotherapy today and where its commitment and allegiances may rest.

Whereas observance of morality turns a person into a *bourgeois*, one who sees himself as an autonomous 'I', self-consistent and not readily aware of his own internal divisions and contradictions, the practice of ethics turns a person into a *citizen*, one who is able to feel and express solidarity and civic responsibility on a wider scale and beyond the confines of his native soil. Whether or not these are explicitly stated, a bourgeois understanding of therapy is firmly based on principles such as stability, comfort and the maintenance of normality. Idiom and theoretical orientation may vary but the unmistakably traditionalist element soon becomes apparent. For instance, a terminology may be used that employs tenets of genuinely transformative therapeutic approaches (e.g. empathy, unconditional positive regard, positive therapeutic change) but at closer scrutiny these are revealed to be either decorative or treated as items that can be duly measured (Bazzano, 2016b). In some cases, the use of humanistic lingo covers over a fundamental obeisance to the current master narrative of neoliberalism, i.e. the assumption that it is desirable to measure, apprehend and even *control* human experience.

I am deliberately using the term 'bourgeois' instead of the more anodyne 'middle class', as the latter often denotes 'lifestyle', reasonable affluence and a generic sense of belonging. The link between the two expressions is nonetheless apparent, with 'bourgeois' offering us, I suggest, wider genealogical context and even a hint of faintly sinister commotions just beneath the bourgeois comfort sealed by home ownership, fashion and consumer choice. As a class, the bourgeoisie is characterized by unbending, monotheistic devotion to money at the expense of anything else, drowning 'the most heavenly ecstasies of religious fervour, of chivalrous enthusiasm, of philistine sentimentalism, in the icy water of egotistical calculation' (Marx & Engels, 1848, pp. 15–16). What used to be called personal worth was transmuted into exchange value, 'and in place of the numberless indefeasible chartered freedoms, has set up that single, unconscionable freedom – Free Trade' (ibid).

Conversely, an *ethical* therapeutic practice turns one not into a bourgeois but a *citizen* (Bazzano, 2015) not in the sense of the privileged, narrow-minded dweller of a nation state with high average income, but in the sense Hannah Arendt (1988) gives to the word. As I understand it, this is a notion of a life spent outside the narrow confines of the self (both in terms of the limited life span of finite existence and in terms of a life lived with others) and focused on the common good, not just the good of one's tribe of belonging. The notion of citizenship provides sufficient ethical ground on which self and other, client and therapist, can meet with respect, dignity and in a spirit of solidarity and cooperation, without recourse to those heightened moments of encounter and imagined mutuality and equality cherished by the *cult of the relationship* and the Philosophy of the Meeting currently predominant in psychotherapeutic literature of all theoretical orientations. I wholeheartedly echo Levinas when he says:

> One may wonder whether clothing the naked and feeding the hungry do not bring us closer to the neighbour than the rarefied atmosphere in which Buber's Meeting sometimes take place.
>
> *Levinas, 2008, p. 12*

Crucially for our times of 'audience democracy' (Müller, 2014), with many of us becoming accustomed to applaud or boo and drop a vote or two into the hat of an officious-looking chancer, citizenship is at variance with hazardous notions of warmth, intimacy and so-called 'authenticity' (the latter manipulatively exploited by political leaders and populist movements everywhere on the rise), which, psychotherapy culture has helped foster and even glorify. Instead, citizenship favours the principles of *cooperation*, *friendship* and *civility*. For Arendt (1998), the values of authenticity and warmth cannot really become political: they are but cheap surrogates for fairness and civic responsibility.

An ethical form of therapy inspired by civic responsibility and unsentimental respect for the other will then be a form of hospitality, with the therapist grounding her practice on how to become a *good host*.

Becoming a host

What makes a good host? First of all, the recognition that an entirely self-sufficient existence is a delusion: no one is entirely self-sufficient; no one can exist in isolation. Second, hospitality is active, in so far as the attributes of concern and care do not dwell automatically within the domain of 'Being' but have to be actively pursued. The most important point has to do with the fact that the host must first of all be a guest. My native Italian language has one and the same word to describe host and guest: *ospite* (incidentally, this does not mean that Italians are necessarily better hosts than others). When I say that the host must be first of all a guest, I mean that in receiving the guest, the host is himself received by his own dwelling hence fully understands his own condition of guest in his own dwelling.

What do we mean when we say 'welcome'? Is there perhaps an assumption that this dwelling, this house, this territory is mine and that you, the guest, the other, the client are welcome to enter it for a while? Last year I worked with a client who was in the process of moving house, leaving London, where he has lived and worked for many years. It struck me how poignant his reflections were on the fact that the houses and lodgings that see us through births, marriages, children, separation and death very often keep on much longer than we do. I thought, with Rilke: who made us like this, that no matter what we do, we always look as someone who is about to leave?

A cup of tea

There is another, more fundamental, point as to why hospitality is crucial to human interaction and hence to psychotherapy: it is only through hospitality that individuality comes into being. Summoned by another, called to respond, the response creates me. Called to respond, I step into that shared domain that the neurologist and philosopher Kurt Goldstein (1995), forerunner of Gestalt psychology and a man inspired by Goethe, calls the *immediate*.

The Zen tradition emphasizes the beauty and simplicity of the tea ceremony. This does not need to be mannered or overly precious. Offering a cup of tea to the guest involves both guest and host. Both need to be present to the interaction. The offering, and the acceptance, is also immediate, and both step into a shared domain, the in-between, a realm beyond the mere dialogical sphere, a place of coming-into-being, made possible by a suspension of judgement – not a technique or a strategy but the unadulterated modality of encounter – increasingly rare now that technology provides us with greater, better and smarter opportunities to be indifferent to one another.

Psychotherapy and the Dharma

There are several threads linking counselling and psychotherapy to Zen practice. One of the most important is the aspiration to offer genuine hospitality. What is hospitality? And why is it crucial to both psychotherapy and Zen practice?

A Zen practitioner is inspired by the Dharma (the body of teachings given by the Buddha); by embarking on the path, he/she aspires to become a bodhisattva, a word which literally means 'awakened being'. In its long history from early iconography to the present day, the figure of the bodhisattva has gradually shed the otherworldly garment of Zen archetype in order to assume the features of an ordinary human being. Accordingly, if it once described someone akin to a saint or a person to whom a special revelation had been granted, the term can now be read existentially, i.e. someone who has developed an aspiration to be useful to others. A bodhisattva has realized the unsatisfactory nature of life and has acknowledged the inherent suffering of the human condition: rather than chasing after enlightenment, special knowledge or the ability to perform wonders, he or she aspires to act with wisdom and compassion for the benefit of all beings. Rather than a Platonic archetype outside everyday reality, he or she is an ordinary person like you and me, living and breathing in the phenomenal world. Rather than the carrier of special messages from some higher dimension, the awakened being cultivates spaciousness in his heart/mind so as to make room for the presence of another human being.

There are some similarities here with Christianity, particularly with the unswerving way it is expressed by Søren Kierkegaard. Inspired as well as haunted by the biblical figure of Abraham, in his book *Fear and Trembling* (Kierkegaard, 1985) he comes up with a mesmerizing creation, a figure he calls the *knight of faith*, someone who paradoxically renounces and embraces the world. Kierkegaard's spirituality was grounded in everyday matters yet harboured a tremendous faith which could be appreciated, I believe, as a fundamental *trust without an object*: not in a belief system, a particular person, a theoretical approach or even in oneself but focused instead on a neutral sense of agreement with the process of living-and-dying.

Some therapists would perhaps define this faith as trust in the actualizing tendency: this notion, now under attack in a landscape which places great emphasis on neo-Darwinism and evolutionary psychology, is nevertheless valuable in renewing a pledge in favour of the ineffable nature of life in general and human life in particular.

As a consequence of this pledge, a counsellor might strive to host both the 'positive' as well as the 'negative' aspects of a client, bracketing the desire to see positive change taking place in its more obvious manifestations. Upholding a more neutral yet benevolent attitude towards different Gestalts may in turn help the client be a better host/container of her own emotions and feelings, including those which are troublesome, painful and disruptive. Rogers, of course, had a phrase for this: unconditional positive regard (Rogers, 1980) a notion that has been variously understood and often misconstrued.

Right-brain and left-brain responses

Our individual response to the presence of another human being certainly awakes similar perplexities, to which we might respond in a variety of ways. One way would of course be a 'left-brain' response: cognitive, geared towards encouraging the client to implement positive changes and a certain degree of control over his/her life. Another way, if I were to try a translation of Keats' powerful poetic insight into the language of science, would be a 'right-brain' response. We know that, broadly speaking, the right-brain rules over empathy and inter-subjectivity, emphasizes the journey over the arrival, asserts the primacy of perception, and resists a reduction of lived experience to mere utility (McGilchrist, 2009). We now recognize that interdisciplinary developmental research (as evidenced by pioneering neuro-psychoanalyst Allan Schore (2011)) suggests that:

> the evolutionary mechanism of creation of a right brain-to-right brain attachment bond of social-emotional communication and the maturation of affects represent the key events in infancy more than the emergence of complex cognitions.

One significant upshot is that effective therapy needs to be right-brain to right-brain communication (Panksepp, 1998), something which might call for a redress of the balance after three decades of dominance of cognitive approaches and neuro-behaviourism.

An act of generosity

A Zen practitioner is committed to the practice of the six paramitas, or 'perfections' – the first of these being the practice of generosity. By this very willingness to open up to others, he/she is granted admission to the legendary palace of truth: as it turns out, the most direct way of accessing it is not by esoteric practices and special yogic tricks, but through an act of relinquishment, an act of generosity: instead of an exotic search for mystical revelation, the Buddha invites us to make adequate room for the other. By leaning out of one's imaginary self-bound existence, one discovers spaciousness.

A therapist too makes room for the client, and in this way makes available the remarkable gift of unconditional hospitality. In his masterpiece *Minima Moralia*, Theodor Adorno (2005) argued that we moderns have forgotten how to give presents: we are no longer able to give something for nothing, let alone the gift of one's heart and mind, the gift of what Carl Rogers (1980) liked to call *presence*. That a genuine gift has become such a rare thing gives even more significance to the practice of psychotherapy. Years of training, placement work, self-care and professional development can then be seen as all geared towards honing and refining this subtle capability: to genuinely provide space in one's heart and mind in order to receive another. Perhaps what we are trying to cultivate as counsellors is negative capability, to use the felicitous term employed by the great English poet John Keats (2005) in a letter of 1817. Keats defined negative capability as the talent for 'being in uncertainties, mysteries, doubts, without any irritable reaching after fact and reason' (p. 71). He saw it as an intuitive, insightful way of relating to the world which respects its ineffable, unfathomable nature rather than desiring to capture it and 'understand' it.

'Potlatch'

A topic that sometimes comes up in supervision is that of money. Some supervisees own the fact that it crosses their mind when considering, for example, what aspect influences the nature of their interaction with their clients. Does the monetary transaction affect the therapeutic relationship and if so in what way? Do some of us therapists cling for dear life to our clients for fear of not being able to pay the rent? Do we measure the value of what we offer by the sum we charge? And what is the client really saying when he writes a cheque at the end of a session? Is psychotherapy a transaction like any other? I believe that what the therapist provides is a most unusual gift. I give myself for an hour – unconditionally, without judgement, with an open mind and an open heart. This gift, I believe, is unbearable, i.e. it indebts the receiver, who in turn is prompted to give something, not in return but as a gift in its own right. In this day and age, that gift is money. One could say that this *is* a transaction, but to see it thus is seeing the therapy hour in fast-forward. If we do the opposite for a moment, and slow the sequence right down, what we might see is two distinct acts of gift-giving. In fact, it could be argued that the above applies to any human encounter and operation that involves money, particularly when the parties involved invest it with meaning. I would go one step further: it could be applied to any human transaction where the meaning is inherently there even when the two parties are now cognizant of it. This form of mutual gift-giving is what societies grounded in a gift economy untainted by commodification called *potlatch*. I feel it is important to disentangle therapy from the prevailing view that sees it as a deal between consumer and provider, buyer and seller. Not out of a misguided sense of purity or a stance of high-minded ethical superiority in relation to the sweat and dust of the marketplace, but simply because reducing what comes to pass between a therapist and a client to a transaction fundamentally misrepresents it. The Zen tradition has something to impart in this regard. Since the Buddha's times the teachings are given freely. It has been customary to give a donation for what has been received: this is called *dāna*, the meaning of which is generosity. It is impossible to repay someone for the gift of oneself, so we offer ourselves – money is then the explicable token of our willingness to give.

It has been argued that therapy is a form of potlatch (Žižek, 2008). The term, loosely translated as 'gift', refers to the primary economic system practiced by indigenous people of the Pacific Northwest coast. Theirs was a gift economy rather than an economy based on profit. It was banned in the late nineteenth century at the urging of missionaries and government agents who considered it a 'worse than useless custom' (Cole & Chaikin, 1990, p. 15) – in their eyes a profligate, fruitless practice and even contrary to civilized values. It was widely practiced much later, during the heyday of May 1968, within the Situationist International network, a cultural and political movement which gave us art and architecture, inspired social insurgence as well as seminal philosophical works such as Guy Debord's *The Society of the Spectacle* (Debord, 1983), where we read of the 'parodies of real dialogue and gift-giving' (p. 89), of alienated existence, and conversely of how uncommon and precious authentic dialogue and gift-giving can be.

It is easy, from our supposedly more sophisticated, at times cynical, 'post-modern' perspective to see these modes of exchange as naive. The fact remains that a real gift is not only rare, but quite difficult to match; it even creates a subtle (and not so subtle) obligation. The gift of therapy is in a sense most unusual; perhaps the client's payment represents a way — our accepted way as modern westerners — to respond to this extraordinary gift. Of course this gift is remarkable only if the counsellor has practiced the ways of hospitality.

Active and reactive

The second bodhisattva vow states: 'Afflictions are inexhaustible, I vow to put an end to them'. Stephen Batchelor (2015, personal communication) translates the original word in the text, *tanha* (usually rendered as desires, cravings and more broadly as afflictions) as *reactivity*. Reactivity, as he sees it, is embedded in our organism, it is what arises when an organism comes into contact with its surroundings. It may manifest as craving, aversion or indifference. There is a connection between the second vow stated above and the second noble task: to let go of 'suffering', of what rises up. In other words, not giving in to tanha or letting these natural phenomena be without reacting gives the practitioner greater freedom and the avoidance of aridity, i.e. an existence lived in reactive mode.

I have found this angle interesting as I believe there are wider implications that go beyond the individual human organism and are at work in nature itself. There are *active* and *reactive* forces, the balance of which plays out in the human individual as part of a greater whole. 'Reactivity' in this context is part of the wider presence of reactive forces which lean towards self-preservation, homeostasis and 'well-being' — a shrinkage of experience — when we are faced with the magnitude and sheer unpredictability of becoming.

The other forces are active, their tendency variously described as a process of 'self-overcoming' (Nietzsche, 1995), actualization (Rogers, 1951) or as a bid for freedom (Whitehead, 1978).

Whether Dharma practice itself is in the service of active or reactive forces — whether, in other words, it turns out to be an essentially self-protective undertaking or an act of generosity, is an open question. This has to do, I suspect, with the ways in which different epochs are able and willing to access and translate the Buddha's teachings, and with how much practitioners are open to take the teaching into their hearts.

What would it mean for a culture and a human organism to align themselves with *active* forces present in nature or at least to hold a precarious and precious balance in their favour? Would this stance be in some way more consonant with a notion of ethics that is not subject to the principle of self-preservation?

The left-to-die boat

I remember my surprise in seeing first hand and for the first time Hokusai's 1831 famous painting *Under the Wave off Kanagawa*. At 26cm x 38cm, this is a small painting indeed, and I don't really know why I expected it to be a lot bigger. Something else surprised me: I had seen photos and reproductions of the painting hundreds of times, yet I had overlooked each time the boats struggling in the rough sea under the wave. They are not invisible, but you will have to spend a little time with the painting to notice them. Their presence is, to my eyes, silently resistant. The people in them keep sailing, Hokusai seems to suggest, despite the stormy sea.

It is easy, gazing at the beauty of the tidal wave and at Mount Fuji on the horizon, to overlook the danger the brave men and women in the boats are facing. To miss their presence – however tiny and near-invisible, enmeshed as they are in the turbulent mass of water – is to miss the painter's intention entirely. When we eventually notice them, the painting takes on a whole different meaning. It becomes more than an accomplished composition of blues and whites, of blacks and greys. The beautiful wave is a threat to the lives of the boatmen. To see the beauty of the world and ignore its anguish is to fall into the aesthetic fallacy. To imagine that disaster strikes elsewhere, away from familiar shores; that cruelty and neglect befall others in faraway places is both a convenient and an expedient way to keep calm and carry on. But it is becoming increasingly difficult to ignore the harsh reality.

In March 2011 a boat with 72 refugees left the Libyan coast for the island of Lampedusa, near Sicily. It soon met rough water and was cast adrift for weeks with no water or food.

> Distress calls ware sent out by a satellite phone on board the boat, and were received and forwarded to concerned authorities. The boat encountered helicopters, naval ships and fishing vessels, all of whom ignored its distress signals. Eventually, the boat, caught between ocean currents, drifted back to the Libyan coast. All but nine of the 72 passengers died.
>
> *Raqs Media Collective, 2016, p. 96*

Painters and poets of the past often depicted sea storms and shipwrecks. To gaze at these paintings and read these poems is to realize that a seismic change has taken place in our attitude to ethics. In Turner's 1805 *The Shipwreck*, the viewer can spot a ship sinking in the distance and a few fishing boats coming to the rescue of the sailors who have been caught up in a storm. Turner was probably inspired by reading 'a re-issue of an epic poem from 1762, also titled *The Shipwreck*' (Raqs Media Collective, 2016, p. 95) written by a sailor, William Falconer. There is a photograph of the 'left-to-die boat', taken by a French aircraft and sent to Rome Maritime Rescue Co-ordination Centre: people in the boat are clearly visible even if the picture is unfocused. It is a stark contrast to Turner's *Shipwreck*. The two are not really comparable, not only because one is a painting, the other a photograph but also because one depicts a spontaneous rescue operation while the other documents the technological proficient indifference of our age. Another comparison could be drawn between Turner's painting and a contemporary artistic piece that also draws on shipwreck, Weiwei's famous pose as the drowned Syrian child refugee

Alan Kurdi. The Raqs Media Collective (2016) ask the following, achingly relevant question:

> Is it better to be a fisherman ready to go into the storm to rescue a ship-wrecked sailor than to be an artist pretending to be a celebrity pretending to be a drowned child?
>
> *p. 97*

The fishermen in old paintings and poems are ready to do the decent thing. European navies facing the escalating refugee crisis are instructed to lessen the amount and rate of rescue operations. The assumption behind this decision seems to be that it will discourage people who are fleeing war on land by attempting to cross the sea and reach Europe:

> The logic of this argument goes something like this: 'Refugees attempting to cross by sea know that it is dangerous to make the marine crossing, however they continue their attempts out of the hope that in the event of danger, they may be rescued by ships patrolling the area; once word gets around that people will be left to die in boats rather than be rescued by naval ships, fewer people will want to make the crossing in the first place.'
>
> *Raqs Media Collective, 2016, p. 96*

The above logic allows us to forget that we are not responding to the situation in front of our eyes. It leaves us off the hook; it allows us to be unethical in a civilized fashion. However difficult (and ultimately impracticable) genuine ethics may be they are valuable as aspiration and motivation. It may sound strange, but I do like to think of Zen practitioners and therapists as those fishermen in old paintings and poems. I like to think of us as *bodhisattvas*. This is not setting an impossible, saintly ideal but providing an archetypal source of inspiration, that is aligned with the notion of citizenship discussed above, a notion that is necessarily more expansive than the narrow nationalisms we are sadly getting more used to nowadays, one that was reflected during Theresa May's speech at her party's conference in Birmingham in October 2016. May, who is Britain's prime minister at the moment of writing, came out with a turn of phrase that is as catchy as it is controversial: 'If you believe you are a citizen of the world, you are a citizen of nowhere' (May, 2016). But a bodhisattva *is* a citizen of the world, not perhaps in the sense of a globe-trotting multi-millionaire entrepreneur, but in the case of someone whose sense of ethics goes beyond the narrow confines of her backyard, soil and nation state. And when you think of it, a bodhisattva is also a citizen of nowhere, both inhabiting now-here and a 'place', this transient life that is a nowhere in terms of its ultimate insubstantiality.

The bodhisattva is not a rescuer in the sense of someone who rushes in because she does not trust in the inherent wisdom of the other. Instead, summoned to respond one simply shows up and does what is required, i.e. *acts in response*. The bodhisattva is an archetype. But an archetype (as we've seen in Chapter 1 in the story of Kanzeon and the samurai) is not a figment of our religious imagination or a hologram in a Platonic realm of ideas. It manifests concretely in everyday interactions between ordinary people like you and me. It turns up next to us and within us.

References

Adorno, T. (2005). *Minima Moralia: Reflections from a Damaged Life*. London: Verso.

Arendt, H. (1998). *The Human Condition*. Chicago, IL: The University of Chicago Press.

Bazzano, M. (2012). *Spectre of the Stranger: Towards a Phenomenology of Hospitality*. Eastbourne: Sussex Academic Press.

Bazzano, M. (2015). Therapy as unconditional hospitality. *Psychotherapy and Politics International*, 13(1): 4–13. doi: 10.1002/ppi.1342.

Bazzano, M. (2016a). The conservative turn in person-centered therapy. *Person-Centered & Experiential Psychotherapies*, 15(4): 339–354. doi: 10.1080/14779757.2016.1228540.

Bazzano, M. (2016b). Changelings: the self in Nietzsche's psychology. In M. Bazzano & J. Webb (Eds), *Therapy and the Counter-tradition: The Edge of Philosophy* (pp. 9–22). Abingdon: Routledge.

Blanchot, M. (1993). *The Infinite Conversation*. Minneapolis, MN: University of Minnesota Press.

Bull, M. (2016). Great again. *London Review of Books*, 38(20): 20 October, 8–10.

Cole, D. & Chaikin, I. (1990). *An Iron Hand upon the People: The Law against the Potlatch on the Northwest Coast*. Washington, DC: University of Washington Press.

Debord, G. (1983). *The Society of the Spectacle*. London: Rebel Press.

Goldstein, K. (1995). *The Organism*. New York: Zone Books.

Home Office (2016). *Prevent*. https://elearning.prevent.homeoffice.gov.uk/ Retrieved 23 October 2016.

Keats, J. (2005). *The Letters of John Keats*. London: Adamant Media.

Kierkegaard, S. (1985). *Fear and Trembling*. London: Penguin.

Kitano, T. (1999). *Kikujiro*, a film directed by Takeshi Kitano, 121 minutes. Tokyo: Bandai Visual.

Levinas, E. (2008). *Outside the Subject*. London: Continuum.

McGilchrist, I. (2009). *The Master and his Emissary: The Divided Brain and the Making of the Modern World*. New Haven, CT: Yale University Press.

Madison, G. (2009). *The End of Belonging: Untold Stories of Leaving Home and the Psychology of Global Relocation*. London: CreateSpace.

Marx, C. & Engels, F. (1848). *The Communist Manifesto*. www.marxists.org/archive/marx/works/download/pdf/Manifesto.pdf Retrieved 20 May 2016.

May, T. (2016). Speech at the Conservative Party Conference, 5 October, Birmingham. http://standard.co.uk/news/politics/theresa-may-sparks-twitter-backlash-over-citizen-of-the-world-remark-in-conservative-party-a3361701.html Retrieved 11 November 2016.

Müller, J. (2014). The Party's over. *London Review of Books*, (36)10: 35–37.

Nietzsche, F. (1995). *Thus Spoke Zarathustra*. New York: Random House.

Onuzo, C. (2016). When are the refugees of Calais too old for kindness? *The Guardian*, 22 October https://theguardian.com/commentisfree/2016/oct/22/refugees-calais-too-old-kindness-britain Retrieved 22 October 2016.

Panksepp, J. (1998). *Affective Neuroscience: The Foundations of Human and Animal Emotions*. New York: Oxford University Press.

Raqs Media Collective (2016). Object N00476. *Tate Etc.*, 38, Autumn. London: Tate Publishing.

Rilke, R. M. (1975). *Duino Elegies*. London: Chatto & Windus.

Rizq, R. (2016). Big Brother is listening. *Therapy Today*, 27(8): 6.

Rogers, C. R. (1951). *Client-centered Therapy*. Boston, MA: Houghton Mifflin.

Rogers, C. R. (1980). *A Way of Being*. New York: Houghton Mifflin.

Schore, A. (2011). The Science of the Art of Psychotherapy. A one-day seminar. Cambridge Faculty of Education, 8 October.

Viriasova, I. (2016). The refugee's flight: Homelessness, hospitality, and care of the self. *Journal of Global Ethics*, 12(2): 222–239. doi: 10.1080/17449626.2016.1182935.

Whitehead, A. N. (1978). *Process and Reality*. New York: The Free Press.

Žižek, S. (2008). *In Defence of Lost Causes*. London: Verso.

4

PRESENCE, MINDFULNESS AND BUDDHA-NATURE

What is presence?

The humanistic tradition emphasized the therapist's presence as crucial to therapeutic change, as a factor a great deal more important than the acquisition of academic knowledge or the mastery of a particular set of skills. Rogers (1980) famously wrote:

> I find that when I am closest to my inner, intuitive self, when I am somehow in touch with the unknown in me . . . then whatever I do seems to be full of healing. Then, simply my presence is releasing and helpful to the other.
>
> *p. 129*

How to *be* with a client – how to best tune the therapist's self so that we can be more effective – appears to be at least as important in counselling and psychotherapy training as learning what to do, i.e. how to best respond competently to a particular form of distress the client presents us with.

It has been said that developing therapeutic presence enhances the well-being of the therapist (Geller et al., 2010), makes her more attuned and receptive, and increases spontaneity and creativity in the therapy room. In other words, the cultivation of presence unites self-care with therapeutic effectiveness.

Daniel Stern (2004) captured the Zeitgeist a few years back when he wrote about the present moment in therapy and in everyday life. He and his colleagues in the 'Process of Change Group' in Boston wrote of 'moments-of-meeting' as ways that had greatly facilitated therapeutic change. Therapist and client wrote, 'are meeting as persons relatively unhidden by their usual therapeutic roles, for that moment' (Lanyado, 2004, p. 9). Inspired by the phenomenology of Husserl and Merleau-Ponty, Stern emphasized the difficulty of grasping the present because of its fleeting, dynamic nature and unpredictability; our verbal account of it cannot really do it justice, for it becomes lost in our attempts to explain it. The experience of being fully present in the interaction with a client can catch me unaware at times; the experience prompts me to want to be more prepared and attuned.

In a similar mode, presenting a view in tune with the humanistic approach, Geller & Greenberg (2012, p. 7) define therapeutic presence as

> [T]he state of having one's whole self in the encounter with a client by being completely in the moment on a multiplicity of levels – physically, emotionally, cognitively, and spiritually.

And in her account of working with childhood trauma, child and adolescent psychoanalytic psychotherapist Monica Lanyado (2012) stressed the importance of being alone in the presence of someone, emphasizing the creative value of the capacity to be alone, and the importance of peacefulness and stillness in the therapist. Each practitioner will have his/her way of fostering care of self and find greater attunement. My own favourite method is *zazen*, or Zen meditation, something I have practiced for 36 years. What I find particularly helpful is that in Zen the 'now-ness' experienced through sitting silently, although appreciated, is not elevated to a special or mystical status but is processed as part and parcel of ordinary existence. Our day-to-day existence can be perceived as extraordinary if we cultivate different ways of seeing. In this sense, 'ordinary' interaction with our clients can disclose a world of insights. The other useful pointer from the Zen tradition is that one practices *for no reason at all*: not in order to achieve a desired state of mind or to get rid of an unwanted one. At a time when various 'mindfulness' techniques are being utilized as tools for correcting 'unwholesome' behaviour, the Zen perspective inscribes meditation practice in the dimension of non-utilitarian play and acceptance of human imperfections. Doing something with no gain in mind is one of the definitions of play, a dimension that is intimately connected to healing (Winnicott, 1971).

Care of the self

Practising self-care is a commitment to continue to work on ourselves, to prevent the possibility of burnout and avoid the emotional exhaustion and stress that go with listening to the depth of our clients' troubles and dilemmas. Inspired by the ancient Greeks, Foucault saw care of the self as *askesis*, an ongoing practice of mind and body aimed at nurturing our freedom and dignity as individuals and also as a practice directly linked to ethics, i.e. aimed at relating better to others. Much more than eating healthily, resting and avoiding stress, care of the self is geared towards greater self-awareness, which for the Greeks was crucial in fostering in turn participation to the social and political life. Foucault (2000) renders this process as 'the formation of the self through techniques of living, not of repression through prohibition and law' (p. 89). In other words, the person who practices care of the self will adhere to an inner, deeper ethical code *before* abiding by the rules of her profession. Her participation to public life stems from this inner ethical core rather than from adherence to an established code. Foucault maintains that the two dimensions of ethics, inner and outer, the letter and the spirit of the law, may or may not coincide, depending as to whether the rules of a given society are geared towards the emancipation or the normalization of individuals.

The person who practices care of the self will be less willing to deliberately exercise power *over* another human being. The therapist will be aware of the power imbalance implicit in the therapeutic relationship, particularly when considering that 'the likelihood of suffering from psychological distress' can be legitimately associated 'with the individual's position in society with respect to structural power' (Proctor, 2002, p. 3).

I find it remarkable that Foucault openly relates our propensity to exert power over others with our own fear of death. The greater the fear of one's own insubstantiality, fragility and eventual demise, the greater the need to assert oneself through futile and hostile gestures. The poignant, profound lesson inherited from the Greeks – one that uncanningly matches the Buddha's teachings – appears to be that ethics is intimately related to our awareness of mortality and of the impermanence of all living things.

Care of the self for the therapist could today mean maintaining an ongoing practice of mind/body awareness which also allows for a down-to-earth sense of one's own environment: an internal/external awareness, a form of 'introspection' which is also open to the ethical dimension and our dealing with others and the world. A therapeutic practice, which has care of the self at its core, would emphasize that theoretical knowledge and proficiency in techniques are not enough. The therapist's very self is, according to this particular view, the fine instrument conveying presence.

Two to tango

There is, however, an unspoken twist in the above formulation: presence could easily be misconstrued as the exclusive province of the therapist. Cultivation of presence on behalf of the therapist, paired with her 'offering' of the core conditions would then be all that is needed. But this view neglects the sixth and most important of the conditions for therapeutic change hypothesized by Carl Rogers (1957), namely that the client receives 'to a minimal degree' the therapist's 'empathic understanding and unconditional positive regard' (p. 96). The sixth condition would appear to decenter the therapist's role in favour of the reciprocal element of the therapeutic endeavour. I think this is correct. But I would like to push its implication a little further and hint at a *neutral embeddedness* that questions the separate, intrinsic existence of the therapist's, as well as the client's, self. Thus understood, presence can be thought of as *neutral*. I believe the Argentinean philosopher and psychotherapist Claudio Rud suggests something similar when he writes:

> Like everything that happens, this presence is mutually constituted, it is not something that only the therapist offers; it is an event within this mutual

involvement, within the expressive interconnection that is the therapeutic encounter. Therefore, we are not talking about two presences that add up, but *a single one that expresses itself.*

Rud, 2016, p. 5, italics added

I believe there is a similarity here with the Buddha. Sitting under the Bodhi tree, Gautama experienced awakening when seeing the morning star. At that moment, he exclaimed 'How wondrous! I *and all sentient beings* on Earth are awake, endowed with this same bright mind'. He did not say '*I* am awakened' but realized instead that *everything* is. The phrase 'I am awakened' is a contradiction in terms because awakening partly means to realize that the existence of a separate 'I' is illusory. Similarly with presence: of course therapeutic presence cannot be compared to spiritual awakening, but both belong to existence itself rather than to a 'spiritual person' or a skilful clinician.

Is presence an integrative notion?

It is debatable to which therapeutic orientation the notion of presence belongs. It seemed to have been already there with Freud's emphasis on the evenly suspended attention of the analyst, on his recommendation that the physician turns their own unconscious receptively towards the unconscious of the client, fine-tuning themselves as a telephone receiver (Freud, 1958). The practice of the phenomenological reduction, aka *epoché* (suspension or 'bracketing') – putting aside any assumption so as to meet our clients more directly – is a reminder of how the therapist can become more open to presence in the therapy room. Its first advocate was a Greek philosopher called Pyrrho (365–270 BC), for whom it represented a strategy to overcome dogmatism, the latter defined by one of his followers, Sextus Empiricus, as 'metaphysical entities, transcendental realities, in order . . . to . . . "explain" [our lived experience]. All of these realities are . . . unverifiable' (Madison, 1981, p. 301). Centuries later Merleau-Ponty (1964; 2010) extended the practice of *epoché* to scientific and psychological theories in the attempt to free us from our craving for mastery over the intrinsically uncertain nature of life.

How does one 'do' bracketing?

Several questions still remain: having accepted the validity of *epoché*, how do I do it? Do I simply suppress unwanted thoughts, feelings and emotions? What do other therapists do to cultivate presence and put aside assumptions that get in the way of a genuine encounter? How can I be with the intersubjective process in the room? 'Being with' is for me what provides the key, and my temporary, empirical answer is: meditation. For meditation is essentially, in my understanding, being with whatever arises without judgment and with no attachment.

In the late 1970s, as a 25-year-old recently ordained monk in the Geluk school of Tibetan Buddhism, Stephen Batchelor went to a lecture by Levinas on Husserl.

During the lecture, Levinas mentioned the phenomenological practice of *epoché*: putting aside concepts, assumptions and opinions so as to meet reality more directly. 'How do we achieve bracketing?' Batchelor asked, but Levinas had no answer. 'Can meditation help a person be more aware of his own assumptions and so become more open to experience?' The question was to no avail: 'the notion that one might require a rigorous meditative discipline to achieve such bracketing was an entirely alien idea' (Batchelor, 2010, p. 52).

Presence is understood in humanistic psychology as a way of being rather than the acquisition of a set of techniques, yet there *are* methods we can use in order to invite more presence in the therapy room and be helpful to our clients. In this sense, presence can be seen as a discipline inspired by the dimension of play. It prepares the therapist to meet the unknown, the pre-cognitive and the pre-reflexive – the genuinely new.

Presence and absence

This discussion of presence would be incomplete without awareness of its counterpart: absence. In practising the sort of organismic awareness and phenomenological observation known as *zazen*, the 'I' itself becomes diluted, fully present because *absent* as an intrinsic, separate phenomenon. By listening to sounds in the room, in the street and in the sky above, I perceive myself as embedded in this vast phenomenal world, as part of this very moment as it unfolds: a multifaceted, rich and complex totality. This is another way of asserting the relative, *interdependent* nature of the self, what the Buddha calls *śūnyatā*, which, loosely rendered as 'emptiness', refers to this fundamental experience of everything being intimately connected to everything else. Whether or not specifically meditating on death, the meditator opens the gates of perception to the knowledge of his/her own eventual demise. What makes me fully present in the mysterious unfolding of this moment is the awareness of my future absence, of the sequence of my breathing moving towards the final expiration. What makes me more acutely alert to the ceaseless, creative unfolding of living potentialities is (paradoxically?) awareness of entropy.

When we speak of presence, we are therefore also aware of the ghostly, transient nature of our nevertheless vivid existence. The more we are aware of the interdependent nature of our existence, the more our possibility of being present. Paradoxically, the more we are aware that there is not really something called 'the present' (the *fêted* 'here and now' of much spiritual literature), the more present we can be.

Mindfulness apps and the grim reaper

I'm sitting in an overcrowded commuter train to central London on a warm summer day. It's early in the morning: the heat, the voices of passengers huddled together by chance and blind necessity, the vacant, hopeless stares contemplating a toiling day ahead, the frequent braking and accelerating. I am standing next to a young mother and her baby in a pram. At regular intervals the baby cries and each time the mother activates a singing teddy bear and waves it in front of the baby. The song only lasts ten seconds and after a brief pause the baby invariably cries again. My mind drifts. I find myself thinking 'Is meditation a technique for soothing anxiety in adults, as the teddy bear is for this child?' And is it a mistake to think like that? After all, what's wrong with getting a little solace in an uncertain, often frightening world? Then I remember what a student said to me a couple of weeks before at the end of a philosophy class. I had mentioned Buddhism and its vicissitudes in the West in relation to Schopenhauer; 'I've been practicing mindfulness – the student said with a smile while I was getting ready to leave the room – it is a form of Buddhism, isn't it?'

'Yes – I replied – kind of. How are you finding it?'

'Well, it works wonders. I have this mindfulness app and I listen to it in bed after a long, tiring working day. I'm fast asleep before I know it. It's just great. It does the trick. It helps me relax'.

Falling asleep is not, strictly speaking, the purpose of meditation, but relaxation and stress-reduction can be pleasant and positive outcomes of Buddhist practice. The principal aim of meditation (if one can speak of the aim at all in the utilitarian sense here) is neither relaxation nor stress reduction. If anything, sitting practice seems to bring about heightened awareness of our human situation. As we shall see, 'awareness' is not the be all and end all of meditation practice. Yet greater awareness helps us shed some illusions in relation to our inescapable finitude. We realize the certainty of our own death. We also realize that change, or impermanence is inevitable – the way in which death manifests in life.

The Zen tradition speaks of living-and-dying, one word in Japanese (*shōji*). The term is beginning to catch on in therapeutic circle, but in the process it has split into two words living *and* dying. This is not a matter of language only. Living-and-dying acknowledges the presence of the grim reaper in the very midst of life, the cruel beauty of a sunny day, and perhaps the presence of life in death.

A bumpy ride

There is nothing grand or mystical about paying attention, nor does it necessarily require mindfulness training over an eight-week programme. We all have known, from time to time, the pleasure and satisfaction that can derive from unself-conscious absorption in daily activities, be they cooking, sweeping the floor or, as in the case of Alberto Giacometti, producing great sculptures. This kind of absorption is very ordinary and itself reveals the extraordinary in the everyday.

> The more I work, the more I see things differently; that is, everything gains in grandeur every day, becomes more and more unknown, more and more beautiful. The closer I come, the grander it is, the more remote it is.
>
> *Giacometti cited in Dillard, 2016, p. 192*

Presence is a way of being; mindfulness is a set of techniques. It would be more precise to say: mindfulness *has become* a set of techniques. In its original meaning, mindfulness – *smṛti* in Sanskrit and *sati* in the Pali language spoken by the Buddha– means *remembering*. Crucially, this remembering is not an abstract operation but has a context. It is remembering *something*; it is mindfulness *of* rather than a reified, capitalized, stand-alone 'Mindfulness'. We are asked to remember our impermanent human condition and the transient nature of all living things. We are invited to bring our attention to the uncertainty and fragility of life, to what the Buddha called *dukkha* – a term usually translated as suffering or unsatisfactoriness, but whose textual meaning indicates the empty axle hole of a wheel. If you're driving, and the axle fits badly into the centre hole of one of the wheels, you will have a very bumpy ride. In that sense, *dukkha* could be colloquially translated as 'bumpy ride'. In the midst of this rollercoaster we call life (which is not without its moments of elation, joy and serenity), the Buddha also invites us to recognize feelings as feelings, mind as mind, and phenomena as phenomena and to regard the proliferating inventions of our thinking mind with a light scepticism. Adopting this latter stance is, however, a delicate thing as it can easily turn into 'mind control' instead of a natural curiosity into the workings of our inner life and potential understanding of its creativity.

Mindfulness and mind-control

As someone actively involved in the integration of Dharma practice and therapy, I do appreciate the current popularity of mindfulness programmes and their applications in therapy. As part of a scientific – some would say *scientistic* – interpretation of the Dharma, the current mindfulness trend does capture an aspect of the teachings, namely the pragmatic attitude, the Buddha as physician. In literalizing the cure, however, it emphasizes the dichotomy between illness and well-being and largely reinforces our obsession with self-improvement born out of puritanical shame. It seemingly aims to attain a peaceful state of mind removed from the turmoil of the passions and the ruminations of a mind that, no matter how hard one tries, cannot but secrete thoughts. In short, it tries to sanitize the human condition.

Yet the way in which the heightened awareness spontaneously generated by meditative practice is being utilized by the mindfulness movement appears to veer towards 'control', often assumed to be the same as 'self-regulation' and 'affect-regulation'. I have also found striking similarities in the way in which the notion of 'control' is understood in both mindfulness and in a practice such as yoga. Yoga can 'positively affect self-regulation and decrease hyper-arousal' (Ryan, 2012, p. 16) writes one therapist and yoga practitioner, who also quotes yoga teacher Mira Metha, for whom yoga is 'the control of the mind with the goal of spiritual peace' (ibid). In a similar, prescriptive vein, contemporary mindfulness theorists and practitioners write that a criterion for joining Mindfulness-Based Stress Reduction (MBSR) and Mindfulness-Based Cognitive Therapy (MBCT) Programmes is 'at least some willingness to examine the whole question of control over your behaviour' (Maex, 2011, p. 170), and that by being more aware, mindfulness practitioners 'strengthen their cognitive control' (Dreyfus, 2011, p. 47).

For many mindfulness practitioners and writers, the chief aim seems to be exercising control over the arch-enemy, 'unconscious forces' or even 'the unconscious'.

Some writers manage to present mindfulness as control over the unruliness of the natural way the mind unfolds, something interestingly close to the psychoanalytic method of free association which is the one thing that effectively 'subverts' the psychotherapist's 'natural authoritarian tendencies . . . [and] unleashes the disseminating possibilities that open to infinity' (Bollas, cited in Rose, 2011, p. 12). No free wandering of the mind seems to be allowed in mindfulness, presumably because one does not know what 'unwholesome' and 'unconscious' shenanigans one might open oneself to. As Olendski (2011) writes:

> When the mind is deliberately placed upon a particular object (using applied thought) rather than allowed to drift there 'on its own,' or held deliberately upon a chosen object (using sustained thought) even though it may be inclined to wander elsewhere, we are imposing some control on the process and it is no longer entirely conditioned by unconscious forces.
>
> *p. 63*

Control (for some mindfulness writers 'mastery') seems to be the elected province of mindfulness practice, understood as 'freedom from habit, the . . . realization of choice and the realization that mindfulness is not confined to specialized situations or circumstances' (Santorelli, 2011, p. 208). From the 'basic unreliability [of] our experience' (Teasdale & Chaskalson, 2011, p. 92) and the contingent nature of a world of 'mutually interacting shifting conditions' (ibid) the practitioner is invited to build a citadel of mindful control over an unpredictable world. This is laudable and no doubt motivated by the aspiration to alleviate suffering. But something gets lost in the process. As Sharon Salzberg (2011) points out, it is because of our 'three habitual tendencies' of 'grasping, aversion or delusion' that we 'distort our perception of what is happening' engaging in the 'futile and misguided efforts to deny or control our experience' (p. 177). At times, she writes, people 'consider it almost a personal humiliation to be sick, grow old, or to die, as if we should be able to determine not to, as though they had made a grave mistake somewhere. Yet we cannot control it' (Salzberg, 2011, p. 179). In the same way, the mental anguish generated by the contingent and uncertain nature of life may be considerably alleviated but not pathologized and partly redeemed by a prescriptive re-education programme over the course of a few weeks. The fundamental mistake, I believe, is to confuse the notion of control with the more nuanced neuro-biological notion of affect-regulation. The two notions are only superficially linked; there is in fact a wide distinction between control and affect-regulation.

Control, arguably the goal of yoga and of disciplines linked with Hinduism and early 'Theravada' Buddhism (the latter a major influence on mindfulness-based cognitive therapy) aims at restraining the entire sphere of emotions and feelings, what religious traditions refer to as 'the passions'. Control is needed through the cultivation of 'meditative states, the culmination of yoga . . . the fruit of practice arising from stilling the senses and concentrating the mind' (Ryan, 2012, p. 16). For instance, the all-too-human dimension of sex and sexual desire is in this context seen as problematic, intense and challenging. But the life of the passions is also what makes us imperfectly, profoundly human. The paradox here is that many in the West turned towards meditation, Buddhism and Buddhist-tinged ideas in order to find a fresher, less chastising approach to spirituality than the one afforded by the religion of their upbringing (usually Christianity). However, what they found in some cases is an even more puritanical take on the human condition. As we shall see in Chapter 6, despite the denigration of the senses which is, I believe, central in Christianity, the paradox of the human-God – the God *incarnate* Christ – affords more room for a compassionate embracing of our embodied condition than the prescriptive recipes of wholesomeness and control presented by current versions of 'mindfulness' ever really do.

Control and affect-regulation

Control is different from 'affect-regulation' although the two terms are often used interchangeably in both mindfulness and yoga literature. Affect-regulation is not just the reduction of intensity, the reduction of negative emotion, but it also involves an augmentation of positive emotion, necessary for self-organization (Schore, 2001). Moreover, affect-regulation is learned within primary and significant *relationships* in the life of the infant and the adult, rather than by being proficient in the use of techniques. I understand the aim of affect-regulation to be not curbing intensity per se but developing instead buoyancy by widening the range of one's response to life's variegated and unpredictable occurrences.

Mindfulness approaches to therapy are currently fashioned as 'a form of mental training' aimed at reducing vulnerability to 'reactive modes of mind that might otherwise heighten stress and emotional distress or that may . . . perpetuate psychopathology' (Bishop et al., 2004, p. 231). As such, they may contribute to alleviate distress and help the sufferer prevent the occurrence of compulsive or dangerous behaviours. At the same time, it is worth asking whether this stance may also bring about a regrettable loss of intensity. Massumi (2014) defines intensity as *the inassimilable*, i.e. what the self fails to assimilate. The self cannot by definition assimilate experience in its entirety, no matter how hard it tries, for the latter is always greater. Even if the self were to manage that, it would then be left with only a structure, at the most a symbolic hold over experience. Affirming therefore the primacy of the affects and the importance of affect-regulation over the need to control them incorporates intensity, keeps our very humanness alive and does not introduce a potentially draining psychological conflict. The mindfulness practitioner may gain *control* over his/her passions but arguably loses intensity (wrongly and summarily perceived as detrimental to well-being).

Mindfulness: opium of the middle-classes?

The tenets and methodologies of the mindfulness movement have been critiqued for some time by a host of practitioners and researchers (Bazzano, 2014a; Booth,

2014; Purser et al., 2016 among others). The inevitable backlash started with a timely, well-written article in the *Huffington Post* by well-known and respected Buddhist teachers and practitioners Ron Purser and David Loy, *Beyond McMindfulness* (Purser & Loy, 2013, Internet file), which warned of the shadow aspects of what they saw as a new lucrative industry that promises to 'improve work efficiency, reduce absenteeism, and enhance the "soft skills" that are crucial to career success'– and uses the perceived 'hipness' of Buddhist philosophy at the service of corporate values.

It is at times frustrating to discover that experienced practitioners well-versed in the practice of therapeutic presence (for example, Geller & Greenberg, 2012) accept passively the tenets of the mindfulness trend, submit to its reductive ethos, and are overly impressed by the now obligatory display of documented MRI scans of Buddhist monastics and meditators, showing that, well, meditation is good for you. They seem to find this kind of scientific or pseudo-scientific news very exciting. As a Zen practitioner of many years, I do not care to know that when doing *zazen* my central nervous system's circuits and the parasympathetic nervous system are activated and working harmoniously together, nor that my regular practice helps me achieve good satisfactory levels of neuronal integration. In their effort to join the over-enthusiastic consensus on these claims (in support of which little or no empirical studies have been published) humanistic therapists risk forgetting the unique angle afforded by notions such as therapeutic presence and genuine empathy.

Having examined the notions of presence and mindfulness, I would now like to turn to a related idea that is found throughout Zen literature: Buddha-nature. I thought the best way to initiate this discussion is by sketching the life and teachings of the Chinese Zen teacher Huineng.

Huineng's story

No north and south

As with many ancient Zen stories, the life of Huineng (638–713 AD), a renowned Chan master who came to be known as the 'sixth ancestor' in the Zen tradition, is partly legend, partly factual (Yampolsky, 1967). He lost his father when he was only three. Soon after, he moved with his mother to the Nan-hai province where they lived in poverty, selling firewood in the market. One day he heard the verses of the Diamond Sutra recited from a man who was buying firewood from him. In hearing them, he experienced a spontaneous awakening. He asked the man where he came from and where he had learned the verses of the Sutra. The man told him about Hung-jen, a Buddhist priest he had just paid a visit to, and who presided at Feng-mu shan, a thriving training centre for monastics and lay people in the East Mountain. He had repeatedly encouraged his students to chant the verses of the Sutra as a way to see into one's own nature and become a Buddha. This was enough for the young Huineng to make immediate preparation and travel to Feng-mu shan. He saw it as a sign of destiny. Once there, he met Hung-jen, also known as 'the fifth ancestor' and had his first interview with him. The ensuing dialogue reflects some of the gruffness one expects from Zen encounters.

'Where do you come from and what brings you to this mountain?'

'I am a commoner from the Ling-nan area of southern China. I have come this long way only to pay my respects and learn the teachings of the Dharma'.

'I see, you are from Ling-nan! A real barbarian then! There is *no way* you can become a Buddha, no matter how hard you try'.

'It is true, southerners and northerners are different, but Buddha-nature has no north and south'. Other people came by at that point, and the dialogue was interrupted. Hung-jen sent him to work and soon he was busy in the threshing room (Yampolsky, 1967).

Dust and mirror

Several months passed. Then one day Hung-jen gathered his students and asked them to write a verse that demonstrated their level of understanding. If one of them had awakened to the fundamental meaning, he would receive the Dharma transmission. Not one of his students dared to act; they felt their understanding could be no better than the head monk's, Shen-hsiu. For his part, Shen-hsiu was conflicted between, on the one hand, wanting to show his understanding and, on the other, not being seen as claiming the transmission for himself. So he went to write his verse on a board at midnight, when no one could see him. The verse said:

> The mind is like a clear mirror. At all times we must strive to polish it, and must not let the dust collect.
>
> *Yampolsky, 1967, p. 130*

He then went back to his room, unseen by anyone. Shen-hsiu's view, illustrated in his verse, reflects the teachings found in a classic Buddhist text generally attributed to Asvaghosha, *Awakening of Faith in the Mahayana*. In essence, this perspective is not dissimilar from the view popular today, according to which awakening means complete freedom from misleading thoughts, what is known in Chinese as *linian*, 'freeing from thoughts'. It is not wholly dissimilar from the view popularized by the 'mindfulness' movement that arguably focuses on a latter-day version of Buddhist quietism: the modern term is in this case *affect management* or – 'improved affect tolerance' (Bishop et al., 2011, p. 234), a practice that is furthermore removed from the essentially collective practice of the Dharma and is apprehended instead as 'a process of . . . awareness that involves observing the . . . flow of *private* experience' (Bishop et al., ibid, p. 234, italics added)

Shen-hsiu's interpretation hierarchically discriminates between pure and impure (privileging the former). It also favours 'motionless over motion, the true mind over the ordinary mind, the whole (*ti*) over the function (*yong*), even transcendence over immanence' (Wang, 2006, p. 131). We would achieve emancipation, according to this view, by greater absorption into a pure mind and a quiet state, which is precisely what deconstructive Chan disparages as quietism and 'Zen sickness'. But let's go back to the story.

No dust, no mirror

In the morning, Hung-jen, the fifth ancestor, read the verse posted by Shen-hsiu, called his disciples, burned incense before the verse and encouraged everyone to recite the verse and meditate on it. A while later, he summoned Shen-hsiu and told him that his verse, although not bad, showed insufficient understanding; it was, he added, as if you have come to the threshold but did not go inside. He needed to think over it, he said, and in the next couple of days come up with something better. Meanwhile everyone in the monastery was reciting Shen-hsiu's verses as instructed and one day Huineng, who during all this time had been working away in the threshing room, heard it from a fellow practitioner who was passing by. He asked, and was told, where the verses came from, then said: 'I have been working here for the past eight months and haven't been to the meditation hall yet. Please take me there so I can pay my respect and light incense before these verses'. Because he was illiterate, he asked someone to read it to him. There and then he composed a verse and asked the same person to write it down for him. It said: 'Awakening has no tree; the mirror has no stand. Self-nature is at all times clean and pure; how can the dust collect anywhere?' His statement erases the notion of Buddha-nature as a *thing* (Wang, 2006). It destabilizes the artificial division between Buddha-nature – the mirror – and the ordinary, deluded mind – dust. Like Shen-hsiu, Huineng too is aware of Asvaghosha's treatise but he draws from a different notion, that of *wunian* or 'no thought'. He does not criticize Shen-hsiu's notion of 'free from thoughts' by *praising* thoughts. He elaborates instead a meaning that emphasizes the stream of thought, the stream of life and indicates *non-abiding* as the fundamental condition for human existence (Wang, 2006). Interestingly, in his verse he does not speak of 'Buddha-nature' but uses different terms, 'self-nature', at times translated as 'human nature' – moving away from a notion elevated to a 'pure realm' separate from that of the bodymind of ordinary sentient beings like you and me. Incidentally 'self-nature' 'does not indicate anything that exists in and by itself, or self-identity' (Wang, 2006, p. 134); human-nature is *empty*.

Huineng advocates neither freedom from nor attachment to thoughts, but a middle path that acknowledges our reality as thinking beings, and yet invites us to greater freedom from our conditioned 'mind-loops'. Huineng's encouragement is still valid today, if one considers how often in contemporary mindfulness literature one feels a chastising tone towards 'ruminative thinking', 'unwholesome thought patterns' and the like. Instead, we are reminded that there is a continuum, not a gap, between sentient beings and Buddhas, between the deluded mind and the mind of enlightenment. Let us now move to the last part of Huineng's story.

'I have come this long distance'

Everyone was amazed at the profound insight shown by this illiterate labourer. The fifth ancestor too immediately realized Huineng's depth of understanding. At first, however, he told the assembly that the verse did not show a full grasp of the essential meaning. But at midnight he went to Huineng's room and transmitted Dharma to him. Then he told him to flee the monastery at once, for people there would be jealous of his accomplishment and would do him harm. 'Take the robe that symbolizes the transmission' Hungjen told him, 'go south, and share the Dharma with others'. Huineng took leave and after two months arrived at Ta-yü-ling, where he learned that he had been pursued all this time by several people who wanted to kill him and take his robe but who all later desisted but for one monk, whose name was Hui-ming, known for his violent temper. Hui-ming caught up with him and wanted to kill him. Huineng handed over the Dharma robe and said: 'I have come this long distance just to seek the Dharma; I have no need for the robe' (Yampolsky, 1967, p. 134). Hui-ming, the story says, was affected by this disarming statement and asked Huineng to give him spiritual instructions. Having done that, Huineng then sent him to the north to convey his understanding to others. Later Huineng established his own training centre in Ts'ao-ch'i.

Human nature and the transformative tendency

The Chan tradition acquired the Confucian notion of inherent goodness in human nature, which is quite different from the notion of human nature within the western tradition. It focuses on the 'existential changeability . . . of each living human being' (Wang, 2006, p. 134) rather than on the postulation of a metaphysical unchanging substratum called 'human nature'. 'Nature' is similarly examined in a pragmatic and dynamic fashion, its meaning linked to 'directionality, relationality, and existential-practical development' (ibid). This is a useful distinction when considering, for instance, a notion such as the actualizing tendency (a key tenet in person–centred and humanistic therapy). There are various interpretations. My own sense is that an emphasis on the existential potentialities of the human being towards positive transformation does not require the metaphysical ballast provided by the notion of a 'formative tendency' that is supposedly at work in the cosmos. The temptation to weave elaborate descriptions and explanations is great, and I certainly can't claim to be immune to it. I find it useful to stay close as much as I can with the task at hand (therapeutic work), restrain from building mythologies and cosmologies and above all remember that each new metaphysical postulate is at best a new attempt at description rather than a truth statement. I also find in this regard Claudio Rud's reading of the formative tendency as *transformative* tendency very useful (Rud, 2016), as an ongoing, non-teleological process of *becoming*. Seen in this light, therapeutic intervention would then be focused on healing rather than speculation, as evidenced in the Buddha parable of the poisoned arrow found in the *Majjhima Nikāya Sutra*. A man is wounded by a poisoned arrow, so goes the story, but he is unwilling to let the doctor remove it right away. He needs to know who struck the arrow, to what cast he belonged, whether his skin is white or black. He also wants to know what type of arrow: bamboo, hemp or milk-sap tree? Was the arrow feathered from a vulture's wing, or perhaps from a heron's, a peacock's or a hawk's? Before knowing all this, the man would die.

To conceive of human nature as dynamic and in constant transformation opens the door to actualization, to becoming what one is. This is what Huineng calls 'seeing into [one's own] nature'. The person who does that

> does not abide either inside or outside; he is free to come and go. Readily he casts aside the mind the clings . . . and there is no obstruction to his passage.
>
> *Yampolsky, 1967, p. 150*

The post-secular condition

The notions of presence, mindfulness and Buddha-nature discussed so far in this chapter share, to a degree, a preoccupation with the secular domain. They all aspire to, or at the very least hint at, a potential transformation that can take place in the everyday. They all constitute, despite their profound differences, articulations within what several thinkers called a post-metaphysical world. That we live in a post-metaphysical world has been true up until the end of the twentieth century. But is it still true today?

Contemporary thought evidences a gradual yet momentous shift taking place in the humanities during the last two decades – namely a reconsideration of and even a return to religion. Many still hold the view that secularism is a sufficient substitute for religion, that it represents a cutting-edge view at the forefront of human thought, and that it constitutes a more direct and accurate description of human experience. Yet at the very heart of secular thought, from phenomenology and post-phenomenology to currents of thought in the making, we are witnessing a resurgence of the sacred. The latter emerges from infinity rather than totality, from a horizontal observation of phenomena rather than vertical metaphysical assumptions. We have seen intimations of this in the accounts of some of the most incisive thinkers of the second half of the twentieth century, from Derrida, Cixous and Levinas to Deleuze. Derrida's writings on Kierkegaard, Levinas's analysis of the other, Deleuze's re-evaluation of a deeply religious thinker such as Spinoza – all pointed in this direction, paving the way for current exciting developments of thought such as speculative pragmatism and the new materialisms.

Hearse in the fast lane

My own personal experience that somewhat relates to this, dates back to April 2004, at my father's funeral. We had driven the whole length of the Italian peninsula from Turin, where my father lived in his last years, to his native Benestare, a tiny village at the foot of the Aspromonte Mountains in Calabria. I sat next to the driver in the hearse, my father's body in the coffin behind us. We travelled at high speed for fear of arriving late to the funeral. To the other drivers crossing our path it must have been a strange and even terrifying sight to behold: a hearse bearing a big cross on its roof zooming at a hundred miles an hour, driven by Bobo, a tall, large gentleman who was, besides, an Elvis enthusiast and an Elvis impersonator. Predictably, by the time we were approaching Naples, there was an engine failure. Bobo managed somehow to exit the motorway and hobble to a garage but the men working there took a look at the vehicle and refused to do the job. I didn't know at first what on earth was going on as I saw them confabulating with their manager and Bobo who later explained everything to me. A while later, he removed the cross from the hearse's roof and the mechanics speedily got to work. The coffin with the dead body inside, the large gilded cross on the hearse: they couldn't just act as if everything was normal. Superstitious nonsense, some may say. Fear of the numinous and terror of the grim reaper induced by dogmatic, simplistic Catholic faith, others may add. And what's more, unpractical, paralyzing, inefficient behaviour, an excuse, perhaps for idleness and self-indulgence. Maybe so. In any case, we started back on our journey, the gilded cross duly reinstalled. By now we were late for the funeral – very late. By the time we arrived, it was late afternoon. I learned that the bells in the village church had summoned the mourners at the appointed time. They had waited for hours then went back home. At our arrival, many hours later, the bells tolled again. They all patiently came back. A young priest officiated, a couple of people made a short speech, moving, direct and simple. I felt overwhelmed. By the time I shook their hands I was choking with sadness, deference and a strange joy. Here I was, the educated Zen secularist and existentialist who had put religion aside long ago – humbled by the sincere humility of what surrounded me, reduced to mumble thanks by the silent wisdom of the soil, by the power of heartfelt religious sentiment.

A conversion? Not quite. The genuine affection these poor villagers had for my father, the austere simplicity of the ceremony, with the earnest priest just out of puberty intoning with a sad smile the *requiescat* for the dead. Everything made absolute sense to me. Religion, I thought, holds this small, deprived community and semi-abandoned village (with generations of their young working and studying miles away – New York, Germany and Northern Italy) in the same way a shamanic ceremony will connect the loved ones with the departed, in the same way a conference or a symposium will honour a dead philosopher.

Days and months later I resisted, as I still resist, the temptation to rationalize my experience of that spring day in southern Italy. There is much I could say to explain it away; I could effortlessly draw a list of factors that contributed to the vacillation of my secularist certainties. The thing is, I welcome moments like this as one welcomes the taste of nectar. It does not matter in which direction they are pointing: I get burned either way. They unsettle my hard-earned sense of certainty. They reshuffle the cards of my identity kit. And this in turns connects me to one of the important things I have learned in my formal Zen training: to keep moving, to not get stuck anywhere. It is said of Taizan Maezumi that when he was invited by a humanistic group of militant atheists to give a talk on Zen, to their dismay he talked non-stop and very convincingly of the profound, unmistakable truth of God's existence. Next day, at an interfaith event held in a Church, he spoke eloquently of the notion of God being a consolatory fairy-tale for the faint-hearted who could not stand the tangible reality of death and decay.

Zen and the art of sleep

The secularization of Dharma practice is closely link to its 'privatization': like prayer before it, the link to a community of practitioners in the same temple, church or synagogue is slackened in favour of a distinctly (essentially Protestant in flavour) solitary communion with the deity (or non-deity). Something is gained but something is irremediably lost. Depending on temperament, our greater sense of autonomy will come with either austere striving towards self-improvement and greater abnegation or, in most cases perhaps, with a self-satisfied sense of practising a 'spirituality' that can do without the cumbersome presence of others. This is because the presence of others variously provides solace, mirroring, useful irritation as well as amity on the path.

Meditation, realization and embodiment

Is it possible to live without an ideal? Is it desirable? Is it conceivable to put aside notions of 'essence', of an originating factor that is supposedly capable of explaining life and the world? If we were able to put aside 'essence' and 'ideal', what we are left with would be *just this*: thusness, ordinary life as it manifests, as it becomes at each moment.

Zen practice can be understood as the perfecting of a craft that helps us renew our aspiration to pay heed to life in its fullness, from the standpoint of life itself. Of course, this is never fully realized. Only a deluded person can claim to view life from the perspective of life itself – or a self-proclaimed 'enlightened' person, which is but another name for a deluded individual. The art of Zen training is based on a threefold schema: a) meditation; b) realization; and c) embodiment. As we shall see, this does not describe a linear, developmental process but an ongoing loop that feeds on itself.

a) *Meditation (zazen)* is an ongoing form of psychosomatic practice. By assuming the posture, we manifest the Buddha within. What distinguishes Zen from other Buddhist traditions is the fundamental unity of practice and realization. The intrinsic paradox here is that it takes years of diligent practice in order to come to the realization that it was all there in the first place. We need to run fast in order to stay still, to paraphrase the Red Queen in Lewis Carroll's *Alice in Wonderland*. *Zazen*, practiced daily, at times intensively during retreats, also helps us becoming familiar with ourselves – or, if you prefer, it provides solid enough an anchor that allows us to face ourselves without hindrances or distractions. In my own experience, the best and most direct way to do this is to practice *shikantaza* (just sitting) with no particular object of contemplation. This ostensibly simple practice cuts to the chase. It is the doing of non-doing (*wei-wu-wei*). It undoes the intricate doings of the ego-self, the comings and goings that weave the net of self-identification. By having no goal and no object, *zazen* is also eminently non-utilitarian, and allies itself with other non–utilitarian practices such as play. I have called this practice an 'inglorious activity' (Bazzano, 2013a), echoing the great Roman poet Virgil who said the same about poetry.

In short: there is nothing to gain from practicing *zazen*. If anything, it is a way of giving oneself, and of giving oneself up. This is not supine surrendering, nor is it allied to the *Gelassenheit* of fashionable pseudo-phenomenological thought, which historically resulted in a philosophy of passivity and much worse, collusion with murderous regimes. Quite the contrary: when the self recedes, the 10,000 things advance, as Dōgen says – which brings us neatly to the next point, realization.

b) *Realization (kenshō)*. It may have become clear at this point that the distinction between practice and realization is artificial – at best, a form of necessary didacticism. And yet there is something specific about the realization that needs to be said. *Kenshō* is the Great Death in Zen. I have not experienced it. Allow me to add: I also don't know whether I have experienced it. And if I had, I'd keep quiet about it. I wouldn't go around advertising my breakthrough, or claim I have reached this or that level of spiritual accomplishment, a practice known in ancient Zen lore as *walking around with dog shit on the tip of one's nose*. The sensible thing is to wipe it off, not parade it. The regular practice of *zazen* does bring insights but these need not been worshipped as gilded milestones on the way to the mountain top. Clinging to my precious insight is adding brownie points in my Buddhist pedigree: a pointless activity.

What is *kenshō*? What is it meant by the breakthrough people experience at some point during their practice? There are several possible answers to this question, depending on whether one understands Zen practice in a *logocentric* or *differential* fashion, two perspectives which will be examined in more detail in Chapter 7. For the time being, it will be enough to say that when sitting in *zazen*, doing nothing, one gradually becomes aware of the vast world of phenomena one inhabits, to the point where rigidly held distinctions between the self and the world begin to fall away. A novice will quite understandably experience this as a portentous event; he or she will almost inevitably cling to it tooth and nail. In some odd way the event (what may be described as a momentary seeing-through the insubstantial nature of the self) becomes a vital ornament to that very self. This state of affairs may go on for a while until one day one hopefully realizes that the experience one had was not such a big deal after all. In fact, there is something quite ordinary about a fluidity and interpenetration of self and world. How could it be otherwise? After all, we inhabit the world. We are part of it. How did we ever dream it could be any other way? The sensation I feel in my body right now belongs to the very same sea of phenomena as the water stream or the sound of a passing car. To know this intimately, with one's skin, bones and marrow is what realization is. Every text in existential phenomenology worth its salt will at one point or other describe this deep correlation of self and world. It will mention *epoché*, the suspension of those cherished opinions and beliefs that help maintain our self-boundedness. But I have yet to come across a text in phenomenology which points at a psychosomatic practice which would allow one to experience and know this intimately.

c) *Embodiment.* When it finally begins to dawn on one that the breakthrough experience during that particular retreat or meditation session wasn't such a big deal after all, one is ready for the third step. Many a young lover believes he or she was the first person in history ever to experience the wondrous ecstasy of love. But only a conceited person would persist in that belief. After his *kenshō*, Hakuin Zenji (1686–1769) said that no one had ever experienced the same depth of awakening he did, not even the Buddha. But he did not go on claiming that, though in our day and age a whole industry has flourished that is busy selling water by the river, with many a self-propagandist promising enlightenment over the weekend.

Embodying the insight means finding ways to ground it, to be able to express the Dharma with one's body/mind: this very body is the Buddha (Bazzano, 2013b). We find the ground again in our concrete, finite and bodily existence. We find a way to say 'I' again, yet holding our self-identification lightly, honouring its important nominal function in the scheme of things whilst knowing all along that its importance is relative. Embodying the experience of awakening is also closely linked to the notion of integrity, which I understand as resisting the compulsion to metaphysical claims beyond my necessarily limited, situated perspective. This may be illustrated by a well-known image. At the beginning of practice, the practitioner is said to see mountains as mountains and rivers as rivers. At the moment of embarking on a committed spiritual practice, everything stays in place: here it's me, there it is the world. At some point, when practice deepens and reaches a point of self-combustion, mountains are no longer mountains and rivers are no longer rivers. Self and world interpenetrate. The breakthrough we experience and the corresponding insight dramatically reshuffles our perception and our way of being in the world. The experience is disorienting, exhilarating, and at times alarming. It may be tempting to stay there and from those dizzy heights declare one's authenticity and awakening. But *who* exactly is claiming this great insight that there is no self but the same very self? This is, sadly, the place where many of us get stuck, whether under a transpersonal, integral or spiritual banner but all articulating in different ways a *developmental* view of the spiritual and psychological experience. If, on the other hand, the insights experienced during a breakthrough have been grounded/integrated/embodied, then mountains are again mountains, and rivers are again rivers. The 'transpersonal' or mystical dimension is shed in favour of ordinary life and every day existence. Samsara is nirvana. This very body is the Buddha; this very earth is the lotus paradise. Above all, embodiment means one experiences life and the world from a perspective, from a limited, situated vantage point that is one's body/mind. We go back to where we started, but having gone on a journey of discovery that loosened the grip we normally hold to our *place* and our *identity*. From here, the process starts again, circularly: back to square one, to a limited perspective, then on to a new realization and again back to embodiment and integration. Climbing the mountain, reaching the rarefied air of the peaks, enjoying the view and then beginning the descent down to the valley, to the marketplace, to the dust and sweat, to the buy and sell, the cries and whispers of history and the world. What I find unique in Zen is this affirmation of the world and a constant reshuffle of the scene. There is no resting place, either in the personal or the trans-personal, in the spiritual or the material dimension. The word I suggested for this understanding of the Dharma is *mundane* (Bazzano, 2014b). Zen practice is mundane in that it is *of the world* and does not shun what religious thought normally decides to see as despicable. This is why Zen cannot be said to be a 'non-dual', practice at least in the sense in which the term has been used in recent years. There is no going 'beyond' but instead a full affirmation of the mystery of *this*.

A note on tradition

For all the encumbrance of its paraphernalia and the seeming perpetuation of hierarchy, tradition (or even better ritual, the repetition of a practice weathered through centuries) is a natural ally to *anamnesis*, our imaginative stretch in conceiving the very real existence of life before our coming into the world. This is itself impediment to the exaggerated importance conferred to the self and its petulant demands. The deep bow taken in front of an altar, the settling into the *zazen* posture: through ritual I enter a living stream that has been flowing for centuries and will continue to flow, each living being injecting new life into it and being simultaneously rejuvenated by the great Zen River, the wayward tributary to the Ocean of the Dharma. It is possible to dismiss ritual, rebel against it in the name of individual freedom. I have done so myself. But it would be a pity to reduce a millenarian practice to a set of techniques at the service of the modern-day consumer. In this way the precious opportunity at the heart of the practice – the chance to look deeply into the nature of the self – is lost. There was a world before me and there will be one after my demise. And there is a stream that flows uninterrupted this very moment, unaffected by my presence, by my joys and sorrows, thoughts and emotions. Practice means to step willingly into this living stream.

References

Batchelor, S. (2010). *Confession of a Buddhist Atheist*. New York: Spiegel & Grau.

Bazzano, M. (2013a). In praise of stress induction: Mindfulness revisited. *European Journal of Psychotherapy and Counselling*, 15(2): 174–185.

Bazzano, M. (2013b). This very body the Buddha. *Sexual and Relationship Therapy*, 28(1–2): 132–140. doi: 10.1080/14681994.2013.770143.

Bazzano, M. (Ed.). (2014a). *After Mindfulness: New Perspectives on Psychology and Meditation*. Basingstoke: Palgrave MacMillan.

Bazzano, M. (2014b). Mindfulness and the good life. In M. Bazzano (Ed.), *After mindfulness: New perspectives on psychology and meditation* (pp. 61–80). Basingstoke: Palgrave MacMillan.

Bishop, S. R., Lau, M., Shapiro, S., Carlson, L., Anderson, N. D. & Carmody, J. (2004). Mindfulness: A proposed operational definition. *Contemporary Buddhism*, 12(1): 230–241.

Booth, R. (2014). Mindfulness therapy comes at a high price for some, say experts. *The Guardian*, 25 August. https://theguardian.com/society/2014/aug/25/mental-health-meditation Retrieved 13 November 2016.

Dillard, A. (2016). *The Abundance: Narrative Essays Old and New*. New York: Ecco Press.

Dreyfus, G. (2011). Is mindfulness present-centred and non-judgmental? A discussion of the cognitive dimensions of mindfulness. *Contemporary Buddhism*, 12(1): 41–54.

Foucault, M. (2000). *Ethics, Subjectivity and Truth*. London: Penguin.

Freud, S. (1958). *Recommendations to Physicians Practicing Psychoanalysis*, Standard edition, 12. London: Hogarth Press.

Geller, S. M. & Greenberg, L. S. (2012). *Therapeutic Presence: A Mindful Approach to Effective Therapy*. Washington DC: APA.

Geller, S. M., Greenberg, L. S. & Watson, J. C. (2010). Therapist and client perceptions of therapeutic presence: the development of a measure. *Psychotherapy Research*, 20: 599–610.

Lanyado, M. (2012). *The Presence of the Therapist: Treating Childhood Trauma*. London: Routledge.

Madison, G. B. (1981). *The Phenomenology of Merleau-Ponty*. Athens, OH: Ohio University Press.

Massumi, B. (2014). *What Animals Teach Us About Politics*. Durham, NC: Duke University Press.

Merleau-Ponty, M. (1964). *Sense and Non-sense*. Evanston, IL: Northwestern University Press.

Merleau-Ponty, M. (2010). *Phenomenology of Perception*. London: Continuum.

Olendski, A. (2011). The construction of mindfulness. *Contemporary Buddhism*, 12(1): 55–70.

Proctor, G. (2002). *The Dynamics of Power in Counselling and Psychotherapy: Ethics, Politics and Practice*. Ross-on-Wye: PCCS Books.

Purser, R. & Loy, D. (2013). *Beyond McMindfulness, The Huffington Post*, 7 January. http://huffingtonpost.com/ron-purser/beyond-mcmindfulness_b_3519289.html Retrieved 13 November 2016.

Purser, R., Forbes, D. & Burke, A. (Eds). (2016). *Handbook of Mindfulness: Culture, Context and Social Engagement*. New York: Springer.

Rogers, C. R. (1957). The necessary and sufficient conditions of therapeutic personality change. *Journal of Consulting Psychology*, 21: 95–103.

Rogers, C. R. (1980). *A Way of Being*. Boston, MA: Houghton Mifflin.

Rose, J. (2011). What more could we want of ourselves! The letters of Rosa Luxemburg. *London Review of Books*, (33)12: 5–12.

Rud, C. (2016). The philosophical practice of Spinoza and the person-centered paradigm. Presentation, WAPCEPC *Conference* 20–24 July 2016, New York City, Cuny Graduate Center, 23 July.

Ryan, J. (2012). Yoga for the mind. *Therapy Today*, 23(8): 14–17.

Salzberg, S. (2011). Mindfulness and loving-kindness. *Contemporary Buddhism*, 12(1): 177–182.

Santorelli, S. F. (2011). Enjoy your death: Leadership lessons. *Contemporary Buddhism*, 12(1): 199–217.

Schore, A. N. (2001). Effects of a secure attachment relationship on right brain development, affect regulation, and infant mental health. *Infant Mental Health Journal*, 22(1–2): 7–66.

Stern, D. (2004). *The Present Moment in Psychotherapy and Everyday Life*. New York: W.W. Norton & Co.

Teasdale, J. D. & Chaskalson, M. (2011). How does mindfulness transform suffering? *Contemporary Buddhism*, 12(1): 89–102.

Wang, Y. (2006). The Chan deconstruction of Buddha nature. In J. Y. Park (Ed.), *Buddhisms and deconstructions* (pp. 129–144). Lanham, MD: Rowman & Littlefield.

Winnicott, D. W. (1971). *Playing and Reality*. London: Tavistock.

Yampolsky, P. B. (1967). *The Platform Sutra of the Sixth Patriarch*. New York: Columbia University Press.

5

WHY ZEN IS NOT TRANSPERSONAL

Silence and giggles

A while ago I was invited to teach a class on 'transpersonal psychotherapy' on a humanistic integrative course, standing in for a tutor who was unwell. I was surprised at first, as I don't describe my work as transpersonal. Then I remembered that it is taken for granted that if you are a Zen practitioner and a therapist, the transpersonal label will fit you like a (luminous, ethereal) glove. This is understandable: no other psychotherapeutic approach openly embraces contemplative practices and spirituality. So I cast my doubts aside, tell myself that it will be an opportunity to explore with the trainees the things which are at the margins of most therapeutic training: the links between the two dimensions of meditation and relating, speech and silence, psychotherapeutic theories and the key tenets of Dharma practice. Sometime later, my sense of ambivalence resurfaces when a quick glance at the handouts the tutor I'm replacing left for me makes me gasp. They draft arbitrary maps of consciousness; chart the latter's supposed evolution from self-awareness to giddy 'cosmic consciousness'. They speak of quadrants, levels, and transcendent dimensions; they mention the spirit world, ghosts and reincarnation – all of these as a given. I decide to put the handouts to one side and invite participants to sit with their eyes closed or half-closed. I invite them to be aware of their posture – to notice the ordinary rhythm of the breath, inhaling and exhaling. Speaking slowly, I remind them that some time in the future each of us in the room will exhale for one last time. I urge them gently to attend to this moment, to be aware of their own presence and that of others in the room. Notice the temperature in the room, I add, register the atmosphere we are creating together just by being here. Some of them start to giggle. I realize that even for therapists-in-the-making the experience of sitting in silence for a few minutes feels strange. I wonder how they would cope with those moments in the therapy room when silence inevitably falls. Would they rush in to fill it? After 15 minutes or so I present a few ideas and open up the discussion. Most participants expected an exploration of the mystical, the extra-sensorial and the transcendent. Inevitably perhaps, given the title of the day's training, the group process veers towards subtle energies, seeing ghosts and whether a counsellor can become a conduit for 'higher energies'. I try to be congruent and admit that I don't really know what the transpersonal means though many writers and practitioners seem so sure about it. I invite them to remain present to their experience and honest about what they don't know. I invite them to be more comfortable with not knowing, to consider the vastness of the mystery that we are and that surrounds us. Some make connections between what I am presenting and mindfulness – the little meditation exercise we did reminded some of them of a mindfulness course they've done in the past. I feel heartened by this, reading it as a welcome move away from talk of disembodied entities and the spirit world. At the same time, I am not flattered by the comparison as I don't identify what I do with 'mindfulness' either. I tell myself that it does not really matter what we call it. Even if I don't manage to convey the difference between Zen and mindfulness, I'll be happy if these trainees will go home considering this single notion: how to *be with*: with one's experience as it arises, and with their client's. This is all I concentrate on in the next couple of hours during skills practice. As the day progressed, it appeared as if most of us have learned something. Some have been able to sit with discomfort without being discomfited. For my part, I have learned to adapt in trying to convey my enthusiasm for Zen practice to a group of people who were new to it.

Sitting by the window on the train on the way home as it gets dark, I can't help but notice a feeling of dissatisfaction creeping up. How on earth will I ever be able to convey both the depth and the simplicity of Zen without cheapening it or distorting it, without making it pliable to facile notions of spirituality?

Being human

A familiar theme in vampire and science-fiction movies sees the otherworldly hero or heroine long for the human condition, for the murky rainbow of emotions and feelings as for the uncertainty that comes with the knowledge of being a mortal body. Angels, and devils alike, long for the tang of frosty wind on their ghostly, sulphurous features. They long for the turning of night into day and the brief comeliness of dawn. Although they are at home with eternity, they seem to crave knowledge of time; they yearn to learn entanglement in worldly torments and delights.

In Wim Wenders' seminal film *Wings of Desire* (Wenders, 1987), former angel Damiel learns to be human, gawkily negotiating our perishable domain with his now imperfect, perishable body. He buys a cup of coffee, burns his lips, but the experience delights him. It is a bitter cold morning but to him the cold is bliss: being a mortal body this once, on a chilly morning in Berlin is delightful. This may be due to my inordinate fondness for the hot dark brew, but I find the sight of a former angel taking pleasure in burning his lips on a cup of coffee on a winter morning agonizingly beautiful. In the sequel, *Faraway, So Close!* (Wenders, 1993), his companion Cassiel, an angel keenly interested in human vicissitudes, finds himself suddenly human when he sweeps down to catch a child who had fallen from a balcony. He becomes human, that is, through a spontaneous act of charity. For different reasons, both angels surrender their exalted state and their proximity with God's radiance so as to become merely human.

The focus of the Buddha's teachings is entirely on our peculiar, transient presence in the world and on our cohabitation with others who happen to reside here. Those beings who belong to higher realms are not to be envied, as their lot does not permit them to attain liberation: only an imperfect, finite being like you and me can become a Buddha.

In Zen teachings there is a profound appreciation of the everyday, paired with studied ambivalence, a reluctance to settle on either spiritualism or materialism. I remember having a bad day a little more than ten years ago in Salt Lake City, Utah. I was there to do intensive Zen training and was giving myself a really hard time. I had agonizing doubts about the nature of the teachings I was getting; I saw them as too 'transcendent' and clashing with my own predilections. I had had little sleep in the night ruminating over this and in the morning Daniel, one of the assistant teachers, started his talk by reading a section of Molly Bloom's funny, tender, passionate, unpunctuated soliloquy in Joyce's *Ulysses* (Joyce, 1969). I wanted to cry with joy. And so I did. This wonderful and famous passage is one of the most life-affirming texts I know of. Hearing this celebration of sensuality and free association in the meditation hall, all of us sitting cross-legged in austere black robes, was an incongruously exhilarating experience. For a brief moment, it gave me back hope in formal training.

The everyday ridiculous

Anxious to offset the established categories of religious discourse and the undeniable appeal these still hold for many, secular Buddhism has substituted the notion of the absolute with that of the sublime. Doing away with what it sees as the traditional fallacy of dividing the absolute from the relative, self-declared secularists speak of the everyday sublime. They rightly emphasize how mystifying our being in the world truly is; they draw attention to the often-overlooked strangeness of the everyday. They rhapsodize on the breath-taking wonder of the phenomenal world. This is very effective: it redirects the mystical gaze from the quasi-mystical fixation that imagines that truth, good and beauty dwell in a metaphysical rather than a physical realm. It invites us to appreciate this life and this world.

My objection to this stance is its penchant to overlook the brokenness, anguish and absurdity that sit alongside goodness and beauty. In emphasizing the everyday sublime, it bypasses the everyday ridiculous as well as the absurdity of the everyday. It also risks bypassing the fundamental violence, hatred and injustice that humans have inflicted and continue to inflict on other humans. My objection to the rhapsodizing secularists echoes the very same which were raised against

Pascal: so enraptured is the ecstasy, so beautifully expressed the anguish, it averts our gaze from the very real suffering of the world. It also distracts us from effectively entering the path, whose first step is our willingness to acknowledge the reality of *dukkha*, the dissatisfaction and suffering that is inherent in existence.

To *aestheticize* the everyday is to provide us with an enticing alternative to the more conventional solution offered by pious Buddhism but one that is ultimately not entirely different from the latter. Neither of them truly addresses the anguish of our human predicament. The secular path is often a *literary* solution to anguish, one that I am admittedly sympathetic to. There is a lot to be said for the ability to distil terse, scintillating prose from the dregs of affliction. It is admirable when anyone succeeds in sublimating fear and hatred into art. But we are still a long way away from the cessation of suffering advocated by the Buddha. It can also 'anaesthetize us to the real presence of others, who then become objects in a poignantly beautiful tapestry of life; (John Mackessy, personal communication, 2016).

Shortcuts to ecstasy

There are direct and indirect associations with the spiritual dimensions that trans-personal therapy talks about and the use of psychoactive substances in therapy. This is not new: Psychoanalysis, it has been argued, was steeped in psycho-pharmacology (Clemens, 2013), with Freud effectively being one of the founders of psycho-pharmacology. He sponsored drugs long before the 'listening-to-Prozac' craze began, and this was because he *was on* drugs. Influenced by Aschenbrand's studies on the effects of cocaine on the human body, after completing his medical studies in 1884 he became interested in cocaine, and came to believe that it could be effective in the treatment of morphine addiction and alcoholism. He recommended it to his friend Ernst Fleischl-Marxow, who was addicted to morphine. Within a few days 'Ernst couldn't stop using the substance and he eventually died as Europe's first official cocaine addict' (Clemens, 2013, p. 31). Freud's research on cocaine was exposed 'as outrageously unscientific . . . and the Viennese medical establishment heaped opprobrium upon Freud's name and work' (ibid.). The debacle proved valuable in the long run for it made possible Freud's turn from neurology to psychology.

Later on, on the wave of the Ken Kesey's 'Merry Pranksters' (Wolfe, 1968), substances such as LSD have been applied to therapy with mixed results in the 1970s. For years after that the practice has remained somehow associated with, and circumscribed to, the domain of transpersonal psychotherapy. It has seen some kind of resurgence lately with therapeutic experimentation that involved MDMA, commonly known as ecstasy (Solon, 2016), a psychoactive drug whose desired effects include empathy and euphoria.

Not all of these experiments are positive and life-enhancing. My client Simone is an experienced humanistic therapist with a keen interest in the transpersonal. One day she came to see me after a weekend spent in Austria doing experiential group work that included, alongside regular therapeutic practice of encounter and dyad work, the taking of MDMA. As soon as she got there, Simone felt unsafe and regretted her decision to join. This was not so much in relation to MDMA but had to do with the facilitation itself, which Simone at first thought was unsteady and lacking in transparent communication and as time went on, manipulative and domineering. At the beginning she tried to bracket her apprehension and decided to trust that whatever happened, she had it in her to deal with it. Later she learned that along with MDMA, the facilitator had also given some LSD to participants, without telling them. By the time the cocktail kicked in, Simone was lying on her yoga mat listening to the facilitator saying in a monotonous, irritating voice: 'you are resisting, Simone! Do not resist!' She could also hear fellow participants around the room moaning, laughing and groaning at various degrees of elation, confusion and distress. At this point, despite being high and despite a clear feeling of being trapped in some kind of a nightmare, she somehow found the strength to shut out the jarring voice that kept repeating: 'Do not resist, Simone. Do not resist!' She also managed to pull away gently from the engulfing embrace of the co-facilitator who pressed on her with her very large breasts. She dismissed the facilitator's suggestion that it was Mother Earth Herself surrounding her in her sweaty embrace. She was furious at herself for what she perceived as her own gullibility and misguided openness – above all for not trusting her gut feeling at the start when she felt that the place was not safe, that the facilitators were dangerous, incompetent fools. She managed (not without difficulty, considering her altered, delicate state of mind) to shield herself within a visualized self-protective membrane; she kept telling herself again and again that she would be fine, that despite her vulnerable state and the unbearable pressure she was going to steer a way out of this. By the time she managed to get up and was about to go out into the courtyard for a breath of fresh air, she found the exit blocked by the facilitator who said: 'You can't go out! It is your resistance! Do not resist the experience!' By now Simone had regained some of her composure and mental lucidity, despite the lingering effects of LSD and MDMA. She wanted to challenge the facilitator but felt intimidated by his physical strength and aggressive demeanour. She had mixed feelings. The facilitator was clearly dangerous and could do a lot of damage to vulnerable participants. But Simone also felt tickled to laughter. There was, she said, 'something pathetic about the guy'. She felt that his attempt to gain respect and a sense of authority by attempting to dominate others in such a primitive, blunt manner was disturbing but also comical.

The weekend came to an end, and Simone was glad to have survived it. The next day, back home, she felt strangely elated. She had proved to herself that she had stamina and had learned an important lesson about the more experimental fringes of the transpersonal and, more generally, she had learned to trust more her own instinctual doubts and differentiate them from simple prejudice. It made her rethink some of her own assumptions, namely, about unchecked power dynamics inherent within spiritually tinged groups that willingly elect a leader who is supposed to have achieved a 'higher state of consciousness'. The facilitator spoke and acted from an alleged place of knowing that was never challenged. The entirety of the pseudo-therapeutic proceedings depended on the passive acceptance from the group members of his guru status. Simone also reflected on the arbitrariness and recklessness of using psychotropic substances when not paired to an informed, tried and tested psychotherapeutic practice.

Chemical Platonism

It appears, rightly or wrongly, that many of the tenets within transpersonal psychotherapy are directly or indirectly inspired by the use of psychotropic and hallucinogenic substances. I know for a fact that some of these 'journeys' can be useful to some people at a particular point in their life. At the same time, this type of experimentation leaves the door open to behaviours and practices that the psychotherapeutic tradition has worked hard to overcome for decades. On a theoretical level, the temporary, artificial opening of the doors of perception provided by psychotropic substances has led exponents of transpersonal psychotherapy to the conceptualization of a spiritual dimension that is envisioned outside psychology's reach. At times the experience leads to deeper appreciation of the phenomenal world, of the extraordinary within the ordinary, of the *mysterium tremendum* concealed in the interstices of everyday activities. More often, however, the intense experience brought about by imbibing LSD or MDMA leads to theorizations that assume the existence of an eternal dimension behind and above the everyday. Despite, or in fact because of these conjectures, the wild experimentations often end up confirming the most conservative views parcelled out by the philosophical and religious traditions: eternalism, logocentrism and an all-pervading, watered-down Platonism – all visible behind the veneer of new terms and definitions.

Given my own history, it would be hypocritical of me to chastise the use of psychotropic substances, even though I have stopped imbibing anything (other than the odd glass of Malbec) since June 2003. I do hope my stance does not come across as moralistic, as this is far from my sensibility. What I object to is the eternalist philosophizing often found tagging along accounts of psychedelic experiences and the neophyte's certainties on the 'illusory' nature of death, the interconnectedness of all things in the cosmos, the truth of reincarnation and the tangible presence of the numinous source. I also realize how refreshingly earnest this mystical stance is compared with the more casual popping of pills for weekend escapist consumption.

Everyone's experience is of course different and the apparent forcefulness with which I express my view on the matter is not meant as dismissal of other perspectives. But if my own experimentation in this area taught me anything of value, this has to do more with uncertainty than certainty, learning greater openness, valuing not-knowing rather than a new source of knowing. It may well be that each of us is in some way predisposed to a particular kind of experience, and that the archetypal forms we more or less consciously keep within our horizon of perception influence, or to some extent even direct, our experience. Some of us feel reluctant to translate the bewildering array of phenomena that constantly emerge, linger and fade into the home of the identity-principle or that of 'Being'. Others perceive the 'ten thousand things' as chaos and find comfort and even 'ground' in a holistic view that sees the Many reduced to the One. When a metaphysical position becomes too entrenched, one of the likely outcomes is denigration of the phenomenal world and its inherent richness and complexity. When experience with psychotropic substances becomes too easily translated into facile categories, the experiencer begins to sound evangelical.

'I knew it all along'

A couple of times during therapy, Roberto recounted his first experience with LSD. He travelled to Stonehenge on a summer day, and arrived there by the evening. After taking acid, he sat in silence throughout the night. In the early hours before dawn, he found himself talking to a young Japanese woman who, so it appeared, had sprung out of nowhere. It wasn't a 'normal' everyday small talk, Roberto said, but one that was 'full of resonances and deep hidden meanings'. Minutes before the sun began to rise, he felt a surge of warmth and energy within his body, as if he was welcoming the appearance of the burning star not only as this individual being in a young man's body but as the Earth itself: 'as if I myself was the Earth'. The young woman said sweet things to him that seemed infused with ancient wisdom. 'Listening to her, I became an old Taoist sage, my face lined, with a pointed white beard. The pervading feeling was a sense of knowing, of having accessed a source that was true, profound and at the same time devastatingly uncomplicated. 'I knew this all along' he thought. The ancient setting, the sun rising on a summer day, the benevolent, enabling presence of the young woman – all conjured up, he felt, to the making of a truly inimitable experience.

I listened with great interest to Roberto's story. I noticed his tears, and felt how taken by the experience he truly was. I registered how much it had meant to him. He treasured the event, regarding it as a milestone, a turning point in understanding himself and the world. For my part, I felt sympathetic to him and in some sense I even partly identified with his experience, reminiscent of my own youthful ventures in the area. I bracketed as I could my natural surge of sympathy. Admittedly, it was more difficult to suspend my own assessment of the experience and excruciatingly difficult not to dispute some of the conclusions Roberto drew from it. Years of practice, however, taught me that one cannot bracket away and momentarily suspend one's own being. This is also not desirable as it seriously gets in the way of congruent communication. I remember thinking whether any of his transcendental insights had survived the cold light of day, whether the iridescent richness of his cosmic journey had held out the re-encroaching of routine on the proverbial Monday morning at the office. I tentatively enquired about the aftermath, managing to phrase some of my thoughts. It turned out that Roberto's weekdays that followed had felt greyer and even more devoid of meaning than they had ever been. One obvious way of understanding this trajectory is in terms of the 'lows' that inevitably follows the 'highs'. In Roberto's case, given his real hunger for higher meaning and a deeper connection with others and the world, the 'low' also propelled him further to read and study a range of spiritual texts. His hope was to find a metaphysical description or explanation to substantiate his intuitive grasp of his experience with LSD – a way to reshape his own *idiom* (Bollas, 1996).

At this point in our exploration, I began to see my role as helping Roberto clarify, articulate and build trust in his idiom with or without the borrowing of second-hand metaphysics. My own unstated preference is for an articulation that keeps in check the rush for ready-made philosophical answers and has greater trust in the associations that naturally arise to orient and complement one's unique experience. In this sense, the therapist's task is crucial in assisting the emergence of *authorship* in a client – finding one's 'voice', making sense of one's experience. There is a difference between the more widespread understanding of therapy as an essentially hermeneutical practice and one that is focused on authorship. The first is based on description, at best, and in some cases borders on interpretation, the second on ethical respect for the autonomy of the client and the decentering of the therapist's role. The question then is no longer how to describe/interpret but *how to create space for authorship to emerge*. This is an important point that merits a little more clarification.

Authorship, idiom and 'therapist as idiot'

Existential psychotherapist Spinelli (2007) advocates a descriptive stance intriguingly portrayed as *the therapist as idiot*. This notion has been met with bewilderment, even hostility, and is often apprehended either literally (which ignores its wit) or strategically (as a crafty move to facilitate therapeutic contact). I am familiar with these responses; they are the ones I hear every time when, working with groups, I find myself solemnly advocating the idiotic stance. I suspect my own version differs somewhat from Spinelli's. My own source comes from Zen: without meaning to be flippant, one could reasonably say that becoming a fully fledged idiot is the very essence of Zen training. In Zen literature 'idiocy' is at times described as blindness, and the trainee is encouraged to travel all five degrees:

> *Bonkatsu* is ignorance plain and simple, our ordinary deluded state in the shopping mall of samsara. Then there is *jakatsu*, a sort of articulated, well-informed and academic stupidity: we can't experience life simply because of the amount of learned garbage we have accumulated over the years. Next, we have *mikatsu*, the blindness of one who is devoted to practice but is still deluded – too attached, perhaps, to a literal understanding of the teachings. Then there is *shōkatsu* – we begin to grasp that there is nothing to grasp, nothing to see. At last, there is *shinkatsu*, 'true blindness, the point when all talk of liberation and delusion is utterly meaningless.
>
> *Bazzano, 2016, p. 90*

Encouragement to pursue 'advanced idiocy' also comes from Merleau-Ponty. In his unfinished, posthumously published *The Prose of the World* (Merleau-Ponty, 1973), he speaks of the subject (the person, the individual etc.) as being themselves a *new idiom* who in turn invents new modes of expression. Language itself is opened up to a new singular form that is unique to a particular human experience. This process is at first unavoidably subjective, and inescapably 'narcissistic'; it stutters as it struggles to articulate its own idiom – creating a language rather than applying the given one – what some cognitive scientists would refer to as 'first-person report' (Varela, 1996, p. 332), and obliquely close to what Ted Hughes (2008) partly referred to as 'poetry':

> The real mystery is this strange need. Why can't we just hide it and shut up? why do we have to blab? Why do human beings need to confess? Maybe if you don't have that secret confession, you don't have a poem – don't even have a story, don't have a writer.
>
> *p. 287*

The therapist tunes into the idiotic/poetic (incarnate) language of the client and then offers his/her own idiotic responses – idiotic because they are not *interpretations* but further *associations*, elaboration of a singular idiom. This idiotic exchange may be also described as taking the risk of communication, which is the very heart of genuine encounter, our real chance to pursue 'truth' via engaged conversation rather than the unveiling of a supposedly pre-existing 'Truth'. This is the very heart of rationality, broadly understood:

> [We]are rational not because what[we] say and do has a transcendent guarantee, but simply because . . . [we] can still, if [we] make an effort, communicate with and understand one another.
>
> *Madison, 1981, p. 299*

And then there is stupidity. I remember a poignant remark made by the great, late novelist William Gaddis:

> I constantly try to call attention to what my mother had told me once at some paranoid moment of mine: You must always remember that there is much more stupidity than there is malice in the world.
>
> *Gaddis, 2007, p. 302*

What is stupidity in this context? The attempt to translate the essentially unfathomable human experience (some may call it 'existential unconscious') into measurable, quantifiable data, which is one of the elements of the current zombiefication of experience and obliteration of the humanities operated by neo-liberalism and neo-positivism.

Instead of an opening of language that makes room for and tries to express experience (which is how language is renewed), the meaning of experience is *made to fit* (*incastrato* in Italian) within the clunky iron grip of data. This is eminently boring – as any editor or reader of academic psychology journals will tell you – and deeply uninspiring. It also fails to foster the research and the advancement of understanding it is supposed to promote. It is a disservice to the subjective experience of the client and, equally important, to the therapist's presence and interventions – what some cognitive scientists would refer to as third person description (Varela, 1996).

I don't know how far Spinelli takes his idiotic stance. His idiocy may well be strategic, much like 'non-directivity' with some person-centred practitioners who choose not to take literally the essentially ethical demand implicit in the principle of non-directivity. Personally, I aspire to maintain the stance in all 'phases' of therapy, continually searching for new idioms that may help rewrite the very meaning of therapy. In other words, I claim the right to be an idiot all the way.

On interpretation and 'spiritual authority'

I don't believe my own views on these matters are better or truer: they are, more simply, the closest thing I am able to construct that congruently reflects my experience. I found it, of course, heartening to realize that the latter is somewhat confirmed by certain worldviews and a particular ontological stance. What I find disturbing is to learn that within the field of spirituality and/or transpersonal therapy, the exploration undertaken by a client or a trainee is often met with the imposition of an interpretation. The latter, rather than being simply offered tentatively as the therapist or trainer's own impression and association, is bestowed as accurate and true and its truth validated by the assumed spiritual authority of the therapist/trainer. It seems that the egalitarian spirit pioneered by people like Rogers, or the rigorous stance of ongoing associative work championed by practitioners such as Bollas, are overridden by a regression to the crude pronouncements of an assumed and arbitrary authority. The following example may help to illustrate this.

At one of our morning sessions, Gabriel, a transpersonal therapy trainee, wanted to talk about a dream he had the previous week. It had stayed with him, he said, and there were a few 'entangled knots' that puzzled and even worried him, despite the fluent – if unsolicited – interpretation offered by one of his trainers, a respected transpersonal practitioner. Or maybe, Gabriel added after a pause, *because of* the interpretation. He now wanted to revisit the dream and see what came up this time, if anything. I made it clear that I was not going to give an interpretation, but that I was nevertheless keen to hear his account of the dream.

I find myself at a wedding, Gabriel said. To his surprise, he realizes the wedding he is invited to is his own. He feels embarrassed and clumsy; he is unprepared; his suit, he notices to his dismay, is torn. He is waiting in a crypt, anxious and irresolute. He now catches a glimpse of the bride: she is grey, faceless. There is a certain elegance about her, but no life; 'she is bloodless', Gabriel says. Looking into the next room, he notices that the wedding reception, bizarrely already underway before the wedding has even taken place, is shabby and utterly devoid of colour. It looks like an old sepia photograph. There are a few sandwiches on the table, bottles of beer and wine; no decorations, no music. No one is dancing or even smiling; no felicitations or speeches. A few people stand around in a sort of living room next door, holding plastic cups, exchanging platitudes and inanities. The whole dream, Gabriel says, is suffused with a sense of disappointment and displacement; he has been flung there without being consulted, placed there by a series of bizarre circumstances outside his will. The sadness he felt on waking up was overwhelming, amplified by the realization that what in his mind should be one of the most joyful events in his life is instead so dismal.

The interpretation given by his transpersonal trainer focused on Gabriel's supposedly 'undeveloped feminine side'; it critiqued his 'rational, masculine side that was no longer serving him'. It also pointed at unresolved issues Gabriel had 'brought into his present situation from the accumulated karma of past incarnations'. These included his 'high expectations as one who had been a man in many lives' which translated into chronic inability to accept the 'wondrous ordinariness of his present existence, the mystery in the everyday', in turn linked to his unwillingness to 'accept and fulfil the commitments in his life symbolized by the wedding reception'. The interpretation, bequeathed on Gabriel with oracular certainty, was then sprinkled with a set of tasks he could perform on a weekly basis in order to 'purify the negative karma'.

As he related the above, Gabriel rolled his eyes in mocking disbelief. But his tone betrayed mixed feelings, and a fundamental uncertainty due to the fact that the trainer who had interpreted his dream was well respected. I suggested that we respectfully put aside the interpretation and together take another look at the dream and see what emerged. What gradually came up was a different picture: more tentative, exploratory in tone, and focusing on different details present in the dream. Above all, the strong feeling that slowly began to materialize in Gabriel's recounting of the dream was his anger at being pushed in to a situation in which he had to perform according to a pre-established norm, even though he was neither ready nor willing. The rather forceful interpretation he had been given strangely echoed this general feeling of coercion. Hesitantly at first, but with a growing sense of confidence, Gabriel said that his reluctance was not 'mere adolescent rebellion' against 'mature commitments' but healthy refusal to join in a 'dull parade of norms and ritualized behaviours'. The soggy sandwiches, the warm beer, the faceless, grey spouse: no, he didn't want to be there. He didn't have to oblige. He could choose something better; he could make his own attempts and 'devising a ceremony'; he could make his own mistakes and at least have a sense of greater freedom and dignity.

You have to say something

A common reading of Zen is of a tradition that privileges silence over expression. I have come across this on a regular basis during my time working with trainees and colleagues, and not only among those with little knowledge of Zen. The assumption is that silence is better at conveying an experiential dimension that is either pre-verbal or transcendent, beyond words. There are striking similarities here with therapy, particularly with the kind of psychoanalytic psychotherapy influenced by Winnicott who 'would wait in silence for long periods in order to encourage the dismantling of the patient's false self-defence and the emergence of the true self'. Less concerned with the *meaning* of implicit contents, he 'tended to regard . . . verbal associations as a defence against the essential formlessness of human existence' (Nettleton, 2016, p. 89). The problem with this stance is the merging of the client within a maternal dyad. The client is deprived of the possibility of articulating his/her idiom and individuated experience through free association and exploration. Risking a generalization, I would venture to say that the message conveyed by the Winnicottian analyst may be that the pre-verbal maternal dimension recreated in the therapy room is more important than the articulation of the client's independent creation of meaning. The Zen tradition found expedient ways to escape the danger of turning Dharma practice into an attempt to return to the peace and indistinctiveness of the womb and/or the oceanic experience. It did so in two ways: first, by introducing kōan study, (*gong' an* in Chinese, *kongan* in Korean) which meant that students would not only be obliged to shift from 'just sitting' (*shikantaza*) to intense concentration on insoluble existential riddles but they also had to come up with 'answers' when going to formal interviews with a teacher. In other words, they had to say something, and say it existentially, not just as theoretical answers that show sophisticated knowledge, but by bringing their hearts, bodies and minds to it. Second, it did so by the shaking up of the watery dimension of the quietist contemplation via an emphasis on the bodhisattva ethical practice. Peace of mind and enlightenment take second place in relation to the practice of generosity and active engagement with the world. Indeed, the practice of meditation (*zazen*) itself can be understood as an offering of oneself to the world, carried out with no intention of gain, including silence, oneness or any other desired mental state.

On James Hillman

Long before training as a therapist, I had been captivated by the writings of James Hillman whose astounding breadth of vision culminated in the formulation of archetypal psychology (Hillman, 1983; 1997) – a rare occurrence, in my view, of a genuinely perspectivist (some would say polytheistic) stance in psychology. With its placing of *archetypes as phenomena*, Hillman echoed a position already championed by the existential psychoanalyst Rollo May (1969). He shrewdly avoided the metaphysical canards of either placing archetypes *outside* phenomena in a world of Platonic ideas or in the realm of Absolute Spirit. I mention Hillman here because his highly nuanced position is by far (in my opinion) the richest, most creative and interesting within the wide transpersonal field. Speaking of his book *The Soul Code* during an interview, he said:

> My book is about a third view. It says, yes, there's genetics. Yes, there are chromosomes. Yes, there's biology. Yes, there are environment, sociology,

parenting, economics, class, and all of that. But there is something else, as well.

London, 1998, Internet file

That something else he defined defiantly, unfashionably and single-mindedly as 'soul'. Crucially for Hillman, we are *inside* soul rather than soul being inside us. 'Soul' decentres the ego-self; it also decentres the human within the world. For 'soul' it's not the individual soul some religions talk about, but a collective soul, the soul of the world, *anima mundi*.

Hillman's roots were firmly in Jungian analytic psychology, and later developments in his thinking led to the creation of *Archetypal Psychology*, a 'third generation' derivative of the Jungian school in which Jung is the source but not the doctrine— an orientation that not only took on board changes occurring in society at large – feminism and pluralism among them – but also moved away from a Platonic understanding of archetypes, astonishingly stating that *archetypes are always phenomenal*, belonging to the ordinary world rather than some 'spiritual realm'.

His emphasis was on 'soul' – ineffable, often expressed through art and indeed symptoms – rather than on hierarchic, divisive and dualistic notion of 'spirit' and the 'spiritual'. Hillman's thought is too mercurial, and too profound to be easily categorized. His philosophy is the philosophy of the *Knight Errant*, who does not belong to any church and has no credo or dogma to defend, who is allied to the god Hermes (Mercury) and under the spell of mercurial power.

At the heart of Hillman's polemic was the medicalization of psychology and psychotherapy. In the same interview quoted above he said:

> When the medical becomes *scientistic*; when it becomes analytical, diagnostic, statistical, and remedial; when it comes under the influence of pharmacology – limiting patients to six conversations and those kinds of things – then we've lost the art altogether, and we're just doing business: industrial, corporate business.
>
> *London, 1998, Internet file*

Equally shrewd was his critique of the existentialist thinkers who, for better or for worse, influenced psychotherapy (the convoluted and tyrannical mixture of capitalized abstractions and abject concreteness in Heidegger, the myth of the heroic individual in Sartre). Equally fierce and articulate was his appraisal of humanistic psychology, in curbing the buoyancy and exaggerated expectations of ego-driven 'self-actualization'.

Above all, the greatest emphasis in Hillman's psychology seemed to be on the *plural* nature of the psyche – not in the sense of a bland pluralism but in the more profound, elemental sense of *polytheism*, i.e. the acceptance of many gods, or many perspectives within the psyche, even of those who are labelled as 'pathological'. If his mentor here remains Jung, the unspoken influence is certainly Nietzsche, a thinker who practically invented perspectivism and clarified the importance to deeply honour every aspect of 'our' psyche.

Hillman injected beauty and poetry into the therapeutic endeavour; he was an attentive listener of the collective subliminal, of what is *sub limine*, at the edge of awareness.

Presenting, as he did, a 'third way' in psychology meant being inevitably misconstrued by both 'materialist' and 'spiritualist' factions: the former all-too-easily dismissed him as bordering on 'new age' esotericism, whilst the latter understood his definition of soul too literally. But 'soul' in Hillman – a connoisseur of languages, including ancient languages – is a rendition of *psyche*. Hillman was inspired by his favourite thinker Heraclitus (535–475 BC), for whom the limits of soul could not be discovered even if one travelled every road in the world – such is the depth and breadth of its meaning. The astonishing thing about Heraclitus, whom Hillman considered to be the first psychologist, is that his fragments show no trace of the Platonic (and later Cartesian) division between mind and matter, soul and body.

I am inclined to think that because of its subtlety, literary and artistic sophistication and sheer mercurial nature, Hillman's archetypal psychology does not truly belong to the rather facile dogmatism of what goes under the name of transpersonal psychology. However, it is true that his writings are foundational in some transpersonal training courses either in their magnificent, undiluted form or in a more popularized form (Moore 2004; 2012), and for that reason I am grateful to my 'transpersonalists' colleagues. I hope to be proved wrong, but Hillman's writings are ignored across humanistic, psychodynamic and even (orthodox) Jungian trainings. They are heretical in the best sense of the word and hence do not fit within current psychological orthodoxy.

What does 'human' mean?

I am not immune to the lure of the eternal. If by the sea I hear the waves and make that sound the main focus letting every other sound and sensation recede, the word 'eternity' emerges unaided, unwanted. I welcome it reluctantly. The sound of this wave – and the next, and the next after that – is contingent; it emerges and vanishes. Compared to my being here – momentary, a mere dot in the infinity of a deserted beach in the early hours of the morning – the sea is eternal.

One early morning I stand aside inside Grand Central Station and gazing at the painted constellations on the ceiling, looking at the crowd sliding by hurried and hushed and smart, I'm filled with joy at so much beauty – the mock sky and artful streaming of commuters, their forthright walk in the mouth of a river forever on the move, the strange joy of a speck in the stream.

And yet, I find myself strongly resisting any categorization of the 'eternal' that seemingly bypasses our transient human experience. I was surprised to hear a transpersonal therapist say during a recent lecture that the word 'human' is made up of two sources, *hu* (divine) and *mana* (mind). I had assumed, and still do, that the origin is the Latin *humus*, the organic component of soil which is found in words such as 'humility', which intimates at a grounded awareness of mortality, hence of our limitations. I was baffled to discover that *hu* is Celtic and *mana* Sanskrit – too very dissimilar cultural traditions arbitrarily fastened together. The point of contention is not merely linguistics: it affects how we conceptualize human influences, how we understand our condition, how we articulate our experience and our work with our clients. For some, it appears, the only way to grant dignity and grandeur to the human dimension is by endowing it with the spark of the divine mind. The difficulty with this stance is that it often results in implicit denigration of the existential human dimension. But a chief characteristic of our lot is humility born out of the knowledge that as humans we belong to the soil, existing in an ontological continuum with other beings such as animals (who from time immemorial are shunned by all transcendental-ists and conservative religionists) as well as with the very *oikos* we humans inhabit – that 'environment' which we blatantly plunder and pillage out of a sense of superiority as humans endowed with a superior glint of the 'divine mind'.

References

Bazzano, M. (2016). Planting an oak in a flower pot. In B. Chisholm & J. Harrison (Eds), *The wisdom of not-knowing* (pp. 83–92). Axminster: Triarchy.

Bollas, C. (1996). *Forces of Destiny: Psychoanalysis and the Human Idiom*. London: Free Association.

Clemens, J. (2013). *Psychoanalysis is an Antiphilosophy*. Edinburgh: Edinburgh University Press.

Gaddis, W. (2007). The art of fiction. *The Paris Review Interviews*, 2: 272–305. London: Canongate.

Hillman, J. (1983). *Archetypal Psychology: A Brief Account*. Washington, DC: Spring Publications.

Hillman, J. (1997). *Re-visioning Psychology*. New York: Harper & Row.

Hughes, T. (2008). The art of poetry. *The Paris Review Interviews*, 3: 268–304. London: Canongate.

Joyce, J. (1969). *Ulysses*. London: Penguin.

London, S. (1998). *On soul, character and calling: A conversation with James Hillman*. http://scottlondon.com/interviews/hillman.html Retrieved 16 November 2016.

Madison, G. B. (1981). *The Phenomenology of Merleau-Ponty*. Athens: OH: Ohio University Press.

May, R. (1969). *Love and Will*. New York: W.W. Norton & Co.

Merleau-Ponty, M. (1973). *The Prose of the World*. Evanston, IL: Northwestern University Press.

Moore, T. (2004). *Dark Nights of the Soul: A Guide to Finding your Way through Life's Ordeals*. London: Piatkus.

Moore, T. (2012). *Care of the Soul: An Inspirational Programme to Add Depth and Meaning to Your Everyday Life*. London: Piatkus.

Nettleton, S. (2016). *The Metapsychology of Christopher Bollas*. Abingdon: Routledge.

Solon, O. (2016). My therapist gave me a pill: Can MDMA help cure trauma? *The Guardian Weekend*, 17 September. https://theguardian.com/society/2016/sep/16/mdma-ptsd-therapy-trauma-maps-medical-study Retrieved 26 September 2016.

Spinelli, E. (2007). *Practising Existential Psychotherapy: The Relational World*. London: Sage.

Varela, F. J. (1996). Neurophenomenology: A methodological remedy to the hard problem. *Journal of Consciousness Studies*, 3(4): 330–350.

Wenders, W. (1987). *Wings of Desire*, DVD. Berlin: Axiom.

Wenders, W. (1993). *Faraway, So Close!* DVD, 140 minutes. Berlin: RTM.

Wolfe, T. (1968). *The Electric Kool-Aid Acid Test*. London: Penguin.

6

THIS BODY, THIS EARTH

Incarnate practice and ecopsychology

Red light Zen

A Zen abbot disrobed and left his monastery for a year of wandering. One day he happened to walk near a brothel in a neighbouring town. He stopped and asked if he could work there. As it happens, we need a receptionist, he was told; was he ready to start work right away for food and lodgings but no pay? He accepted and started the same day. Very few took any real notice of his presence at first, apart from the hurried businessmen, workmen and travellers who would give him a passing glance, a complicit wink perhaps or a guilty smile when slyly entering and exiting the house. Occasionally, the women working there would come down to reception in between clients to have a smoke and a chat. Days went by and soon he became a friend to all of them. They liked him, he was ordinary and inconspicuous, and they were surprised at his genuine interest in their lives. They may have been puzzled by his seeming lack of sexual curiosity and desire. Sometimes he'd ask them if they were happy. What was it like to do their job? He heard all about their families and the towns they came from. For their part, the women began to like his serenity and simplicity. They became curious about him and his past. Who was he? Where had he come from? So he told them, and then invited them to visit the monastery. One by one, they all went there. Arrangements were made to host women in the monastic community – quite a revolution for those days, the story says. And one by one the women took the monastic vows. The official story ends here, making it a tale of redemption, a journey of conversion from the suffering and delusion of worldly attachments to the contemplative and ethical life, and perhaps, in the light of our discussion, a tale of transformation from the relative to the absolute perspective. But I have heard of the existence of a postscript to the story. It would appear that some five years later, once the nuns had completed a cycle of thoroughgoing Zen training, the abbot suggested that they now go back to the brothel.

I don't know what readers will make of this tale and of the twist at the end. It may well be that going back to the previous job is not the end of the story, and that what counts here is the unsettling of our unilateral and predictable ways of understanding the psychological and spiritual transformations. Perhaps the tale points at the intrinsic unity between samsara and nirvana, delusion and liberation, the examined and the unexamined life. Perhaps it invites us as practitioners to consider the flipside of any preferred position we have reached and to keep moving on the path: to opt for the monastery if we mistakenly believe that happiness can be found in the brothel; and to 'get down' to the dusty whirlpool of the world if our practice has become a little too precious, a little too pure. As often with Zen, the disorientation its teachings produce, points towards greater appreciation, as Hakuin Zenji points out:

> Truly, is anything missing now? Nirvana is right here, before our eyes. This very place is the Lotus Land, This very body, the Buddha.
>
> *Hakuin Zenji, in Waddell, 2012*

Learning from phenomena

The dharmas are boundless. I vow to learn from them.

Paradoxically for a philosophy and a religion that is associated in the popular imagination with the bodily practice of meditation and yoga, contemporary applications of Buddhism seem to deviate somewhat from the reality of the body. In fact, more fertile connections are to be found in Christianity, stemming from the notion of Christ as God *incarnate*, made flesh. The use of bodily, even sexual, imagery was common practice in counter-reformation Catholicism, a famous example of which is Bernini's orgasmic *St Teresa of Avila*. In the Renaissance, artists rendered depictions of the Christ's genitalia, none of them gratuitous or sensationalistic but appreciative of Christ's humanity, of 'God [becoming] an entire man, and therefore a sexual being; his sex, like his dependence on his mother's breast, is a pledge of that full humanity' (Kermode, 2001, p. 169). Paintings by Ludwig Krug (1520) and Maerten van Heemskirk (1532), various renderings of Crucifixion and Pietà 'suggest large erections which may have been intended to symbolize resurrection' (Kermode, ibid, p. 169).

This may sound strange at first to those who received a Christian education peppered with a good measure of denigration and mortification of the human body. And yet in relation to key notions such as embodiment, a large section of the psychotherapy tradition is indebted to the phenomenology of Merleau-Ponty who in turn drew his important notion of the body subject from the work of Christian existentialist Gabriel Marcel (2012), who spoke of God incarnate. Incidentally, the above is, among other things, a case of how ideas and practices travel *across* systems of belief and theoretical orientations with no particular group or tribe legitimately entitled to claim exclusive ownership to any of them.

The seeming paradox here is that on the whole the bodily humanity of the man-God Christ comes across more strongly than that of the human philosopher-sage Buddha. Jesus is prone to all too human existential despair on the cross, fearing abandonment from the Father moments before his surrender to the divine will. Depending on whether the interpretation is religious or secular, Gautama Buddha is either gradually elevated to omniscient being or to moral superhero (Bazzano, 2013b).

The Zen tradition reinserts the body at the very centre of its practice, the ground of which is *zazen*. Realization is arrived at via the senses. This means that the equivalent of religious revelation is accessed via a clearer perception of phenomena and the world of becoming. 'The *dharmas* (phenomena) are boundless; I vow to learn from all of them': this is the orally transmitted third bodhisattva vow, chanted during dawn *zazen* and on other occasions along with the other three vows. A *traditional* interpretation sees 'dharmas' as the religious teachings in all of the traditions. It invites us to be receptive to the wisdom and compassion present across various mythologies and cultures when we come across them. It encourages in us the practice of humility (not thinking that Buddhism is superior to other religions but being respectful of other practices and beliefs). A *counter-traditional* reading of the third bodhisattva vow understands dharmas as all phenomena. Great teachings are present in the sound of the waterfall, the colours of leaves – even the sound of the traffic at rush hour. A thought (whether 'positive' or 'negative'), a sensation, the myriad sounds of the world at every given moment: they can all be doors to a clearer perception. Openness to 'that which arises' (the etymological meaning of 'phenomenon') simultaneously makes us aware of two things: a) the limitations of our everyday perception; and b) the infinity of experience.

A metaphysical striptease?

According to the philosophical tradition, truth is *aletheia,* or unconcealedness. Some have wittily described this process as metaphysical striptease (Massimo Barbaro, personal communication, 2009). But no striptease is needed in the case of a counter-traditional reading, partly because the notion of (one) truth is itself under fire, and partly because a phenomenon is not *just* appearance but carries within itself a wealth of multiple meanings and connotations – if only we can make ourselves open to receiving them. All one does in this case is *stay with* the experience and (in the case of therapy) help the client articulate an idiom that will begin to express it. This approach is largely found within Zen and phenomenology. The advantage here is that when dealing with the religious experience in therapeutic work, one is able not only to discuss (when deemed necessary and helpful) doctrinal points, but more importantly the very heart of the experience.

For my client Marina, who was raised a Catholic in her native Spain, going to mass on Sunday is still important, despite the fact that she harbours doubts (and consequent worries) about key articles of faith such as the transubstantiation, i.e. the belief that the bread and wine given at communion become the body and blood of

Christ. What worried her even more is the fact that each time she would not attend mass, on that particular week 'something bad would happen'. It didn't help much that she knew intellectually that this logic was superstitious and did not make much sense. We began to explore phenomenologically her going to mass and what emerged were two things: a) she felt it gave her a precious moment of quiet reflection; and b) on certain occasions, she was filled with a 'tangible, pleasant and meaningful' sense of shared community. Given her family commitments as well as the very demanding nature of her work, there was no other time in the week where she could experience the above. In relation to the sense of shared community she sometimes experienced, she mused whether this was a kind of transubstantiation in itself – in this sense the presence of the Christ made manifest by the community of believers. I felt unexpectedly moved by this, and I'm not sure whether this was a reflection of her intensity of feeling, activation of my own past, or a mixture of both.

The body as the great reason

What is really this thing we call 'me'? Is it a mental substance, a 'mind'? Would it be accurate to say that, in essence, 'I am my brain'? Even if I acknowledge that the brain is crucial in allowing me to relate to the world and combine all the complex activities of my sense organs, is it right to assume that consciousness is indistinguishable from the brain? Once in a while, I like to ask students and trainees whether they see themselves as *having* a body or *being* a body. The ensuing discussion is often captivating. Some, often people with medical knowledge and background, will readily say 'I *am* a body'. Others (usually the majority) will say 'I *have* a body'; they will sometimes add that the idea of being a body has an unpleasant ring; they find it somehow indecorous to identify with something that is perishable, that is prone to sickness, old age and death. What often emerges from the discussion is that despite the apparent disagreements both answers entertain the dual assumption that the body is constituted of *matter* and that we know what matter is, for instance something physical and perishable, a 'thing', unless it is animated by mind, or spirit, or both.

I do not have an answer to the kind of existential and philosophical questions formulated above. When transposing them to therapy, one thing seems to emerge with sufficient clarity: the positive change and healing that may take place are not solely mental occurrences but involve the totality of the *bodymind* and perhaps something else besides. There may be fundamental shifts in the way clients *think* about themselves and their place in the world, but for changes in consciousness to have a stable and lasting effect they are usually paired with an organismic shift. Consciousness itself cannot be arbitrarily uncoupled from 'matter' or phenomena. As we shall see, both genuine phenomenology and Zen point in this direction. An insight or realization is not only an intellectual but also a sensory occurrence. Furthermore it would be philosophically unsound to separate consciousness from phenomena and allow it to hover above 'matter'.

As a rule, the notion of the self (or subjectivity), discussed in Chapter 1, is either unduly substantiated or summarily circumvented. We either get bogged down in it, or else we shun it in favour of loftier concepts. For this reason, Merleau-Ponty's position is highly unusual in western philosophy and even among phenomenologists. He formulated the fertile notion of the *body-subject* (Merleau-Ponty, 2010), an effective way forward from the double impasse of Cartesian subjectivity and the disembodied notions of spirituality.

The task is to work *with* subjectivity and find an emancipatory way of conceiving our being in the world, of constructing an 'irregular cosmology . . . of our finitude and imperfection' (Nussbaum, 2003, p. 661). In this sense, incarnate subjectivity is none other than 'the finite mortal individual, democratic citizen, equal to and among others, who contains the world within himself by virtue of his resourceful imagination and his sympathetic love' (ibid, pp. 656–667). It also opens a path for refashioning our relation to nature and rethinking ecology outside the golden cage of anthropocentrism (Bazzano, 2013a).

Naturalizing the human

There are similarities and electrifying associations between aspects of Zen teachings, Dōgen in particular, and the writings of Nietzsche (Bazzano, 2006). One area where the two have strikingly similar things to say is in relation to the human body. A constant theme in Nietzsche is that of the naturalization of the human, a process that requires a steadfast rejection of Platonism and, to some extent, of the western canon itself. In his *reversal* of Platonism, Nietzsche depicts the body as the great reason and the spirit as the small reason. In this configuration, 'spirit' becomes a tool or a vehicle for the body. Similarly, in Dōgen, we find a strong emphasis on the primacy of somatic practice. Instead of opposing rationalism with spiritualism, both Dōgen and Nietzsche invite us to descend into the concrete yet fleeting reality of our mortal body. I don't think it is easily realized how dramatic this shift of perspective truly is even today (Kōgaku, 1991), despite the fact that practices such as body psycho-therapy – alongside somatic practices such as Yoga, Tai Chi, Chi Gong and others– have gained greater popularity, signalling on the whole an acceptance of the essential unity of the mind and body. Yet on some level we are still (knowingly or unknow-ingly) worshiping the thinking subject, Descartes' *cogito*, still deemed to be the fundamental principle of philosophy, and famously crowned by Kant (2007) in his 1781 *Critique of Pure Reason* as the highest principle in the process of under-standing – a statement that both neglects sensory experience and sees the thinking subject as the measure of all things.

The shift towards the body and the body-subject or incarnate subjectivity is not mere embracing of the physical and situated reality we find ourselves in, for if it were so we would still need to postulate a 'thinking I' that benevolently includes an essentially separate and external thing, the body. Implicit in this stance is the basic error of reason: to attribute agency to a self or subjectivity. But if this notion is evaded and the error amended, what we are left with is *pure becoming* – what is naturally perceived by a purely somatic self.

The reason why some accounts of this shift towards the body often sound vertiginous and even mystical is because, I believe, we are unaccustomed to perceive becoming from a somatic self. Culture and education within the tradition is entirely dependent on the idea of the thinking self and by extension on the idea of the soul. It is not easy to retract or even revise a habitual stance when confronted with a practice and a culture that effectively undermines some of our cherished beliefs. Take the notion of spiritual attainment – or *satori*. Although Zen literature describes attainment as happening via the body, when filtered through the lenses of the western tradition this is interpreted as the realization of the immortal and the eternal, as the adept having reached a permanent, unadulterated state outside becoming.

The idea of the soul is very seductive and so is its by-product, the notion of a separate thinking self. Being lured into the potent idea of the individual soul – as many Dharma practitioners inevitably do – has at times the effect of turning the Buddha's teachings into another eternalist religious perspective. Remaining attached to the notion of a separate thinking self has another (opposite and complementary) result, inspired by secularism: it turns the teachings into a toolkit of moral control of those passions that risk overwhelming the self. I believe this is what happens with the mindfulness movement, which by and large promotes a body/mind practice useful in attempting to manage the inevitable unruliness of contingent existence and of troublesome emotions.

My critique is not intended as dismissal: both the transpersonal/mystical and the mindfulness/secular styles catch glimpses of the Buddha's teachings. It goes without saying that both are legitimate, even though I happen to disagree with them. The transpersonal/mystical reading of the Dharma relies on the 'absolute' and more esoteric aspect of the teachings. It catches the Buddha's freedom from what binds us in concentric circles of craving and servility. But it flies on wings of wax too close to the sun, without the somatic, grounded practice that allows for a steady crossing of the great water. I have heard and read practitioners within the transpersonal/mystical perspective claim attainment, 'self-actualization' and 'self-realization'. But the very statement 'I have attained', by reinstating the self at the centre, turns the whole spiritual quest into a narcissistic undertaking.

Zen and nature

Zen re-naturalizes the human and de-humanizes nature. What are the implications of these statements? And what do we mean by 'nature'? Nature is *shizen* in Japanese, a term that does not point to something objective out there, outside the domain of human experience. Rather than as a noun, the word is used as an adverb and adjective. Our western notion of *natura* is on the other hand aligned to the notion of *physis*, a term associated, from the third century on, with natural, immutable and universal laws – and opposed to *nomos*, which can be summarily rendered with nurture, custom, convention etc. This conventional view of nature derived from *physis*, the physical world, though still prevalent today, is not the only perspective. But the cultural dominance of the west has meant that for instance the notion of *shizen*, which was originally different, is now aligned with 'our' notion of natura and physis. Rather than a place we inhabit (*oikos*, from which 'ecology' comes), nature becomes what surrounds us, the peripheral 'environment', the environs of human-centred existence. Rather than being part and parcel of us, nature is a field out there that we may or may not care about.

From what I understand, a certain element of ambiguity fortunately still remains in the word shizen; this is reflected in the Zen tradition which translates the Taoist notion of wei-wu-wei, the doing of non-doing, as *mui shizen*, which can be understood as 'living in tune with nature' the Zen equivalent of the western notion of *eudaimonia* – virtue, happiness or the good life.

The genuine person lives a life of simplicity, unregulated and unfettered, a life of 'free and easy wandering'. This is a notion of virtue that is quite removed from the notion inherited after 2,000 years of Christianity. It is extremely difficult to translate notions such as 'non-doing', 'genuine person' and 'free and easy wondering', into a western philosophical and psychological frame. My own sense is that we would do well to deconstruct some of the western foundations *before* (or at least while) endeavouring to acquaint ourselves with the Dharma. We are fortunate in that at the very heart of the tradition, there existed and still exists a counter-tradition (Bazzano & Webb, 2016). We would also do well to remember that even the most consistent system of philosophy produced in the west carries within it, when we read it attentively, its own undoing.

No-view

Creating space is essential if anything new is to arise. A well-known Zen story tells that the Japanese Zen teacher Nan-in (1868–1912) received a visit from an important academic who was used to commanding obedience and respect, and who wanted to know about Zen. The teacher served tea, and kept pouring the tea in the professor's cup. The tea overflowed, and the professor exclaimed: 'You are spilling the tea all over! Can't you see the cup is full? No more will go in!' 'Like this cup' Nan-in said, 'you are full of your cherished opinions and conjectures. How can I introduce you to Zen unless you empty your cup first?' (Senzaki & Reps, 1998)

The above story is usually interpreted as an invitation to clear the mind from excessive academic verbiage in order to make it 'empty' and be more fully present in the 'here and now'. This reading is partly correct. It beautifully illustrates the anti-intellectual streak in Zen that discourages ruminative thinking in favour of a more instinctive, intuitive, and heart-centred stance on life. A variation on this reading points towards the *suspension* or *epoché* of whatever constitutes our fundamental stance on life in favour of entertaining a view that is positively other or, as some would say, a 'no-view'. One doesn't need to be a philosopher or even to have read philosophy to hold a philosophical stance or worldview. The sum of generalized attitudes accumulated along the way (both our experience and our attempt to be shielded from experience) constitutes our philosophical stance. To be invited to suspend it can open up a new horizon.

Ultimately, there is no real purpose to Zen practice, no particular goal to be achieved in the future. And yet if we look closely into our own motivations, we may recognize that there *is* an underlying aspiration. This may be the *negative* aspiration of *not* wanting pain and suffering, or the desire to be alleviated from the particular burden we may be carrying at one time or another. The same applies to therapy, with the expectation of healing and integration explicitly or implicitly present from the very first session. People will define aspiration differently. Some – and I count myself among them – will even be suspicious of the word. In contemporary political commentaries, 'aspiration' has become synonymous with social climbing and a code among reformed parties of the Left for reaching out to the centre ground and the middle classes. Aspiring to be what I am not is also a recipe for neurosis, particularly if my aspiration is to move 'beyond biology'. Stephen Batchelor (2005) has written eloquently about the ways in which a meditator is ensnared by Mara, a mythical figure in Buddhist iconography that can be loosely linked to Satan. Many interpreters understand the Devil's clutches as akin to those of biology. 'Instincts' and 'desires' have to be curbed; they are seen as trappings and distractions on the path to liberation. This is true of course for compulsions, obsessions and other hindrances to one's well-being. The practitioner can only benefit from sidelining and discarding these. Her life will be freer and the organism's energies able to be directed towards wisdom and compassion.

Culture and civilization

It would be justifiable, however, to detect in the anti-biology rhetoric of some Buddhist-inspired teachings a flight from our embodied condition and our conti-nuum with animals and other forms of life. Animals often get a bad press in Buddhist texts. They have come to symbolize our greed and violence, our fraught defence of territory. The animal realm is, among the six realms, associated with instinct, straightforward one-sidedness, a certain amount of intelligence clouded by dumb-ness. It is also associated with ignorance, stubbornness and humourlessness. Chögyam Trungpa gives the example of the otter:

> An otter, who already has his prey of fish in his mouth, swims through the water. Suddenly, he sees another fish swimming, a bigger, fatter one. He forgets that he already has a fish in his mouth and he jumps towards the other fish – but the first fish slips away. So he loses both the first and the second fish.
>
> *Trungpa, 2004, p. 221*

In transcribing the passage above, it did cross my mind that one of my own traits is the tendency to pursue what I perceive as advantageous to myself and that consideration for others is not always a priority. Yet I hesitate to describe these traits as 'animal-like'. Not only does it sound unfair to animals; it also confirms the anthropocentric prejudice that is one of the hallmarks of most religions and systems of thought. This is being rectified in much contemporary thinking by an affirmation of the unbroken continuum between the human and the animal domain alongside a revaluation of the intelligence, resourcefulness, and playfulness of animals as part of a general frame of creative evolution (Acampora & Acampora, 2003; Derrida, 2008; Lemm, 2009; Massumi, 2014; Bazzano, 2017). This is not a mere understanding of humans as animals, as more reductive theories would have us believe. The human difference (as the difference of every particular domain) is strongly emphasized while recognizing that all living beings are within a continuum. Nor is it a Darwinian move of shrinking humans to size only in order to place them at the peak of the evolutionary line. Taking on board contemporary philosophical discussions on the human–animal continuum has far-reaching implications. One of these is that actualization – in Zen parlance, becoming a Buddha – means manifesting and inhabiting more fully one's intrinsic animality. This is the province of *culture*, understood in the Nietzschean sense, i.e. opposed to *civilization*. The first is cultivation, freedom from moralizing; the second is taming, a morality of repression (Lemm, 2009). The first fosters organismic awareness and greater freedom; the second is a process of indoctrination into the herd-culture of stale, received knowledge.

The animal presence in the human evoked here is not merely symbolic but directly intertwined with the life of the organism. It is an urgent attempt to leave behind anthropocentrism, the fixation that sees the human (*anthropos*) at the centre of nature. It is an attempt at decentring the human subject, the person, an entity that can no longer be thought of as the ground upon which the wider political dimension rests (Cadava et al., 1991). In this sense, both Zen and therapy would ideally provide spaces for culture, i.e. for the cultivation of both instinctual courage and advanced artistry, the combination of which is crucial in retrieving 'ancestral animality from the prehistoric wild' (Acampora, 2003, p. 3). This task is twofold. It is first of all *diagnostic*, in the sense of uncovering animality under the layers of theology and morality and in this sense this is akin to Darwinism (though, crucially, without the latter's eventual elevation of the human). It is also *therapeutic*, an ambitious attempt to heal our civilization of (human) animals who have become 'spiritually sickened by [having been made] all-too-humanly tame' (Acampora, 2003, p. 2). This vision calls for nothing less than a *feral philosophy*, for the revitalization of wild animal energy, which has waned while suffering centuries of 'over-civilizing ideologies and institutions' (Acampora, 2003, ibid).

Can therapy ever be instrumental to this arduous task? My own view is rather pessimistic, for two reasons:

a) For too long we have been dominated by 'the priestly type' whose successful and perverse endeavour to extirpate the passions in the name of morality has granted a 'false overcoming' (Lemm, 2009, p. 20) i.e. the very opposite of cultural achievement.

b) On the whole, therapy as a profession continues to exhibit a propensity to comply with dominant ideologies – in our day and age, neoliberalism. Among the many nefarious influences neoliberalism is having on the world of counselling and psychotherapy, there are two, intrinsically linked, which are pertinent here: the *commodification* of human experience and the *control* and regulation of the domain of affect.

At the same time, as Rollo May already suggested a few decades ago, the therapy space may well be one of the last remaining domains where this sort of exploration can take place (May, 1969). A clinical example may help to illustrate this point.

'Go for it brother!'

When my Argentinean client Mateo was about 6 years old, he had what he called 'a powerful experience' and his 'first sense of achievement'. It took place in the pampas of the Santa Fe province, with cattle farming in huge open fields. Twice a year, some 20 men would ride to the end of the fields and bring all the cattle to the ranch for vaccination. Mateo loved horse riding and was keen to take part whenever he could. At times, when two groups of cattle were joined, each with one bull, intense bull-fighting would ensue. This would be managed by the older Gauchos: they'd come in with their horses and whips. On one occasion, while the cattle were being led by the men (including 6-year-old Mateo) towards the ranch, one cow suddenly deserted the group. Mateo's older cousin winked at him encouragingly and said 'Come on brother, go for it!' Mateo turned his horse and rode it towards the cow, 'my whole bodymind one with the galloping . . . I became one with the horse, entirely focused at bringing back the cow'. He succeeded and 'one by one, the older Gauchos greeted me with a special, double handshake and congratulated me with a gaze of manly recognition'.

We had come to this story while exploring how he experiences his strength and power as a man in everyday life. Reflecting now on this vivid experience, he saw it 'as a kind of ritual', adding: 'the sensation of power and achievement is still very present with me'. At times he found an immediate, if somewhat obscure, correlation between the 'potent stir' experienced as a 6-year-old boy and his current sense of sexual power and strength. It was nonetheless 'difficult to contextualize this experience in my own life' he said, despite having no doubts about 'the very real impact it had on me'. He also felt the experience was akin to a 'ritual scar', a sort of rite of passage. We explored how this may have influenced the construction of his masculinity. Mateo wondered whether he was coming a little closer to understanding a notion that had baffled him for years, Nietzsche's *will to power*. Could this mean 'power as a vital, positive force, not necessarily linked to the customary meaning of power *over*, of oppression and domination?'

I felt deeply impacted by this particular session. Mateo found it 'very enlightening'. It represented a shift of sorts and led to a deeper exploration of masculinity. He presented, I felt, a predicament that I found echoed time and time again in the narratives of some male clients, namely the difficulties in reconciling an exuberant sexuality with the social constraints that demanded the domestication of their vital energies. In Mateo's case, this did not create significant inner or outer conflicts. But for others this struggle often becomes a harrowing internalized psychological friction that greatly impairs their well-being and their sense of self.

The link Mateo made to Nietzsche may have been fortuitous but it proved stimulating. His point about understanding power as strength and vitality, rather than domination over another, reflected a breakthrough in his awareness. It also provided us, if not with an interpretative key, at least with a wider anthropological context.

How to avoid capture

There is much that animals can teach us, if we were able to even temporarily bracket human hubris. For instance, animal inspiration instructs us on how to survive the primal mum and dad theatre without becoming, as the English poet Philip Larkin mused, irretrievably fucked-up. In Kafka's *Metamorphosis* (Kafka, 2009), becoming-animal is a way to endure the constraints of the Oedipal family. Here creativity is survival and *at one* with instinct, for the two are 'inextricably entwined' (Massumi, 2014, p. 39), despite the canonical view that sees creativity as a sublimation of instinct and redirection of the latter into the symbolic domain. The unity of creativity and instinct also provides us with the essentials of a *feral philosophy* (Derrida, 2008) that is useful to the naturalization of the human.

In tune with Nietzsche's correct emphasis on the deed at the expense of the doer (*no doer behind the deed*), we also find an appreciation of 'noncognitive primary consciousness [or] thought in the act, flush with vital gesture' (Massumi, 2014, p. 39). Closely linked to the above is a debunking of a sacred cow to which all therapeutic orientations genuflect in sycophantic adoration: the notion of *agency*, in favour of a transindividual process of vital becoming. The *subject* of psychology gives way to a '*subjectivity-without-a-subject*' (ibid, p. 41, emphasis in the original), which in turn 'may be considered spiritual, if by that is simply meant intensely, relationally enlivening' (ibid). This then linked to the notion of the *mental pole* proposed by A. N. Whitehead (1978), a non-substantive mode of activity that co-creates and cooperates with its complement, the *physical pole*. There is no mediation between the two, nor are they the 'properties of a substantial being [but rather] they are constitutive modalities of events in the making' (Whitehead, 1978, p. 108).

Linked to the above is another vital lesson animals teach us: to make language play, or to make instinctive use of it: 'the vital gestures of animal play display a reflexivity-in-the-act that really produces the conditions of human language' (Whitehead, ibid, p. 45).

Above all, animals teach us how to avoid capture: for them, this means not being shackled by the alternatively cute and demonic lenses of anthropomorphism. For humans, this means not falling into a trap of our own device, i.e. anthropomorphising the human by forgetting that we exist in a continuum with animals. And there is another important aspect of avoiding capture, and it has to do with the philosophical/psychological enterprise as such. 'Capture' here can mean several things: the regression to ontological certainties after the painstakingly radical work of post-structuralism; the supine acceptance of neo-liberalism in the way we operate as therapists/trainers/writers, lulled into believing that our work is still progressive merely because it utilizes a jargon of authenticity and false objectivity.

Of pets and cockroaches

There are times when Gina, a woman in her early thirties, sees her desire for orderliness in her home as problematic. This is because the odd argument would flare up with some regularity with her new boyfriend who has a more casual attitude to this. Sure, he can be a bit messy at times, she says, but on the whole he is cooperative, does his bit with the housework even though this doesn't come natural by him. Recently she began to wonder whether she is being a little too strict and even, in her words, 'obsessive' about it. True, she does like to live in a clean, tidy place but feels that sometimes this desire takes over and makes her tense, particularly at weekends when they are supposed to relax and spend time with one another. The other week – five months into our work together – she recounted a dream set in Naples in the home where she grew up. She had woken up that morning with a warm summery feeling; her dream was luminous, she said, full of light and of joyous, indefinite noises. Later, on the way to our session, the atmosphere of the dream still with her, she remembered an episode from childhood. One summer day – she might have been six or so – her mother told her in a serious voice, that it was important that she and her brother (with whom she shared a room) kept the room really tidy. No sweet crumbs on the floor, she had said, otherwise cockroaches would show up from nowhere. It must have been from then on, she now wondered aloud, sitting across the room, that she developed a fear – no, not fear, *terror* – of cockroaches. And she also wondered whether there may be a connection of sorts: was her obsession with tidiness connected to the terror of cockroaches? Now, conventionally roaches are not pretty or cuddly as pets are, but did they *stand for* something, she speculated, i.e. disease, disorder, contamination? She had understood her mother's injunction as the law, as the necessary entry into the civilized community, in this case her family. She found it curious though that her brother didn't develop the same obsession with tidiness or, for that matter, a similarly intense fear of cockroaches. In fact, she added, her brother could be a bit of a slob – she smiled as she said this, adding 'my brother can be really messy, *gloriously* messy, messy big time'. She laughed out loud; her affection, even admiration for her brother was palpable. As for Gina, she understood the law, she accepted the law. Every sensible person would, wouldn't they? Even though, well, it could make a person boring and conventional. In any case, she was OK with it deep down, it was, after all, her ticket to the civilized world; no place for cockroaches there, none at all.

I nodded, noting aloud the good things earned by her acceptance the law: a sense of stability, order, and a clear space around her where she could work and study for her literature degree. Then I asked her hesitantly if there was, well, something she had *lost* by, as it were, shutting the door on cockroaches – or rather, I rephrased, was there something, if anything, to which she was denying access? Don't think so, she said, somewhat defensively. In her early to mid-twenties she had certainly *invited* chaos, disorder and instability. She had been a bit wild, had gone through her sex, drugs and rock 'n' roll phase. At this point, our dialogue veered towards the theme of transgression. Had she been transgressive then, she wondered, and asked herself what this word 'transgression' meant to her, a desire to trespass, to ignore boundaries, to, say, reach out and kiss someone I happen to be talking to, she said, like I want to do sometimes at work? To feel their mouth and face and tongue and sweat; a conscious but crazy decision I never take, she said, of course I don't, I mean, it would be totally nuts, right? Though I savour the feeling of what could be, of what that could feel like. But the rest, the drugs she had taken then, the occasional blackout, not much of a taboo-breaking that really, if this is what this is all about, she said, taboo and the law, breaking the taboo by transgressing and so forth. She moved on to talk about Kafka's (2009) novella *Metamorphosis*. I mentioned Clarice Lispector's *The Passion According to G.H.* (Lispector, 2014). We both felt that something important was being processed and explored. We were tiptoeing around a chasm, the literary references drifting in and out of our conversation providing us not with diversion but with larger historical echoes, confirmation and amplification of her experience, reflected here in the counselling room, the reverberation of something so hard to put into words.

Human–animal continuum

Visiting a San Francisco zoo in the early 1970s, Gregory Bateson observed two monkeys playing with one another and noticed how their playing was similar to, though not the same as, fighting. At first, as Brian Massumi writes, the observation included himself, the human observer, but then fails to return to this in the rest of his essay

> It is as if, against everything he says about play and reflexivity and language, [Bateson] reverts . . . to the unreflexive assumption that the animal and its evolutionary relation to the human can simply be denoted, the presence of the human observer absent-mindedly placed under erasure.
>
> *Massumi, 2014, p. 65*

Incidentally, this absent-mindedness is also at the heart of a philosophy now in vogue, *speculative realism*, which applies this convenient expurgation of the human subject in its allegedly objective observation of 'things' in the world.

In opposition to this reactive human tendency, Massumi draws our attention to a continuum of mutual inclusion: 'of the human in the animal, and the animal in the human' (Massumi, 2014, p. 65). This stance goes against the 'rigidly exclusionary operation' (ibid) found in the zoo as much as in the laboratory, crucially allowing for recognition of grey areas or 'zones of indiscernibility' (p. 49) between one species and another. This notion even made the news a few years back in *The Guardian*:

> Genetic tests on bacteria, plants and animals increasingly reveal that different species crossbreed more than originally thought, meaning that instead of

genes simply being passed down individual branches of the tree of life, they are also transferred between species on different evolutionary paths. The result is a messier and more tangled 'web of life'. Microbes swap genetic material so promiscuously it can be hard to tell one type from another, but animals regularly crossbreed too – as do plants – and the offspring can be fertile . . . 'The tree of life is being politely buried,' said Michael Rose . . . 'What's less accepted is that our whole fundamental view of biology needs to change'.

Sample, 2009, Internet file

The tangled web of life

Not only is the human in a continuum with the animal; animality and life itself simply cannot be rigidly separated from the non-organic. From the writings of Charles Darwin to the filmic musings of Terrence Malick the notion of the 'tree of life' – namely the idea that genes are solely and neatly passed down individual branches – is still resilient. However, another image is now beginning to appear, that of the tangled '*web of life*'. In philosophy, the first inkling of this came with the work of Deleuze and Guattari (2004) who suggested a rhizomatic rather than an arboreal imagery. A term used in botany, 'rhizome', stands for a horizontal, frequently underground stem sending out roots and shoots from its nodes. It resists the vertical organizational structure of the root-tree system. Unlike the vertical and linear connections (the tree and its roots in the ground) for Deleuze and Guattari a rhizome is ground-less, multiple and mutualist – the latter attribute taken from interaction between species, as in the example of the orchid and the wasp (Deleuze & Guattari, 2004). For Claudio Rud, this represents 'a movable, transitory interaction impossible to explain by the term identity' (Rud, 2009, p. 36).

There are, of course, differences between species, between humans and animals, but both exist on an animal continuum. This calls for a need to go beyond anthropomorphism – not only when applied to animals but, crucially, to ourselves. We need to question thoroughly:

> our image of ourselves as humanly standing apart from other animals; our inveterate vanity regarding our assumed species identity, based on the specious grounds of our sole proprietorship of language, thought, and creativity.
>
> *Massumi, 2014, p. 3*

New materialisms

It is an act of human arrogance to assume that animals do not have emotion, thought, creativity, desire or subjectivity. It is our self-satisfied way of relegating animals 'to the status of automatons' (Massumi, 2014, p. 51). New and exciting developments in political ecology and philosophy (Bennett, 2010; Coole & Frost, 2010) depict vibrant networks of transformation activated both within and without humans and effectively redress the balance, not only in terms of the relation between the human and the animal, but more generally with regard to how we traditionally perceive what we dismissively call 'matter'.

In actual fact, Bergson's vitalist philosophy (Bergson, 1944) had already taken important steps in this direction, but it was later sidelined and dismissed in favour of neo-Darwinism. Yet Bergson paved the way decisively for the transcendental empiricism of Deleuze (1966) and for those thinkers who later developed what came to be known at the beginning of the twenty-first century as *New Materialisms*, an interdisciplinary movement that mounted a formidable critique of anthropo-centrism. It invited us to rethink subjectivity, by drawing attention to the role of non-human energies within the human. Crucially for therapy, it also underlined the self-regulatory abilities of various non-human processes within and without the human.

A multimodal outlook

I remember the dismay I felt, a few years ago, in receiving the feedback of an anonymous reviewer in response to an article of mine that tried to adapt these ideas to therapy. Expressing what was and still is the uncritically accepted view, the reviewer had referred to Bergson's vitalism as a 'universally debunked concept' and deemed my defence of vitalism indefensible. More specifically, the reviewer's stance explicitly relied on Bertrand Russell's hurried dismissal of vitalism in the name of rationalism, a position that is largely instrumental in perpetuating the mind/body and spirit/matter divide and is at the very heart of the problem. It has been argued that the striking lack of elementary philosophical background (Bazzano & Webb, 2016) and of the rudiments of philosophy of science (Bazzano, 2016) in counselling and psychotherapy courses results in a gullible acceptance of whichever trend dominates the scene at any given time – neo-Darwinism being a case in point, alongside, for example, unexamined, over-enthusiastic reliance on the most superficial aspects of neuroscience. Presenting a different perspective becomes a difficult task especially if it goes against both the general consensus and the vested interests that steer the consensus.

The new materialisms movement rethinks *matter* as *materiality*. Matter is conventionally thought of as inanimate or dead whereas as materiality it is reconceived as 'active, dynamic, self-creative, productive and unpredictable' (Ansell Pearson, 2011, p. 47). The way we think about matter affects how we think of biology and living organisms and a shift of perspective can help instate a *multimodal* outlook (Coole & Frost, 2010), one that actively refuses to accept the mind/matter dualistic opposition inherited by the philosophical tradition. A possible consequence of this can be a salutary move away from the entrenched biologism that is arguably creeping into the humanities and into the world of therapy. The current uncritical acceptance of one particular form of naturalism (i.e. neo-Darwinism) over others may also have a lot to do with corporate interests and pressures from states and government. This stifles the possibility of *multi-naturalism*. The acceptance of multi-modality in the natural sciences would mean welcoming an array of perspectives and opening a dialogue that is sadly lacking because of the demands of globalized capitalism. These require a dumbing-down of scientific research aimed at the maximization of profit for the few. Bluntly put, the empire does not appreciate the fact that hypotheses are fallible, and that a theory can be contradicted by other theories. It wants certainties, and efficient ways for perpetrating its rule, hence it buys a theory and a methodology, and sells them wholesale in its provinces and colonies.

Ecology: the last refuge of the narcissist?

The shift described above – essentially a move away from anthropocentrism – is the essential prelude to any form of ecology or ecopsychology. Ecology begins, in my view, with something like this arresting picture presented by Nietzsche:

> In some remote corner of the universe . . . there once was a star on which clever animals invented knowledge. That was the haughtiest and most mendacious minute of 'world history' – yet only a minute. After nature had drawn a few breaths the star grew cold and the clever animals had to die.
>
> *Cited in Thacker, 2013, Internet file*

Without tempering human hubris and downsizing our role in the great scheme of things, ecology quickly becomes the last refuge of the narcissist: a comforting way to compliment ourselves on the sensitiveness of our beautiful souls; a convenient way to ignore that we too are perpetrators of the planet's tragic ecological unbalance. Perspectives vary widely within the ecological movement and among therapists or meditators who are commendably involved in it. Ecopsychology effectively challenges the holy shrine of the therapy room, unfastening the conventional cocooned space and restaging the encounter within the naturally healing settings of a park, a garden, a country lane and (with equine therapy and related practices) through contact with non-human beings. Incidentally, this brings to mind a Zen teacher under whose guidance I trained for a while and who was fond of taking the whole meditation group outside, under beautiful oaks and gingko biloba trees. The setting certainly enhanced a sense of stillness and connectedness. It also instilled in me at first an implied demarcation between 'pure nature' and the 'corrupted world'. Realizing this, I started thinking, rather perversely, that if it was any good, my *samādhi* (concentration) would and should be there in a McDonald's; and that the discrimination between 'organic' open field and 'synthetic' food joint is a little too precious.

Some of the stances within ecopsychology are problematic: one will find, for instance, the romantic viewpoint that lays blame on Copernicus' heliocentrism and advocates a reorientation towards the Earth, the human and, finally, 'me'

(Sampson, 2011). Some ecopsychologists tend to shore up their particular angle with allusions to 'interdependence' and the Buddha's teaching of *paticca samuppada* (p. 261) or 'dependent co-arising'. This notion, usually understood via the interpretation of author Joanna Macy's reading of dependent co-arising (Macy, 2003) is only one of a myriad of interpretations, adopted by a certain strand of ecopsychology and ecophilosophy alongside Naess' view of the 'ecological self' (Naess, 1989). But an important, often neglected, aspect of *paticca samuppada* is the *relativization* of the human and of the human self. The paradox here is that the self is seen both as unsubstantial (existing only as convergence and falling apart of aggregates) and existentially alone. This aloneness is inescapable (no one else can die my death, no matter how 'interdependent' I might be) and even desirable. This is because one less attractive aspect of interdependence is *entanglement*. I do realize, however, that valuing aloneness and suggesting entanglement as one of the components of interdependence is almost sacrilegious in our current psychological landscape.

Romancing the wilderness

The notion of 'interdependence' introduces *groundlessness* (*śūnyatā*, commonly translated as 'emptiness'), a place where, as we have seen, existential aloneness on the one hand, and the absolute otherness of the world in all its uncertainty, beauty and terror on the other manifest together. 'Interdependence' can be seen as 'an overture to the symphony of groundlessness' (Bazzano, 2009, p. 13), undermining the alleged solidity of the self, rather than a confirmation of a cosy notion of interconnectedness. The emphasis is on all phenomena, including the self, being *devoid of inherent substance* (*svabhāva*), i.e. on all phenomena being *empty*. What is important is that we stop the *reification* (turning living processes into 'things') of phenomena. As westerners, we have only begun to grapple with this radical Buddhist notion which still runs counter to the axioms of western thought and is therefore easy to misinterpret. With McMahan (2008), I believe that one of the main problems has to do with the fact that Buddhism in the west has been transmitted via the German and the English Romantics, the American Transcendentalists and Rousseau. These influences contributed to the currently predominant rendering of dependent origination as 'inter-connectedness', which in turn translated 'nature' and our relationship with it as the romance of the wilderness (McMahan, 2008), even into naive notions of Buddhist Romanticism (Thanissaro, 2002). Crucially, the outcome of Buddhist (and ecological) Romanticism is not a radical deconstruction of the self, a seeing-through its ephemeral nature but instead an identification of the self with a greater Self, in this case an *ecological* Self. I disagree with this interpretation, shared by Buddhist teachers such as Joan Halifax and Joanna Macy (McMahan, 2008) and by *Deep Ecology*'s main theorist, Arne Naess (1986, 1989) who, significantly influenced by Hinduism, writes of 'Self-realization'.

In the age of the Internet, the matrix, and the network, the idea of interdependence is very appealing. This is all very well, but something gets lost in the process; the radically existential nature of the teachings of the Buddha, summoned by ecologists to endorse their theories, is neglected. The Buddha's insistent teaching on the reality of *impermanence* is deeply ecological. He may not wax lyrical about eating strawberries in the sunlight but he does remind us of the transience of all things. This can be a profound and tragic realization, starkly rendered by Gary Snyder (1990) as 'the sight of our beloved in the underworld, dripping with maggots' (p. 110).

Loyalty to the Earth and the 'fully living person'

An incarnate, organismic psychology can greatly benefit from the naturalization of the human that is at the heart of Zen practice and philosophy. Both organismic psychology and Zen gesture towards a reformulation of the human being as *fully-living*, arguably a necessary 'upgrading' of Rogers' notion of the fully *functioning* person (Rogers, 1961), because it registers more accurately the organismic and ecological embededness of the human animal. What I am proposing is an *eighth characteristic of a fully living person*, in addition to the seven characteristics of a fully-functioning person listed by Rogers (1961). This eighth characteristic can be sketched as comprising the following: greater awareness of the 'earth-household'; a reduced sense of our own importance within it; a primary form of loyalty to the Earth to which we inextricably belong. Entertaining the notion of an eighth characteristic would also be a way of reinterpreting Rogers' notion of the *persons of tomorrow* (Rogers, 1980).

First, this entails a clear aspiration to end our war with nature, i.e. building the premises for an articulate critique of the idea of 'cultivation' at the heart of our dominant educational system in the west, designed as 'movement away from natural process . . . [as] a sort of war against nature – placing the human over the animal' (Snyder, 1990, p. 91).

Second, it puts into question dominant notions of spirituality, doubting both the overriding image of a centralized divinity sharply distinguished, as a 'creator', from the 'creature', as well as a hierarchical spirituality which claims a 'special evolutionary spiritual destiny for humanity under the name of higher consciousness' (Snyder, 1990, ibid).

Third, loyalty to the Earth also implies the ability to embrace the dark side of nature, what we often interpret as absurd, brutal and parasitic. This is crucial in relation to those aspects of therapy, ecopsychology and Buddhist practice which tend to overlook the dark side of nature.

Being 'green' or championing 'green issues' has become a decorative badge for corporate culture and so-called green capitalism, with conservationism being central to economic exploitation, profitability and the maintenance of the political status quo. Environmentalism itself originates with colonial expansion (Grove, 1995), as conservation schemes were adopted by colonial governments and swiftly mutated into ways of dispossessing or exerting control over native populations. Parallels may be drawn between the opportunistic and ultimately shallow approach of environmentalism and a form of therapy, arguably predominant today, bent on polishing the surface of the ego-self, providing efficient ways of patching up an ever-elusive solidity and identity. Similarities might equally be found between a deep ecology and an organismic psychology, both motivated by an aspiration to widen the field of inquiry beyond both anthropocentrism and a self-serving ethos.

References

Acampora, R. R. (2003). Nietzsche's feral philosophy: Thinking through an animal imaginary. In C. D. Acampora & R. R. Acampora (Eds), *A Nietzschean bestiary: Becoming animal beyond docile and brutal* (pp. 1–16). Lanham, MD: Rowman & Littlefield.

Acampora, C. D. & Acampora, R. R. (Eds). (2003). *A Nietzschean Bestiary: Becoming Animal Beyond Docile and Brutal.* Lanham, MD: Rowman & Littlefield.

Ansell Pearson, K. (2011). Multimodal. *Radical Philosophy,* 167: 46–48.

Batchelor, S. (2005). *Living with the Devil: A Buddhist Meditation on Good and Evil.* New York: Riverhead.

Bazzano, M. (2006). *Buddha is Dead: Nietzsche and the Dawn of European Zen.* Eastbourne: Sussex Academic Press.

Bazzano, M. (2009). Brave new worlding: A response to Ernesto Spinelli's practicing existential psychotherapy. *Existential Analysis,* 20(1): 9–19.

Bazzano, M. (2013a). One more step: from person-centered to eco-centered therapy, *Person-Centered & Experiential Psychotherapies,* 12(4): 344–354. doi: 10.1080/14779757.2013.856810.

Bazzano, M. (2013b). This very body, the Buddha. *Sexual and Relationship Therapy,* 28(1, 2): 132–140. doi: 10.1080/14681994.2013.770143.

Bazzano, M. (2016). The conservative turn in person-centered therapy. *Person-Centered & Experiential Psychotherapies,* 15(4): 339–354. doi: 10.1080/14779757.2016.1228540.

Bazzano, M. (2017). *A Bid for Freedom: The Actualizing Tendency Updated.* Unpublished manuscript.

Bazzano, M. & Webb, J. (Eds). (2016). *Therapy and the Counter-tradition: The Edge of Philosophy.* Abingdon: Routledge.

Bennett, J. (2010). *Vibrant Matter: A Political Ecology of Things.* Durham, NC: Duke University Press.

Bergson, H. (1944). *Creative Evolution.* New York: Random House.

Cadava, E., Connor, P. & Nancy, J. L (Eds). (1991). *Who Comes after the Subject?* New York: Routledge.

Coole, D. H. & Frost, S. (Eds). (2010). *New Materialisms: Ontology, Agency, and Politics.* Durham, NC: Duke University Press.

Deleuze, G. (1966). *Bergsonism.* New York: Zone.

Deleuze, G. & Guattari, F. (2004). *A Thousand Plateaus.* London and New York: Continuum.

Derrida, J. (2008). *The Animal That Therefore I Am.* New York: Fordham University Press.

Grove, R. (1995). *Green Imperialism: Colonial Expansion, Tropical Island Edens and the Origins of Environmentalism.* Cambridge, MA: Cambridge University Press.

Kafka, F. (2009). *The Metamorphosis.* Eastford, CT: Martino.

Kant, I. (2007). *Critique of Pure Reason.* London: Penguin.

Kermode, F. (2001). The sexuality of Christ. In F. Kermode, *Pleasing myself: From Beowulf to Philip Roth* (pp. 167–174). London: Allen Lane.

Kōgaku, A. (1991). The problem of the body in Nietzsche and Dōgen. In G. Parkes (Ed.), *Nietzsche and Asian thought* (pp. 214–225). Chicago, IL: University of Chicago Press.

Lemm, V. (2009). *Nietzsche's Animal Philosophy: Culture, Politics, and the Animality of the Human.* New York: Fordham University Press.

Lispector, C. (2014). *The Passion According to G.H.* London: Penguin.

McMahan, D. (2008). *The Making of Buddhist Modernism.* New York: Oxford University Press.

Macy, J. (2003). *World as Lover, World as Self.* Berkeley, CA: Parallax.

Marcel, G. (2012). *The Mystery of Being.* London: Harvill.

Massumi, B. (2014). *What Animals Teach Us About Politics.* Durham, NC: Duke University Press.

May, R. (1969). *Love and Will.* New York: W.W. Norton & Co.

Merleau-Ponty, M. (2010). *Phenomenology of Perception.* Abingdon: Routledge.

Naess, A. (1986). The deep ecological movement: Some philosophical aspects. *Philosophical Inquiry,* 8: 10–31.

Naess, A. (1989). *Ecology, Community and Lifestyle: Outline of an Ecosophy.* Cambridge: Cambridge University Press.

Nussbaum, M. (2003). *Upheavals of Thought: The Intelligence of Emotions.* Cambridge, MA: Cambridge University Press.

Rogers, C. R. (1961). *On Becoming a Person.* Boston, MA: Houghton Mifflin.

Rogers, C. R. (1980). *A Way of Being.* Boston, MA: Houghton Mifflin.

Rud, C. (2009). Revision of the notion of identity and its implications in PCA clinical practice. *Person-Centered and Experiential Psychotherapies,* 8(1): 33–43.

Sample, I. (2009). Evolution: Charles Darwin was wrong about the tree of life. *The Guardian,* 21 January. http://theguardian.com/science/2009/jan/21/charles-darwin-evolution-species-tree-life Retrieved 7 November 2015.

Sampson, V. (2011). The darkening quarter. In M. J. Rust & N. Totton (Eds), *Vital Signs: Psychological Responses to Ecological Crisis* (pp. 3–16). London: Karnac.

Senzaki, N. & Reps, P. (1998). *Zen Flesh, Zen Bones: A Collection of Zen and Pre-Zen Writings.* London: Penguin.

Snyder, G. (1990). *The Practice of the Wild.* New York: North Point Press.

Stern, D. (1985). *The Interpersonal World of the Infant.* New York: Basic Books.

Thacker, E. (2013). Lacking a homunculus. *Radical Philosophy,* 181, September–October: 51–54.

Thanissaro, B. (2002). Romancing the Buddha. *Tricycle Magazine.* http://tricycle.org/magazine/romancing-buddha Retrieved 5 March 2015.

Trungpa, C. (2004). *The Collected works of Chögyam Trungpa.* C. R. Gimian (Ed.). Boston, MA: Shambala.

Waddell, N. (2012). *Hakuin's Song of Zazen.* The Zen site. http://thezensite.com/ZenTeachings/Translations/Song_of_Zazen.htm Retrieved 30 November 2015.

Whitehead, A. N. (1978). *Process and Reality.* New York: Free Press.

7

ON DIFFERENTIALISM

Skin-deep

The reader will gather that the argument offered in this chapter is in every respect consistent with the project of deconstruction, by which I mean the deconstruction of metaphysics. This project is not only worthwhile; it is indispensable, despite the fact that the difficulties encountered and the hostilities it engenders are substantial, unwittingly rooted as they are in our elemental, pervasive fear of dissolution of personal identity. This fear is wholly justified: identity *is* openly called into question as soon as we sever the causal link between the originating factor and utterance and, more broadly, between doer and deed.

Zen teachings are often seen as paradoxical, i.e. beyond (*para*) received opinion (*doxa*). They rarely comply with the typical paradigm of most systems of belief and psychological orientations. As we shall see later in this chapter, the logocentric view, central in western science and philosophy, assumes the existence of a fundamental unity between language and reality. It also tends to condense difference, fragmentation and subjectivity into a larger, all-encompassing whole that often relies on logic and reason.

People approaching Zen for the first time often experience as a paradox Dōgen's affirmation of the unity of practice and realization. The paradox deepens as one continues to practice. We don't practice in order to obtain realization but so that realization becomes manifest. We practice because we are already realized. This form of reasoning is outside the normal confines of reason and, more precisely, outside the confines of causal logic. It makes total sense to say that I practice *in order to* achieve realization and that my realization is the fruit of my sincere, committed practice. Similarly, we go to a therapist in order to get better. As a therapist, I will be pleased if the client's presenting issue has been in the course of time dealt with and at least partially resolved. It would be illogical, cruel even, to suggest that malaise and health are one and the same. The 'problem' they may be experiencing hinders them, obstructs their vision and effectively thwarts their potential. Getting to the roots of their fundamental incongruence will, to some extent, free them up in order to become who they really are. This process of healing will deepen the client's experience, allowing him or her to relate to others with greater depth. How can one refute any of the above?

Yet there is a fundamental flaw in this way of reasoning, and this is partly illustrated in a passage by Dōgen where he comments on a famous episode in Zen literature, known as *Bodhidharma's Skin, Flesh, Bone and Marrow* (Heine, 2008). Before leaving China to go back to his native India, Bodhidharma, a Buddhist monk credited with initiating the Chan (later Zen) tradition, gathered a few of his students. He wanted to transmit the genuine Dharma and nominate a successor. To the four students who showed up, he said: 'Tell me how you convey your understanding of the Dharma.'

Dao-fu said: 'One should not cling to words and letters nor abandon words and letters'. Bodhidharma said: 'You conveyed my skin'.

Then Nun Zongchi said: 'To me, the Dharma is the joy of seeing the land of Akshobhya Buddha once and never again'.

Bodhidharma said: 'You conveyed my flesh'.

Daoyu said: 'At their origin, air, earth, water and fire are empty. The five aggregates do not exist. Thus, there is nothing to attain'.

Bodhidharma said: 'You conveyed my bones'.

Finally, Huike came forward, bowed deeply, and went back to his seat.

Bodhidharma said: 'You conveyed my marrow'.

Then he transmitted the Dharma, the bowl and the robe to Huike.

Until Dōgen's commentary came along, it was taken for granted that only the last student 'got it', the marrow suggesting the deepest understanding in a hierarchy where the skin is the most superficial – 'skin-deep' we say in common parlance. The protocol required that Bodhidharma gives the bowl and the robe to *one* student. But in Dōgen's understanding, all four disciples have *different*, equally valid, views of the Dharma. Notions of depth and surface belong to a logocentric view of the world.

In praise of doubt

I often hear fellow Zen practitioners lament the fact that for a tradition fiercely berating reliance on words and letters, Zen has produced a staggering amount of literature. This is not necessarily a bad thing if, to paraphrase Luther, it invites us to open a book and read. Two centuries before its advent, Luther's rallying cry planted the seeds of the Enlightenment (such is the power of literature), and the most articulate proponent of the Enlightenment, Immanuel Kant, was to write: 'thoughts without intuitions are empty; intuitions without concepts are blind' (Kant, 2007, xxxii). Anti-intellectualism has its purposes; it is good to suspend bookish knowledge and go back to incarnate practice, to the austere luxury of 'just sitting'. It would, however, be a mistake to rely solely on 'pure' practice, privileging the meditation hall to the detriment of the library because, in my own experience, this opens the door to mysticism. There is nothing wrong with mysticism per se but we would do well to consider the dangers of mystification inherent to mysticism, as well as reflecting on the fact that Zen does not direct us to a resting place but invites us to balance words and silence, heart and intellect. My present understanding is that it invites us to both recognize the unfathomable, *and* to think and express what cannot be expressed.

I realize this view may be unfashionable; after all, we have inherited the fierce anti-intellectualism of the 1960s and 1970s that 'idealized instincts and feelings, looked down on philosophy and favoured primal screams and grunts over articulate expression and verbalization' (Bazzano, 2006, p. 33). This was done for many good reasons but it has also discouraged independent thought. Taking my cue from Adorno (1978), some ten years ago I candidly thought to have identified the causes for this: the deeply embedded suspicion reserved for shrewd thinking and analysis, and subsequent perversion of the richness and depth of thought to mere problem-solving (Bazzano, 2006). Some of my early forays into 'the meaning of life' after university, from my early twenties to my early thirties in India, had an intense mystical streak, but with age I've grown impatient of hearing the young Wittgenstein's posh-sounding adage quoted to me once again: 'that whereof we cannot speak, thereof we must remain silent' – often a real cop-out that, in my experience, leaves the door open to all sorts of mystifications. It may well be that by disparaging mysticism I'm partly rebuking my younger self – berating his naivety while secretly envying his youth. Yet I have learned that suspending natural doubt and perplexity altogether in favour of the ecstatic, of peak experiences and surrender to charisma, can land oneself in odd places. One brief example may suffice here.

For 12 years, between 1980 and 1992, I learned a great deal as a disciple of the Indian mystic Osho Rajneesh. His dynamic approach to meditation, the exhilarating blend of eastern contemplative practices, bioenergetics and western psychology, the vibrant international community of practitioners he assembled in Poona, India – all made for an invigorating, unforgettable experience. It opened my heart, body and mind; it blew away the dust of Catholicism and paleo-Leninism gathered up until then on my tender soul. Throughout this adventure, I also kept brushing aside the gnawing doubt that the entire enterprise rested on a rather wobbly foundation, namely, one man's claim to great spiritual enlightenment. The joy and elation I felt, however, were too real, and too great. My first 'rebirthing' session gave me an unforgettable vision of agony that turned to ecstasy and made me see the whole of history as a dream, as a flutter of a butterfly's wings. How could I disrupt the depth and joy I experienced by paying attention to boring, 'negative' doubts? Yet these became stronger during the years of temporary relocation of Osho's headquarters in the Oregon desert, a period that I started to refer to, furtively and only in my own private thoughts, as Stalinist – the turning of a spontaneous assemblage of rebels and spiritual seekers into an established, hierarchical and autocratic society. It bugs me that I never paid serious attention to my doubts and quietly went along with the consensus that within the community dictated that doubt is 'negative'. But then again it is very unusual in my experience for a spiritual approach to appreciate the value of doubt. In Zen, doubt is seen as essential, thus actively encouraged rather than discarded. As the Zen saying goes, great doubt, great insight; little doubt, little insight; and no doubt, no insight. For the great teacher Hakuin Zenji (1686–1768), the practice of Zen needs three essential elements: 'a great root of faith, a feeling of great doubt, and a great, burning aspiration' (Waddell, 1999, p. 72).

The Zen tradition is not alone in giving value to doubt and in emphasizing the ordinary aspect of human existence against the deification of teachers and gurus. The Jewish Lithuanian tradition in which Emmanuel Levinas was schooled before his forays into phenomenology, showed profound distrust of the 'charismatic', seeing in those 'forms of human elevation . . . the essence of idolatry' (Levinas, 1990, p. 11). He valued rigorous debate and argumentation as valuable antidotes to notions of 'the Sacred that envelops and transports me', which he saw as 'a form of violence' (Levinas, 1990, p. 23).

Making a good impression

On a basic level, the term 'logocentrism' refers to the widespread belief that language translates reality faithfully and effectively. This is because the dominant view considers *logos* – variously translated as discourse, speech, the principle of reason and judgement – to be a superior way of building a theory of knowledge. But this does not take into account the multiplicities of language and speech.

I grew up in a lower-middle class household in Calabria, southern Italy. My mother was a housewife who received a basic education. Like my father, she was of humble origins. My dad was sent to college thanks to the savings of his father who had worked as a labourer in New York City. My father became a teacher and eventually a headmaster. Both my parents wanted their two children to be well-educated. Among themselves, they spoke the local Calabrian dialect, but when addressing my sister and me they spoke Italian, a sort of equivalent of 'BBC English', a pleasant but neutered language. Some of my peers spoke the dialect; many of the kids I wanted to hang out with were street boys with a rather rough demeanour. I tried so very hard to be like them but most of the time failed miserably. They mocked my attempts to talk the dialect and slang; it didn't sound real to them. I was trying too hard; I hadn't been born in to it, though I understood it well. And it didn't sound real to me either: I felt it kept reality at bay; it shielded me from raw experience and the full sensory impact of the world in and around me. As I remember it, the dialect was gaudy, vibrant and full of vivid images. It had an impressive array of multilayered and intricate swear words. It was exciting; it cut to the chase, and it cut to the quick. Also, the currency of some of its expressions expired pretty fast. Visiting my hometown after a 10-year gap, my old friends gasped at my antiquated usage of slang. 'Oh, no one says that anymore'. On the other hand, the dulcet tones of certified Italian served their purpose: speaking them was paramount if you were to do well or get by at school. At times they conferred a vaguely cultured aura to the person who spoke them, and it was handy for getting a decent job. Failing that, and given the high level of unemployment in the region, you could at least cut a *bella figura*, make a good impression or maybe even try to date the doctor's daughter.

Speaking speech

There is a speech we are born into; it is ready-made, full of definitions and denominations; it is as clear-cut as identity cards. You're male or female, Italian or British, young or old. This speech is functional; it helps the person enter a stream of cultural identity, identify with it and for some even make a home in it. In many ways, this language is a form of useful role-playing. But if we solely rely on a ready -made, supposedly 'neutral' language, the latter can become a prison or a tyrannical guide that we feel we ought to follow blindly (Bazzano, 2014). This type of speech is *secondary* and is effectively the repetition of ideas already expressed: this can be referred to as 'spoken speech' (Merleau-Ponty, 2013, p. 202).

There are times, however, when we struggle to find words for our experience. Now and again our clients find it hard to express what they are going through. The intensity of what is being experienced does not translate easily into language. Maybe there are no words yet for what is happening; maybe new words will have to be created. This does not apply solely to distress, but may refer to experiences of joy and re-enchantment. This is when an opening for a second mode of speech may get underway: 'speaking speech', the emergence of our silent yearning, the temporary apprehension and completion of thought (Madison, 1981). This mode of speech is by nature tentative; it has been called speaking speech (Merleau-Ponty, 2013, p. 202); it does use logical constructs and reason, but aims at expressing some-thing outside the domains of logic and reason. It is almost a new *idiom*, and here the therapist's best stance is in the role of an *idiot* (Bazzano, 2016a; Spinelli, 2016), of one who helps the client to forge a speech that best reflects the emergence of the new, the event-like quality of experience as it unfolds.

Logocentrism and metaphysics of presence

> Man would be erased, like a face drawn in sand at the edge of the sea.
>
> *Foucault, 1973, p. 387*

The other critique of logocentrism that I want to articulate here takes its lead from Derrida (1998). I will begin this discussion by quoting a passage from a pivotal book, first published 40 years ago:

> All the metaphysical determinations of truth, and even the one beyond metaphysical ontotheology that Heidegger reminds us of, are more or less immediately inseparable from the instance of logos, or of a reason thought within the lineage of logos, in whatever sense it is understood: in the pre-Socratic or the philosophical sense, in the sense of God's infinite

> understanding, or in the anthropological sense, in the pre-Hegelian or the post-Hegelian sense.
>
> *Derrida, 1998, pp. 10–11*

What does 'metaphysical determinations of truth' mean? They are essentially decisions, measurements and judgements of truth. All of them are inevitably *logocentric*, i.e. based on a notion of truth as *logos*, as (rational) discourse, of truth described as the expression (signifier) deriving from an originating feature (signified), regardless of what the latter may be (Magliola, 1984). If we accept the above description, then we can see how the entire edifice of the western tradition is logocentric and based on a precise hierarchy that demands of us that we do the following: a) give priority to 'meaning' (or 'sense') and 'inner voice' as 'the binary constituents of meaning' (Magliola, ibid, p. 4); b) choose vocalization as the number one mode of expression; and c) agree that '"writing" occupies the last place' (ibid) in this hierarchy.

Logocentrism is (almost) inescapable, even when the approach one professes is – as is presented in this book – avowedly non-logocentric. This is partly because logocentrism, as represented in the three-point hierarchical scheme above, is inextricably linked to what many of us take as undisputable: a metaphysical notion of *presence* and the principle of self-identity. In this respect *differential* thought of the kind espoused by Nāgārjuna and Derrida is a concerted assault on what we hold most dear: the notion that I am I and that whatever is, is. So it is not at all surprising if it attracts hostility. Nāgārjuna is then labelled a 'nihilist' and Derrida stands accused of being the 'mad axeman of Western philosophy' (cited in Bazzano, 2013).

All conventional ideologies, whether openly or not, value self-identity as 'a binary combination of "originating factor" and "expression"' (Magliola, 1984, p. 5). The I is 'I' as well as 'me', it is at the same time naming and it is named. The entire tradition, from Augustine, through Aquinas and later Descartes and Locke, is dancing to the same merry tune. For John Locke (2015), 'a person can consider itself an itself, or the same thinking thing . . . by that consciousness which is inseparable from thinking and essential to it' (Locke, 2015, p. 239). For William James (2000), considering our spiritual self is a reflective process. And for Husserl (2012; 2013) the meaning of 'I' is realized in the immediate idea of one's own personality.

Logocentrism and metaphysics of presence are in attendance even in theories of identity that are not based on personal identity but that are nevertheless, in Robert Magliola's terms, 'cryptic displacements' (Magliola, 1984, p. 6) of the classical principle.

A middle path

Nāgārjuna's philosophical and existential project is not dissimilar from deconstruction, for he directs our awareness to the intermediate realm between existence and non-existence. He restores the Dharma from metaphysical escapism and logocentrism – both greatly influencing how the majority understand Buddhism in the west. Like the Buddha before him, Nāgārjuna is not satisfied by saying that something *is*. Like the Buddha, he finds it inadequate to say that something is *not*. In the *Samyutta-Nikaya,* or 'Book of Kindred Sayings' (Davids, 1993), the Buddha is asked three times by a student whether there is a self, and each time he remains silent. After the student leaves, Kāśyapa remarks that this may be construed as failure to respond, to which the Buddha replies that if he had told the student that the self exists, he would have incurred the error of *eternalism.* If he had said the self does not exist, he would have made the opposite mistake, that of *nihilism.* Instead, he added, as a Tathāgata (teacher of suchness) I teach the *middle path* that brings to an end the either/or dichotomy between extremities: because of this, that arises; because this happens, that arises.

When reaching this crucial point, all logocentric interpretations of Zen and Buddhism usually go on to announce a 'nondualistic awareness . . . a nondual form of awareness in which the subject/object dichotomy is transcended – or the self/ other dualism is seen through – leaving instead pure, undivided, nondual awareness' (Wilber, 2014, Internet file). Yet this 'nondualistic awareness' is still within the confines of logocentrism, i.e. it harks back to a notion of unity. This is effectively 'a regression to the times before the Buddha, to the logocentric vision of Vedanta and the Upanishads which the Buddha grew out of' (Bazzano, 2016b, p. 149). I have great respect for Vedanta, but it is a disservice to gloss over fundamental differences between traditions. The co-opting of the Buddha's teachings 'within the transcendentalist perspective . . . has a long history [with] two emerging trends' (Bazzano, ibid, p. 148). The first one was 'the need to provide a form of Buddhism . . . more compatible with the social life emerging out of the political stability found during the Mauryan, Kushan and Gupta empires' (Batchelor, 1983, p. 48), and which required 'a greater attempt at symbiosis with the indigenous Brahmanical culture and the presentation of . . . Buddhism within a metaphysical format able to hold its own against the competing Hindu systems' (Batchelor, 1983, ibid.). The other trend was the transfiguration of the Buddha from historical sage/physician to omniscient being, presumably with the aim of elevating Buddhism as a religion to higher levels of specialness.

Singing the world

It is precisely against this process of deification and the baroque paraphernalia that accompanied it that the radical practices of Chan and Zen emerged in the Far East. They were refreshingly free of metaphysical assumptions; they emphasized somatic practice (*zazen*) and indirect, humorous and irreverent *artistic* expression of the Dharma. While the Vedic-Upanishadic tradition emphasises *ātman* (variously translated as self, breath, soul), Zen refutes the notion of substance and highlights instead the fluid nature of reality.

A logocentric reading of the Dharma misunderstands the fundamental Buddhist notion of *śūnyatā* or 'de-void-ness', a term that indicates both 'without substance' as wells as *a move away from void-ness.* Imagine that someone is knocking at my door.

Who is there? The standard 'nondual' logocentric reading will be: the other is me; there is no fundamental distinction between self and other. We are one, tributaries to the same ocean. A variation on this 'unitary' theme may be: both self and other are inherently empty. This is all well and good. It may even be true on the *absolute* level. But I still need to hear the knock, make the decision, get up and open the door (Magliola, 1984). Each of these distinct acts affirms the relative dimension, each of them says: you and I are separate, there is a gap between us, and this gap is the space of ethics, of risk, of empathic awareness and compassion. Gnostic *indifference* is denied, as we trample over the toffee-nosed imperturbability of the sage, sever the fence of spiritual superiority, and come to re-cognize that the phenomenal world can be blissful: we sing the world, our features betraying the lineaments of desire: a veritable act of heresy for all those holy denigrators of life out there.

The four noble tasks

So, in a sense *śūnyatā* (de-void-ness of being), this great canonical term in Zen is nothing but a makeshift word, an utterance in a transactional language. It serves us egregiously well, provided we don't start erecting altars in its name. To be clear, I am not merely saying that 'truth is paradoxical', that Zen teachings are paradoxical. At closer scrutiny, paradox appears to be the preferred trope of logocentrism, particularly within religion, a point stressed by Derrida in 'White Mythology', a chapter in his *Margins of Philosophy* (Derrida, 1984, pp. 207–272). Religion almost succeeds 'where more univocal systems, such as science and logic, necessarily fail' (Magliola, 1984, p. 206n). It does so by misnaming 'discontinuities' by calling them 'contraries' and lumps them together in a 'mystical unity' (ibid), e.g. God is both centre and circumference; the absolute is both presence and absence and so forth.

What I am endeavouring to clarify here is the *unique* nature of Dharma teachings as expounded by Nāgārjuna and subsequently by the Zen tradition. Their uniqueness resides in the vivid presence of the non-logocentric elements within it. I would not be surprised if within each of them one were to find aspects that escape logocentrism, yet the way most great religious traditions have been apprehended is at heart logocentric. This is true of both western and eastern religions. The Vedantic traditions, though by no means constituting one comprehensive doctrine, by and large explain the world in terms of a unified whole. A system of education, ethics and politics, Confucianism is equally logocentric, being essentially a highly sophisticated theory of presence applied to the world. And so are Hinduism and even Taoism, the latter emphasizing the union of opposites. Admittedly within Buddhism too, and Zen in particular, there are significant strands of logocentrism.

There seems to be a factual, inexorable, even plodding logic at work in the Buddha's elucidation of the four noble truths or, as imaginatively rendered by Stephen Batchelor (2015), four noble *tasks*; I must: a) acknowledge that our existence is characterized by suffering, dissatisfaction and turmoil; b) realize that this arises from our reactivity and cravings; c) trust that we can achieve freedom from dissatisfaction; and d) trust that this freedom consists in walking the 'middle path'.

My cravings come from ignorance, which in this context indicates the rather simplistic notion that this thing called 'me' exists truly, inherently and independently.

'Heaps'

An antidote to this is provided by seeing first-hand, through concerted meditative awareness, that all phenomena constantly interact and that there are no such things as essences or substances anywhere. We must see this for ourselves as well as in ourselves. If we do this, we are likely to discover that we too are made of combinations: physicality (*rupa*), feeling-tone (*vedana*), perception (*samjna*), impulse (*samskara*) and consciousness (*vijnana*). The Buddha's description of experience does not give primacy to 'mind' or to the conventional mind–body split, but depicts instead a dynamic process of experience that dissolves the conventional sense of being a mind inside a body inside a world. We realize that we are made of 'heaps' or 'aggregates' and slowly learn to dis-identify with them.

Nāgārjuna's four-cornered logic

Yet within Buddhism, for example with the Abhidharmic tradition, the five afore-mentioned 'heaps' are regarded as real – a possible drift into a form of identity-theory. All phenomena *interact*, I have said earlier. They do not originate and dissolve, but constantly interact. While the Abhidharma sees phenomena as originating and coming to pass, the Prajnaparamita tradition holds to the 'doctrine of non-production of elements . . . a more radical apprehension of the stream of becoming' (Magliola, 1984, p. 92). And it is to this latter tradition that non-logocentric aspects of 'Nagarjunian' Zen thought and practice belong. My contention is that without a little knowledge of deconstructive work in relation to the principles of identity and unity these seemingly elusive aspects of Zen are easily misapprehended. Zen's negative dialectic is often read as pointing to a transcendent unit, to an 'it' that cannot be described, or to *reductio ad absurdum*. But the crucial point here is that although Zen *does* say that 'it' cannot be described, that does not mean that there is an 'it' in the first place. Notions of identity and unity are ingrained in our being, which is why we naturally conflate Zen's negative dialectic with other eastern and western logocentric perspectives. An example of the latter is found in the *Upanishads*, according to which the nature of ultimate reality is *neti, neti*, or 'not, not', neither this nor that: it cannot be expressed, but all along the assumption is that there *is* a fundamental substratum beyond appearance. The Zen path follows instead the 'middle way' traced by the Buddha. In other words, it is not a way to some final truth or a path leading to knowledge. It is instead the end of socratizing, of theory, and of knowing (Sprung, 1978). It is a *practice* of wisdom (*sophia*), not a means to it or a discourse about it. It is an incarnate expression of sophia rather than a longing, a love of (*philo*) sophia. It is also the possibility of finding delight in the mundane, of noticing an everyday gratuitous elation that is not regimented within an all-encompassing identity.

Zen's negative dialectic does not aim at building a metaphysical home in the midst of an uncertain world – at times there will be a *dwelling*, a holding place that later will be abandoned. This is in a sense the meaning of Zen ordination, *tokudo*: becoming homeless, without a metaphysical fixed abode. This is beyond our customary dialectic of dialogical confutation of truths and beliefs. Nāgārjuna *dissolves* metaphysical questions. He does so by expanding the two-cornered logic of the *dilemma* into the four-cornered logic of the *tetralemma*:

> The dilemma will state: 1) A is B; 2) A is not B. The tetralemma will assert: 1) A is B; 2) A is not B; 3) A is both B and not-B; 4) A is neither B nor not-B. While mysticism and spiritual absolutism lingers on the *third* lemma, Nāgārjuna goes beyond. But this 'going beyond' does not gesture towards a unified reality, an all-encompassing 'whole' or 'logos' . . . It does *not* suggest unity of opposites, as expressed, for instance, by Heidegger's thinking of the negative of being, of that nothingness which he sees as identical with Being. It does *not* translate the Buddha's insights *within* the Vedic-Upanishadic (and later Advaita) worldview.
>
> *Bazzano, 2016b, p. 148*

Nāgārjuna does not evoke an eternal *logos*, a permanent metaphysical home untouched by the winds of impermanence blowing through our life. His stance is neither: a) *logocentric rationalism*, nor is it affected by; b) *logocentric mysticism*, but can be described as; c) *differentialist* (Magliola, 1984) though the term is not to be understood hierarchically, i.e. as more valid than the first two but simply as one that is consonant to some practitioners such as myself. My own preference for different-ialism is based on the appreciation of its shrewd rethinking of the relationship between signifier and signified, of its critique of self-identity and its reluctance to be committed to an institution of metaphysical explanation of reality. This discussion is crucial in setting Zen apart from mysticism – whether of the spiritual, religious or supposedly 'phenomenological' variety.

Incarnate phenomenology

The above distinction (between rationalist and/or mystical logocentrism on the one hand and differentialism on the other) is equally important in therapy, especially in relation to sections of avowedly 'existential' humanistic counselling and psycho-therapy influenced by Heidegger (1962). Having his writings enshrined, as some practitioners tend to do, meant that little or no attention is paid to thinkers who built on them effectively while demonstrating its pitfalls. I am referring to Jacques Derrida, but also to writers/practitioners labouring within areas of enquiry com-monly known as post-existentialism, post-structuralism and post-phenomenology who have all been constructively critical of Heidegger's spiritual absolutism and Platonism (Magliola, 1977, 1984; Derrida, 1998; Ralkowski, 2009). Writing about different types of mysticism, Derrida sees Heidegger's notion of *Sein* as belonging to that particular kind of mysticism that recognizes the unity of opposites (Magliola, 1984; Brooks, 2015), an operation that is in fact a 'fatal failure to "match up" the oppositional halves' (Magliola, 1984, p. 199).

In *The Question of Being* (Heidegger, 1958), we read:

> Only because the question 'What is metaphysics?' thinks from the beginning of the climbing above, the transcendence, the *Being* of being, can it think of the negative of being, of that nothingness which just as originally is identical with Being.
>
> *p. 101*

Identity of 'being' with *Being* replicates the theme found in Taoism and logocentric Zen, one that swallows whole the self-identity principle so dear to the philosophical tradition. Finely attuned to Heidegger's critical practice, Derrida deconstructs (*Dekonstruktion* was after all Heidegger's term), drawing on Heidegger's late work *Identity and Difference* (Heidegger, 2002), the mystical notion of unity of opposites, opening the phenomenological inquiry to a multiplicity of interpretations (Derrida, 1998).

What is often overlooked is the fact that this crucial move towards difference and multiplicity is already found latent in Merleau-Ponty's late work (Merleau-Ponty, 1964a). As a humanist, Merleau-Ponty was not inclined to abandon the centrality of the human subject, yet like Derrida (a doctoral student under his supervision), he drew from Saussure's structural linguistics. In his unfinished work *The Prose of the World*, Merleau-Ponty (1964a) describes language as 'less a sum of signs . . . than a methodical means of differentiating signs from one another' (p 31), and writes of signs not as 'representations of certain significations [but as] . . . means of differentiation in the verbal chain' (ibid, p. 31). Both statements, among others, echo Saussure's famous claim that there are only differences in language. Merleau-Ponty's *incarnate phenomenology* sets out to describe these differences from the 'vantage point' of a body–subject who is at all times implicated in the world. This is a long way from Heidegger's logocentric view of phenomenology, which he sees as a prelude to a general ontology. This is because Merleau-Ponty is reluctant to bypass subjectivity, which is for him 'one of those solids that [we] will have to digest' (Merleau-Ponty, 1964b, p. 154). And there is much more that sets his work apart from Heidegger's: its engaged ambiguity, a healthy disinclination to yield to grand statements, the strategic foreswearing (rather than blanket dismissal) of science and technology; and a genuine humility in pursuing an inquiry aimed at clarifying our existence within the confines of our incarnate, social and historical domains. All of this would provide us therapists with a formidable array of philosophical guidelines.

Shift happens: the path of Zen differentialism

Zen itself is not the harbour of purity and spontaneous spirituality untouched by logos that many of us wish it to be. There is a lot of Zen that is logocentric. Even the radical writings of Alan Watts, who did much to popularize a delectably anti-institutional view of Zen in the west, are often imbued with the notion of identity, even of '*Supreme Identity* of *atma* and Brahma, of the Self and the Infinite' (Watts, 2014, p. 72), a standpoint from which 'the world is seen as nothing, as illusion' (ibid).

Even more markedly logocentric are elements of Zen inherited in the west, in turn influenced by the practices and theoretical stances of the *Yogācāra,* known as the school of 'consciousness only' or 'of representation only' (*chittamatra*), which became influential in China particularly after the translation, in the early fifth century, of one of its key texts, the *Laṅkāvatāra Sūtra* and, in the sixth century, of another important text, the 'Mahāyāna compendium' or *Mahāyānasaṃgraha.* For these philosophers/practitioners, 'external' objects of perception are like an illusion, but the mind that perceives them is real. They also maintain that there are two types of mind: 'one that perceives only sense objects; and the other, the self-cognizer, which perceives only the mind perceiving the objects' (Tobden, 2005, p. 370). But the notion of a self-cognizer is absurd; it is akin to that of a 'blade of a sword that cuts itself or [to that] of a self-illumining light' (ibid, p. 371). The Chittamatrins, as these thinkers are often called, see the distinction between subject and object as deceptive, and refer to a nondual consciousness that can see through the deception. This view is echoed by Seng-ts'an, the third Chinese Zen ancestor to whom the poetic text *Xinxin Ming* ('Trust in Mind') is attributed (Soeng, 2004). This text is studded with gems such as 'do not search for the truth; only cease to cherish opinions' (p. 14). At some point we read:

> Things are object because of the subject (mind); the mind (subject) is such because of things (objects). Understand the relativity of these two and the basic reality: the unity of emptiness.
>
> *p. 14*

But 'unity' of emptiness ascribes a *centric* view to the 'ten thousand things' (of which the mind is also one). A non-centric, Nāgārjunian view, would state that 'both objects of knowledge and consciousness exist *conventionally*' (Tobden, 2004, p. 371, italics added), that is, *relatively*. Consciousness is not eternal, nor independent of phenomena. Both consciousness and phenomena exist only relatively. Talk of the nondual is nevertheless all the rage in current strands of spirituality and transpersonal psychotherapy – its popularity partly due to its teleological, as well as logocentric, appeal (respectively: the promise of future attainment in the upward climb towards so-called higher states and the reduction of experience to unity and holism).

An alternative position is vibrantly present in strands of Zen thought and practice. Full of wonderful instances of Nāgārjunian wisdom, I call this stance, after Robert Magliola, *Zen differentialism*. The reader may recall the dialogue between Isan and the monk, described in the Introduction: a great example of differentialism in action. The teacher pulls the rug from under the student's feet several times, so as to incite greater fluidity of perspective. The aim here is to become free from centres imposed on the flow of experiential reality and learn instead how to shift perspectives at will – a perspective of no-perspective. Case 27 of the *Gateless Gate* (Yamada, 2004), a collection of kōans, records a dialogue between Nansen and a monk. The monk asks: 'Is there a truth which no one has taught?' to which Nansen replies 'Yes'. 'And what is this truth?' the monk asks. Nansen replies: 'It is not mind; it is not Buddha; it is not things'. No concession can be found, in this version of Zen teachings, to notions of 'eternal consciousness' *or* crude empiricism; no commitment to either spiritualism *or* materialism. One finds instead skilful, often playful skirting of grand theorizing that has the effect of throwing the inquirer and practitioner back to herself.

Where Zen and phenomenology meet

In a key text of classic Buddhist literature, Nāgārjuna's *Middle Way* (Sideris & Katsura, 2013) the relative and absolute are often referred to as the *two truths*. The relative is understood as the truth *gathered* (in the world), a translation of *saṁvṛti* that is akin to the western notion of empirical evidence but also denotes a conventional, commonly accepted truth. In an ambivalent turn of phrase, the absolute is rendered as the *ungathered* truth, a translation of *paramārtha*, the ultimate or absolute, similar to the western notion of the sublime. Though representing the 'highest truth', the latter is not conceived as separate from ordinary activities. It does not join the chorus of denigration of 'wicked and untrustworthy' everyday experiences and perceptions that is the refrain of religious orthodoxy, nor does it take flight into a notion of Buddhist 'emptiness' which, unhinged from the empirical truth, becomes as dangerous as the clumsy handling of a poisonous snake.

We do need to employ empirical 'relative' truth if we are to live in the world effectively: the chair I am sitting on in order to write these words does not evaporate simply because from the absolute point of view it does not intrinsically exist but is an amalgam of many components that are ultimately empty. Similarly, empirical truth affirms the difference between this and that: to say that gold is the same as grime is untrue in the sense of empirical truth (Streng, 1967). Absolute truth is there to offset our tendency to perceive phenomena as solid objects that exist separately from the world they inhabit. Nāgārjuna's 'Middle Way' affirms a sense of *indeterminacy*: phenomena are 'indeterminable – they cannot exist in their own right' (Magliola, 1984, p. 121). Bimal Krishna Matilal (2006) sums up this position admirably when he refers to the phenomenal world as neither real nor unreal, but as logically and rationally *unresolved*. By definition each phenomenon (its meaning being 'that which appears') is something we definitely perceive and not mere 'illusion'. The world of phenomena we inhabit, even though impermanent, *exists*. If it didn't, all our striving would be utterly pointless. At the same time, the world is never apprehended or resolved. For Merleau-Ponty, it is unfathomable, it forever resists explanation hence our experience of it is ambiguous (Bazzano, 2014). For Nāgārjuna's, everything is subject to *dependent origination*, i.e. everything is indeterminate, 'empty', devoid of absolute value. Merleau-Ponty forswears scientific explanations of the world; he brackets scientism and all theoretical assumptions in order to have a fresh look at phenomenal reality. He also puts aside the dominant view of classical materialism according to which the perceiving subject is one solid object among other solid objects. Similarly, Nāgārjuna does not reject the phenomenal world but invites us to a non-committal stance towards the final validity of the phenomenal world (Matilal, 2006).

Reality itself is deconstructive

Lucid expressions of Zen differentialism or 'deconstructive' Zen are found aplenty in the teachings of Huineng (discussed in Chapter 4) as well as in the *Hongzhou* school of Chan Buddhism. One of the focal points of these critiques is the reification of a notion championed by Huineng, *wunian* or 'no-thought'. This is what a deconstructive practice does best: questioning any new, useful idea once it has fossilized into a dogma. The school criticizes the privileging of 'awareness or "intuitive knowledge" over discriminative cognition' (Wang, 2006, p. 135), and its teachings are best elucidated by Huang Po (Blofeld, 1958):

> [You] students of the *dao* . . . will realize your original mind only in the realm of seeing, hearing, feeling and knowing. Although the original mind does not belong to seeing, hearing, feeling and knowing, this mind cannot be separated from them.
>
> *p. 36*

The above statement cuts through the common assumption that realization is something static and separate from our everyday, ordinary mind. A parallel and equally common conjecture challenged by the Hongzhou School is the separation between everyday activities and our sense of self-identity. With the fixity of our static notion of self beginning to relax, the parallel belief in a pre-existing, self-existing agent behind our action also slackens. Then 'enlightenment' and everyday functioning are seen as arising together in dynamic interaction, both in flux and subject to change. The common misconception of enlightenment is of a permanent state of mind achieved once and for all. This then goes to inform the fantasy of an enlightened way of being in the world. This can be liberating: it frees us from a dependence on gurus and spiritual teachers who claim to have experienced the 'non-dual', as it is fashionably called nowadays in some circles. A differentialist teaching, such as the one proffered by the Hongzhou School, offers a sharp and effective critique of common misconceptions and of logocentric interpretations as a whole. The Zen masters in this tradition know all too well that 'the living process of change and flux will undercut every fixed position and every attachment to self and self-identity. *Reality itself is deconstructive*' (Wang, 2006, p. 140, emphasis added).

The Hongzhou School advocates the difficult and necessary practice of *erasure* – the last thing we want to do. We are invited to put aside concepts that, although useful at some point in the past, have now solidified into dogma. We are asked to disregard those moments of ecstasy and insight experienced in meditation, the milestones on our path which now begin to hinder our direct experiencing of reality through expectation, and lure us into a false sense of spiritual achievement. To be able to teach erasure requires the skilful means of a seasoned and unusual teacher. To be at the receiving end of this sort of teaching requires faith and commitment. The reason is that we normally take it personally (I certainly do) when our cherished insights are put to the test and we are invited to carry on the path as if starting from scratch. In this sense, what deconstructive Zen teaches is also *self-erasure*, not in the nihilistic sense but in the service of a dynamic view of reality that does not allow us either to sleep on our laurels or, for that matter, indulge in our equally cherished list of failures.

The history of Chan Buddhism is filled with examples of deconstructive teachings. Mazu Daoyi (709–788 AD) famously taught that 'the mind is Buddha' (Jia, 2006, p. 171), which helped dispel the notion that 'Buddha' refers to a special state of mind *separate* from our ordinary everyday mind. Before long, his students became attached to the phrase, turning it into a new object of faith. So Mazu began to say that there is *neither mind nor Buddha*.

Dried shit-stick

A similar degree of fluidity is found in the teachings of Linji Yixuan, a Zen master of great renown, and founder of the Rinzai School (Sasaki, 2009). His central notion of *wuyi zhenren*, or 'true person of no status' (Batchelor, 2009; Bazzano, 2010), indicating an important attribute of an accomplished Zen practitioner, was clearly devised as a caution to practitioners for not elevating themselves. Furthermore, in the Confucian era in which it was formulated, '"no status" meant being truly a nobody . . . [emphasizing] . . . both [our] intrinsic human dignity – not justified nor augmented by power, wealth and prestige – as well as the bereft, impoverished, and homeless state of our transient condition as humans' (Bazzano, 2010, p. 61). Soon enough, this same notion was elevated by students to transcendental heights, so one day Linji entered the meditation hall to give his usual discourse and addressed his students: 'Did you know that within your lump of red flesh there is a true person of no status? If you haven't figured this out yet, then just look!' One student asked: 'Who is the true person of no status?' At this point, Linji got up, grabbed the student by the collar and cried: 'Speak! Speak!' The monk tried to say something. Linji let go of him, and said: 'The true person of no status – a dried shit stick!' and went back to his room.

Zen literature presents us with countless interpretations of this rather startling but not atypical incident. My understanding veers first towards the element of surprise and even shock, designed to invite the student to bypass the usual routes of the rational mind when offering an insight to the teacher's question. But there is also something more fundamental at work here. Linji, who made no preference between the sacred and the secular, in the above case extends his lack of preference to what is deemed admirable or despicable. A 'dried shit-stick' is what the ancients used in lieu of toilet paper. Unless, Linji seems to be saying, we are able to see the Buddha in the lowest manifestations, we still have a long way to go.

As with other examples within Chan Buddhism, Linji's teachings are usually categorized as 'iconoclastic', but this is a one-sided interpretation. For if on the one hand skilled Zen teachers pull the rug from under our feet, leaving us to confront reality without filters and crutches, on the other hand they also reconstruct concepts as pointers that aid one's practice. They make use, in other words, of both '*kataphatic* and *apophatic* language' (Wang, 2006, p. 141, emphasis added). Both terms are often applied to theology, the first – from the Greek *kata* (descent) and *femi* (speak) – means something like 'bringing down God in order to speak to him'. The second, from the Greek *apophēmi* (to deny) expresses *via negativa*: 'describing God by negation' or denying that God can be expressed by rational language.

We are not allowed to rest either in negation or affirmation but are imaginatively and sometimes shockingly provoked into maintaining a fluid stance that is seen as more attuned with the dynamic nature of reality. At the level of expression, particularly with the Zen practice of kōan study, this can be summarily rendered with the apparent paradox: 'Say something, even though nothing can be said'.

Unfocused

A skilled therapist will aspire, particularly if practising from a person-centred perspective, to be non-directive. This is a stance of ethical respect for the client's autonomy and an expression of dynamic faith in the human being's inner resources. It is also, in the light of what has been discussed above, the aspiration to suspend explanations about reality, allowing space to notice emergent phenomena: a registering of experience devoid of a centre, a loyalty to non-centred experience – not wholly dissimilar from 'evenly suspended attention' (Freud, 1971). The imposition of a logically organized view of reality is prescriptive rather than descriptive and betrays a misunderstanding of *śūnyatā*. Even when 'well-intentioned', e.g. avowedly relational and/or holistic, it severely curbs the scope and breadth of the therapeutic encounter. Openness to *śūnyatā* evades the common trappings of 'dialogue', 'knowledge' and 'understanding' which are typical of the intersubjective frame. It also eludes the trappings of love and ecstatic union, typical of the transpersonal frame. This is because in the open space of *śūnyatā* there is less fascination with the *person* of the client, and also no fixation with the transcendent 'presence' of the therapist. One could say that there is *no focus*.

In praise of eccentricity

The logocentric tradition holds a stronghold on most branches of knowledge and a sign of its power and ubiquity is that its perspective is often taken for granted as the wise and/or common-sense view. Faced, for instance, with a leaning towards genuine wonder at the multifarious nature of the world that is devoid of a fundamental metaphysical or ontological principle is often deemed inconsequential. Of this nature was the rather sanctimonious critique moved by Henry James, Matthew Arnold and others at the candidly polyphonic verse of the nineteenth-century English poet Robert Browning, whose main fault was, in their view, *eccentricity*, literally understood as the absence of an authorial or metaphysical *centre* (Perry, 2016). Something similar is found, a century later, in the more sympathetic but still harsh critique of Walter Benjamin's gigantic manuscript on Baudelaire by his friend Adorno who saw it as deteriorating into 'wide-eyed presentation of mere facts' (Benjamin & Adorno, 1999, p. 283). Benjamin took that as a compliment, replying: 'you are describing the proper philological attitude' (ibid, p. 292).

Invoking aesthetic principles, as Browning's critics did, may just about justify their critical position. Equally, an appeal to philosophical consistency may give reason for Adorno's criticism of Benjamin's writings. But I find it considerably more difficult to defend the need for a unitary principle within therapy. By definition the latter is an art and a practice that deals with the plurality of *psyche* and the personified difference of each individual client.

A path of radical scepticism

The history of Chan Buddhism is a good example of deconstruction *avant la lettre*. There is a constant process of self-scrutiny at work in this school that confronts head-on our familiar human tendency for *reification*, i.e. for turning any fluid, descriptive notion into a substantial, essential, static *thing*. Some of these deconstructive leanings are particularly strong, as with Huineng (638–713 AD), known as the 'sixth ancestor' of Zen, and with the Hongzhou Chan School. A key Buddhist notion that gets thoroughly deconstructed is that of 'Buddha nature' (in turn originating from the doctrine of *tathātagarbha* or self-originated wisdom), a notion that all other Buddhist doctrines of salvation can be turned into a sacred item. It is refreshing that instead of inflating this notion, as it would be customary for most schools of thought busy overemphasizing their importance, Chan Buddhism is, on the whole, focused on deconstructing it (Wang, 2006). A well-known example of Chan deconstruction at work is Huineng's response to Shenxiu's verse, illustrated in Chapter 4.

The path explored here is one of radical scepticism. What prevents this from becoming either a mere academic exercise and/or cynicism is adherence to an ethical frame. A great example in the Buddhist tradition is Nāgārjuna (150–250 AD), who pursued his radical inquiry within the ethical frame of the Dharma. A rare parallel example in the west is Nietzsche, who created a powerfully deconstructive hermeneutics while living a practically ascetic existence. The widely held view that radical scepticism paves the way for moral relativism and all sorts of evils and shenanigans betrays a pessimistic view of human nature. What we find in both Nāgārjuna and Nietzsche is greater freedom from the metaphysics we have inventively created but that have ended up enslaving us. In their own different ways, both alert us to the fact that there are no extra-linguistic actualities. We create values and concepts in order to make the world habitable. Someone's courage and strength are measured by their ability to endure, even flourish in a world where values have disintegrated. Can one still live and thrive once the illusory nature is revealed of notions such as 'being', 'unity' and their religious equivalents – God or, in Buddhism a reified, ontologically separate notion of nirvana? Yes, because, in the absence of certainties, we need certitude, which can be cultivated by a regular somatic practice and by the discipline of being with what arises without the use of illusory props, including those thought constructions that, no matter how brilliant, end up becoming entanglements. Conceptual entanglements are traceable back to metaphysical assumptions about existence, our attachment to the idea that there is something *sub*-stantial under it all. Equally, it would be a mistake to read this position as a sort of pragmatic empiricism.

Zen and the art of pole-dancing

What does wisdom mean in this context? It may be described as the great affirmation of a phenomenological reality that is devoid of epistemological as well as metaphysical *ground*. An aptitude for embodying the great affirmation distinguishes *prajna* (often translated as wisdom) from both traditional metaphysics and traditional empiricism. Simply put, wisdom here means the realization of the 'unsayable suchness (*tathatā*) of things' (Martin, 1991, p. 105). Phenomenological reality is affirmed despite (and because of) its inexplicable nature. Affirmation does not imply understanding, interpretation, and least of all justification. It simply does not belong to the realm of *logos*, i.e. to the sphere of metaphysical declarations of truth.

Watching a little while ago an interview with Welsh poet and priest R. S. Thomas, I was struck by his definition of Christ as a poet because it coincided with my own long-held view of the Buddha as a poet and a *strong* poet in particular. I do respect the view of the Buddha as the founder of a religion called Buddhism, but find the notion of the strong poet far more valuable. A strong poet is one who introduces (often subtly and imperceptibly) a new vision and a new language. He or she often begins by using the contemporary language and worldviews in vogue but as one listens, reads and absorbs and is impacted by it, one's perspective will begin to shift. A new language begins to emerge which unsettles previous beliefs – even though these may not necessarily be challenged head-on. He is not the only strong poet within the tradition. Starting with Shakyamuni Buddha, the history of the Dharma presents us with several exemplars, the most prominent after Shakyamuni being Nāgārjuna. The strong poets' ability to redescribe the teachings assures their relevance and brightness.

To Nāgārjuna we owe the crucial insights that *śūnyatā* is one with this impermanent life. The uniqueness of Zen, a tradition that has capitalized on Nāgārjuna's teachings, consists in maintaining a fluid connection between the relative and the absolute. But if we were to attach to the notion of emptiness as a new belief, we would probably remain stuck in the absolute domain. This fundamental error is not confined to quasi-theological disquisitions among Buddhist scholars but has tangible implications in other areas. The error is, for example, replicated within sections of contemporary psychotherapy influenced by Heidegger. The latter's notion of *Dasein* or Being-in-the-world, appeared to provide at first a valuable substitute to the Cartesian–Freudian notion of a separate subject. But Heidegger failed to notice the equally important dimension of separation, alterity and what generally goes under the name of inter-subjectivity, leaving love, as Binswanger had it, outside in the cold.

Several cautionary instances equally point at the danger of remaining trapped at the opposite (relative) pole. In some quarters of humanistic psychology we find subjectivity worshipped to the point where it becomes narcissism in the guise of organismic awareness. What is unique in Zen is its emphasis on a playful and unsettling dance between the two poles. This is different from the fashionable trap of 'non-duality' and the claim of having gone 'beyond'. What we find instead is constant, ambivalent oscillation between the subjective and the objective, the relative and the absolute – a refusal, born out of integrity, to take residence in any of the two polarities. When presenting these ideas, the response I often hear is that this perspective is unsettling, for it does not provide the orderly enough structure that is necessary for exploration. This kind of objection is legitimate and although I am tempted to say that structure is a place where nothing ever happens, I tend to reply instead that in Zen practice the structure is provided by the steady somatic practice of *zazen*. A regular practice of meditation and a therapy session settle the bodymind and make it open for the adventurous exploration.

A ready-made metaphysical exploration of experience is not a structure but a surrogate of structure. Regular, stable meditation practice allows the practitioner to perceive 'emptiness' without floundering. He or she will not find a doorway to a mystical plane behind the curtain of the everyday. Emptiness 'merely removes the false veneer of inherent existence' (Batchelor, 2001, p. 39) and ushers in a glimpse of the precariousness of existence. One of the unassuming outcomes of this is that in perceiving emptiness, I am no longer full of myself.

The teachings of the Buddha, Zen literature and the Zen tradition give us inspiration. But they are no substitute for the dedicated psychosomatic practice of *zazen* and the radical ethical practice of generosity.

References

Adorno, T. (1978). *Minima Moralia – Reflections from a Damaged Life*. London: Verso.

Batchelor, S. (1983). *Alone with Others: An Existential Approach to Buddhism*. New York: Grove Press.

Batchelor, S. (2001). *Verses from the Center: A Buddhist Vision of the Sublime*. New York: Riverhead.

Batchelor, S. (2009). True person of no status. Gaia House, Zen Retreat, 13 April. http://dharmaseed.org/talks/audio_player/169/13391.html Retrieved 25 September 2016.

Batchelor, S. (2015). On the four noble tasks. *Upāya Zen Center*. https://upaya.org/2015/02/stephen-batchelor-four-noble-tasks/ Retrieved 12 November 2016.

Bazzano, M. (2006). *Buddha is Dead: Nietzsche and the Dawn of European Zen*. Eastbourne: Sussex Academic Press.

Bazzano, M. (2010). A true person of no status: Notes on Zen and the art of existential therapy. *Existential Analysis*, 21(1): 51–62.

Bazzano, M. (2013). Feeding Sophie. *Self & Society: An International Journal for Humanistic Psychology*, 41(1): 85–86.

Bazzano, M. (2014). The poetry of the world: A tribute to the phenomenology of Merleau-Ponty. *Self & Society: An International Journal for Humanistic Psychology*, 41(3): 7–12. doi: 10.1080/03060497.2014.11084358.

Bazzano, M. (2016a). The therapist as idiot. *Hermeneutic Circular, Society of Existential Analysis*, April: 10–11.

Bazzano, M. (2016b). House of cards: On Ken Wilber's neo-traditionalism. *Self & Society: An International Journal for Humanistic Psychology*, 44(2): 145–156. doi: 10.1080/03060497.2016.1147666.

Benjamin, W. & Adorno, T. (1999). *The Complete Correspondence 1928–1940*. Cambridge, CAMBS: Polity.

Blofeld, J. (1958). *The Zen Teachings of Huang Po*. New York: Grove Weidenfeld.

Brooks, J. (2015). Writing beyond borders: Derrida, Heidegger, and Zhuangzi in Brian Castro's after China. *Neohelicon*, 42(2): 625–638. doi: 10.1007/s11059-015-0309-6.

Davids, R. (Trans.). (1993). *Book of Kindred Sayings Vol. 1: Samyutta-Nikaya*. Melksham: Pali Text Society.

Derrida, J. (1984). *Margins of Philosophy*. Chicago, IL: Chicago University Press.

Derrida, J. (1998). *Of Grammatology*. Baltimore, MD: John Hopkins University Press.

Foucault, M. (1973). *The Order of Things: An Archaeology of the Human Sciences*. New York: Vintage.

Freud, S. (1971). Recommendations to physicians practicing psychoanalysis. In S. Freud (Ed.), *The Complete Psychological Works of Sigmund Freud*. Standard Edition of, Vol. XII (p. 115). London: Hogarth Press.

Heidegger, M. (1958). *The Question of Being*. Lanham, MD: Rowman & Littlefield.

Heidegger, M. (1962). *Being and Time*. New York: Harper & Row.

Heidegger, M. (2002). *Identity and Difference*. Chicago, IL: University of Chicago Press.

Heine, S. (2008). *Zen Skin, Zen Marrow: Will the Real Zen Buddhism Please Stand Up?* New York: Oxford University Press.

Husserl, E. (2012). *Ideas: General Introduction to Pure Phenomenology*. Abingdon: Routledge.

Husserl. E. (2013). *Cartesian Meditations: An Introduction to Phenomenology*. The Hague: Martinus Nijoff.

James, W. (2000). *The Principles of Psychology, Volume 1*. Mineola, NY: Dover.

Jia, J. (2006). *The Hongzhou School of Chan Buddhism in Eight through Tenth Century China*. Albany, NY: State University of New York Press.

Kant, I. (2007). *Critique of Pure Reasons*. London: MacMillan.

Levinas, E. (1990). *Difficult Freedom: Essays on Judaism*. Baltimore, MD: John Hopkins University Press.

Locke, J. (2015). *An Essay Concerning Human Understanding*. London: Createspace.

Madison, G. B. (1981). *The Phenomenology of Merleau-Ponty*. Athens, OH: Ohio University Press.

Magliola, R. (1977). *Phenomenology and Literature*. West Lafayette, IN: Purdue University Press.

Magliola, R. (1984). *Derrida on the Mend*. West Lafayette, IN: Purdue University Press.

Martin, G. T. (1991). Deconstruction and breakthrough in Nietzsche and Nāgārjuna. In G. Parkes (Ed.), *Nietzsche and Asian thought* (pp. 91–114). Chicago, IL: Chicago University Press.

Matilal, B. K. (2006). *Epistemology, Logic and Grammar in Indian Philosophical Analysis*. New York: Oxford University Press.

Merleau-Ponty, M. (1964a). *The Prose of the World*. Evanston, IL: Northwestern University Press.

Merleau-Ponty, M. (1964b). *Signs*. Evanston, IL: Northwestern University.

Merleau-Ponty, M. (2013). *Phenomenology of Perception*. Abingdon: Routledge.

Perry, S. (2016). Against the same-old same-old. *London Review of Books*, 38(21): 32–38.

Ralkowski, M. (2009). *Heidegger's Platonism*. London: Continuum.

Sasaki, R. F. (2009). *The Record of Linji*. Honolulu: University of Hawaii Press.

Sideris, M. & Katsura, S. (2013). *Nāgārjuna's Middle Way*. Boston, MA: Wisdom.

Soeng, M. (2004). *Trust in Mind: The Rebellion of Chinese Zen*. Somerville, MA: Wisdom.

Spinelli, E. (2016). *Practicing Existential Therapy: The Relational World*. London: Sage.

Sprung, M. (1978). *The Question of Being: East-west Perspectives*. University Park, PA: Penn Press.

Streng, F. J. (1967). *Emptiness: A Study in Religious Meaning*. Nashville, TN: Abingdon Press.

Tobden, G. Y. (2005). *The Way of Awakening: A Commentary of Shantideva's Bodhicharyavatara*. Boston, MA: Wisdom.

Waddell, N. (1999). *Wild Ivy: The Spiritual Autobiography of Zen Master Hakuin*. Boston, MA: Shambala.

Wang, Y. (2006). The Chan deconstruction of Buddha nature. In J. Y. Park (Ed.), *Buddhisms and Deconstructions* (pp. 129–144). Lanham, MD: Rowman & Littlefield.

Watts, A. (2014). *The Supreme Doctrine*. Forest Grove, OR: Allegro.

Wilber, K. (2014). Toward a fourth turning of Buddhism, https://integrallife.com/integral-post/toward-fourth-turning-buddhism. Retrieved 15 June 2016.

Yamada, K. (2004). *The Gateless Gate: The Classic Book of Zen Kōans*. Boston, MA: Wisdom.

8

IMPERCEPTIBLE MUTUAL AID

Zen, therapy and the unconscious

'Why don't *you* have a go at it?'

Half way through my Zen training with the *White Plum Sangha*, an international organization founded by Taizan Maezumi Roshi, my own teacher at the time, Genpo Merzel, started devising a method that brought together elements of Zen with the self-help technique *voice dialogue* (Stone & Winkelman, 1989). I was excited at first by the potential for innovation undoubtedly present in the combination of these two strands. I was also intrigued by the implementation of the functional Jungian notion of *personifying* (working with autonomous aspects of the psyche) which voice dialogue implicitly draws on. The latter is part of a generalized attempt across therapeutic orientations to tackle the notion of multiplicity, which the reader might recall from Chapter 1.

During a 3-week intensive retreat in the US, almost exclusively focused on the integration of voice dialogue and Zen, I soon began to feel frustrated by the fact that out of all the wealth of knowledge and expertise western psychotherapy had to offer, my teacher should go and pick what increasingly felt as a third-rate, sub-Jungian bag of tricks. Being at the time even more opinionated than I am now, I had little trouble voicing my discontent at Roshi in front of some other 50 partici-pants. Couldn't we choose from depth psychology, existential phenomenology, or the intelligent quarters of the humanistic tradition? Surely there were more interesting parallels to be found that would enrich comparative work with the Dharma? I can see now how truly staggering my arrogance and insensitivity were at the time. Voice dialogue was, after all, what my teacher knew about western psychology and his intent had been sincere as well as painstaking. Moreover, I myself had no psychotherapeutic training at the time and, apart from a theoretical knowledge of philosophy and psychoanalytic theory, had no concrete alternative to offer. My teacher's reply set something in motion. He simply said: 'If you think you know better, then why don't *you* have a go at it?'

Step after faltering step

A month later I began my psychotherapy training. In fact, interest had been sparked already three years before, when I began sessions with Tony, my therapist. To me, he embodied the principles of his favourite psychologist, Alfred Adler – community feeling, belonging, solidarity – uniquely aligning them with an encyclopaedic knowledge of literature, theatre and films – a knowledge he wore casually, with no ostentation. To my earnestness for all things deep, philosophical and intense, he responded with a lapidary suggestion: 'Less Dostoevsky; more Coronation Street'. His description of our relationship was: 'I'm Tenzing Norgay, you are Edmund Hillary. I may suggest the terrain to you, but you've got to do the climbing.'

Already in Tony's room I had felt, week after week, that Zen practice alone could not take care of life's nitty-gritty. Yes, it would grant me something invaluable, and often hard to convey: at times, it would afford me the panoramic view from an airplane, the exhilaration of flying over the terrain, the buoyancy of being with whatever arises, and the sovereign composure that comes from discerning that no matter how miserable or stuck, this human life *is* the life of the Buddha. At times though one feels the urgency to *walk* the landscape, step by faltering step, pacing the unevenness of the topography and feeling on one's bare skin the inclemency of weather and light and in the process learn that change is worthwhile and possible. My expectation was, and still is, that psychotherapy is a way to walk the terrain step by step.

Mindful contemplation alone is not enough. It does not fundamentally alter the causes of suffering. To truly believe that raising our awareness over our own situation in the world – how we relate to ourselves and others – is enough, is in itself a kind of delusion. It is a form of arrogance born of ignorance, not realizing how entrenched (as well as unknown to the conscious mind) our motivations and emotions truly are. This is the area where problems have arisen in the first few decades of the gradual transmission of Buddhism to the west, with religious practices being translated and transported from one culture to another, from hierarchical, semi-feudal to liberal and capitalist societies. A major way in which inevitable contradictions and dilemmas have been later confronted is by emphasizing ethics against the neglect of the ethical dimension that was rife in the early days of Dharma transmission to the west. This was an important step to take, useful in dealing with abuse of power and sexual misconduct within sanghas. Yet some of the questions I hear some colleagues and fellow practitioners often ask are: Have we now come full circle? Is the need to abide by ethical codes beginning to fetter our work? Are we witnessing the birth of a new puritanism?

Heretical cosmology

I met Allen Ginsberg when I was 21 years old. Well, kind of. With some friends, I had gone to a 3-day international poetry festival at Castel Porziano, a beach outside Rome, where I had the good fortune to hear *viva voce* some of the Beats read their verse, including Gregory Corso (whom we spotted on the same train from Rome),

William Burroughs (who read part of Dr Benway's routine from *Naked Lunch*), and Ginsberg himself. I was a shy and very stoned young man, and when I spotted Ginsberg, I went up to him. What I really wanted to say was: 'I love what you do, I love your poetry. Thank you so much!' Instead, God knows why, I heard myself mutter: 'Er . . . excuse me, got some spare change?'

Some of the poets and writers of the Beat Generation (Kerouac, Snyder and Ginsberg among them) were greatly influential in the 1950s in sparking a sincere interest in Buddhism and Zen in particular. Gary Snyder, poet, activist, eco-philosopher and long-time Zen practitioner, studied Zen formally in Japan. Jack Kerouac gave wide currency to anecdotal Zen lore and conflated in his own original idiom the legacy of Proust and Joyce as well as the visceral urgency of the French existentialists. Ginsberg, a major poet in the American, Whitmanian democratic tradition, practiced Vajrayana Buddhism with Chögyam Trungpa Rinpoche. The Beats represented an important turning point in western culture and a creative response to the sheer gormlessness of the American dream. It is true that they were mostly men, and that their take on Buddhism, particularly Kerouac's, came with generous helpings of naivety and misreadings. Yet it pains me to see current spiritualist consensus read the Beat phenomenon as a regressive route to a sensual Eden and a limbo of pre-egoic regression (e.g. Wilber, 1983).

What pains me most is that in popular spiritually tinged literature a crucial link is blatantly missed: the link between the poetry of *democracy* and the *body* that these poets and writers inherited from Whitman, and contemplative practices. This is an incarnate notion of democracy and is inseparable from the spell of the sensuous and the pain of death, a notion that requires a new, non-eternalist cosmology. This fundamental point is sadly forgotten by large sections of contemporary spirituality but certainly not overlooked by contemporary ethical philosopher Martha Nussbaum:

> Here is a new cosmology that Whitman offers us, to stand over the cosmologies created by philosophical and religious systems: the finite mortal individual, democratic citizen, equal to and among others, who contains the world within himself by virtue of his resourceful imagination and his sympathetic love.
>
> *Nussbaum, 2003, pp. 656–657*

This new cosmology is the *heretical cosmology* of our situatedness, transience and imperfection, one that is ready to discard Plato's world of transcendent forms and the Christian cosmology of Heaven and Hell in the name of 'the curious sympathy one feels when feeling with the hand the naked meat of the body' (Nussbaum, 2003, p. 661).

From guru–disciple to teacher–student

Discussing the teacher–student relationship in Tibetan Buddhism, two practitioners write:

The initial phase of Vajrayana in the west was welcomed by the chaotic ethos of the 1960s which, however chronically befuddled, provided an atmosphere of freedom and open-mindedness. In contrast, the 1980s and 1990s have been characterized by the rise of neo-Puritanism, and the mode of crazy wisdom has been demonized by those whose spirituality is dominated by concepts of political correctness.

Gyamsto & Rolpa'i, in Dorje, 2001,p. xix

In the same passage they add:

The creation of strict demarcations appears to be more important than celebrating wider horizons of possibility . . . [W]henever committees cast votes on to what is authentic, authenticity is likely to be found elsewhere.

Ibid

In Vajrayana Buddhism, the affiliation with the teacher is crucial and often not very dissimilar from the relationship between guru and disciple. There are pros and cons in this particular constellation as there are in its secular equivalent of student–teacher. The shift is not merely structural and/or educational but reflects a fundamental change of ethical attitudes that has taken place over time. If on the one hand the potential for misuse of power is far greater in the guru–disciple relationship, with the modern version of student–teacher what is lost, I feel, is the potential for profound, meaningful closeness that perhaps makes the transmission of the teachings possible in the first place.

Personally, I feel grateful to those who in the disorganized ethos of the 1960s opened themselves up to experimentation and exploration. I'm thinking of the Beats but also of Alan Watts and of the 'crazy wisdom' teachings of Chögyam Trungpa. My own first tentative forays into the vast ocean of the Dharma came a decade after, in 1978, just before the dawn of the age of acquiescence that ushered in the Thatcher and Reagan era and the first stirrings of neo-liberalism. With hindsight, it is a positive fact that some of the features of the early days of the Dharma in the west have been questioned – namely the hierarchical power structures within Buddhist sanghas and the naive surrender to Zen teachers and Vajrayana gurus. It is good that some of the sexual shenanigans have been exposed and the suffering they created has been in some cases healed. But we are still in a time of transition. Western Dharma – with its more secular, democratic emphasis – still relies on the charisma, eloquence and prestige of a handful of teachers. Students and retreatants are still by and large being talked at, and there is very little room for genuinely open, experiential communal discussion and encounter. We have questioned the feudal structures of some Buddhist institutions only to replace them with the equivalent, neo-liberal, 'democratic' model where a transient gathering of paying customers attend week-long retreats and courses so as to recharge their batteries before going back to their accelerated lives. With the welcome disappearance of feudal structure, something else also disappeared: the teacher–student relationship.

I left institutional Zen in 2006 for various reasons. I do not regret this choice. On occasions though I look back at those years of formal training with some wistfulness: I look at the valuable friendships struck within the community and at the whole Zen adventure, from organizing retreats with my partner to travelling to the US for extensive periods of training. Most of all, I treasure the early morning chats over coffee before dawn with my then teacher, Genpo Roshi, on those occasions when I was his assistant. The relationship with a teacher is unique in the world. As I write this, I realize I have never grieved for the loss experienced after leaving the Zen sangha. Perhaps scribbling these words is an attempt to do just that. It's just that life sometimes moves too fast. An old chapter seemingly closes forever before you know it. I am thinking of my 12 years as sannyasin with Osho, in India, then Oregon, then India again: extraordinary, unforgettable – and even before encountering Roshi.

Both experiences have been pivotal in my life. Without surrender to a teacher, I would have never taken certain leaps. I would not be where I am now. Of course, I could not have remained there forever. Leaving the Zen sangha and Roshi taught me greater self-reliance. I found that being an exile, a stranger, a non-joiner can be difficult as well as rewarding. Looking back, I have been in and out of groups and communities with almost cyclical regularity. Perhaps this is a character flaw of mine. But I have found companions along the way, as well as illustrious examples and 'role models'. Spinoza was a double exile – first as a Jew in Amsterdam, then as an individual within his own Jewish community. And Derrida's life tells a similar story. Perhaps being a stranger and an outsider is a condition both necessary and peculiar to philosophers. And this may apply to some therapists too and to the struggle some of us experience with what psychotherapist and writer Julie Webb describes as 'arriving and departing, belonging and not belonging in various communities of therapy'. As unsettling as this can be, 'it seems this is the way it is and keeps some of us, in an important sense "alive"' (Webb, 2016, personal communication).

With the teacher–student relationship going out of fashion in the transmission of the Dharma, we may be now transitioning towards new assemblages and new forms of transmission of practice, but it is hard at present to predict what shape this will take. There are obvious ethical reasons why therapy does not encourage that same level of intimate connection in the teacher–student or therapist–client relationship. At times though an overriding concern about boundaries can positively verge on therapist's under-involvement and in therapy trainings can encourage a sense of 'separation and individualism regardless of how much "inter-connected and inter-subjective" literature tutors throw at students' (Webb, 2016, personal communication).

The lie of giving

The voluntary undertaking known as the third Buddhist precept is a vow to abstain from sexual misconduct. Classical Buddhism limited itself to an explanation of circumstances by which sexual intercourse was considered suitable, and highlighted the principle of non-harm, i.e. avoiding hurting partners and third parties. As a result, each Buddhist sangha across the centuries had to interpret this precept in relation to contingent mores and values of a specific era. This partly explains why determining once and for all what constitutes sexual misconduct is unfeasible. Nonetheless, at one level the whole matter is unambiguous: Robert Aitken (1997) rendered it brilliantly when he wrote of the misuse of sexual intercourse as *the lie of giving*, when the act is really taking. He also said there are many other ways to misuse sex than the sexual act:

> A relationship that involves dominance, exploitation, and passive aggression is an ongoing violation of this precept. [And so is] the drive to tear the other down.
>
> *Aitken, 1997, p. 30*

Sexual misconduct is not limited to breaking the vow of celibacy or to having sexual relations outside a committed relationship, but is necessarily extended to rape within marriage, incest in the family, to misogynist pornography which creates an aggressive and risky environment for women and encourages imbecilic attitudes in men. We also need to extend sexual misconduct to the intolerance and prejudice against gays, lesbians and sexual minorities. If we accept this, then we might recognize that a great deal of sexual misconduct happens *in the name of religion*. I think of Zen as a non-fundamentalist ethical tradition which comes to life in its dealings with the world and the challenges it poses. Some of the more customary trappings of conventionally theistic religion are just not there in Zen or Buddhism: there is no social engineering, no strict rules or injunctions in relation to procreation with its corresponding bias against non-procreative or 'recreational' sex. There is no reason then why, as Buddhist practitioners, we should be afraid of exploring this rich and complex domain, rather than resorting to a dogmatic appraisal of rules or generic appeals to 'conscience'. Con-science has a twofold nature: if on the one hand it is indeed *the sense (and knowledge) we have in common*, a shared manifestation of discerning wisdom, conscience is also public opinion, often manifesting as prejudice and intolerance.

'Sexual scandals' have become a regular, even predictable feature within Buddhist communities but they are not comparable to either the degree or kind of abuse perpetrated by clerics of the Roman Catholic Church. In response to them, we veer towards two types of reaction: we either tend to seize upon the *orthodox* or the *permissive* view. But neither avoidance nor denial (nor, at the other end of the spectrum, unmitigated condemnation) have been useful rejoinders. Both outlooks do not seem to recognize the wider context; both tend to minimize the pivotal role of *power*; both emphasize, via contrasting explanations, the *sexual* component and sidestep, or fail to clarify, the element of *misconduct*.

Anti-sexism and anti-sex

There are interesting similarities between sexual misconduct in Buddhist sanghas and sexual harassment in society at large. Second-generation feminists in the 1970s rightly opposed sexual harassment: theirs was a political stance, centred on human rights and the abuse of power, tackling the misuse of authority usually perpetrated by an older male boss/teacher/employer towards a younger female employee/ student. At its inception, the battle against sexual harassment focused on *harassment* rather than the *sexual*. Cases of sexual harassment and sexual discrimination had been raised over the years because of *harassment* and of *discrimination*. It would appear that attitudes have now drastically changed: in our permissive, liberalized western socie- ties, the battle against sexual harassment has increasingly become hostility against sex itself. It is baffling that the just critique of *sexism*, heralded by both first- and second- generation feminists, has now metamorphosed into the denigration of *sex*.

From the start, feminism has challenged the boundary that separates the *personal* from the *professional* (Gallop, 2002, p. 56), yet the current insistence on professional boundaries has effectively severed the link between the personal and the profes- sional. What is reviled under the current cultural climate is precisely the *sexual*. The philosopher Jane Gallop writes:

> MacKinnon and other feminist scholars and lawyers were successful in get- ting sexual harassment legally defined as sex discrimination under Title VII (covering employment) and, presumably, under Title IX (covering educa- tion). Yet, in the decade and a half since that clear feminist victory, the feminist definition of sexual harassment appears to be fading, giving way to a more traditional understanding in which this behavior is condemnable because it is sexual.
>
> *Gallop, 2002, p. 58*

Fear of the sexual dimension in pedagogy erases the *personal* dimension, a move confirming a fundamental unease and anxiety in grappling with the complexities of erotic dynamics. But a culture which collectively and more or less consciously decides to bypass the eloquent beauty of the erotic does so at its peril; neglecting the tremendous gifts of the incarnate experience of sexuality means neglecting both *dukkha* and *mudita*, both the suffering and the joy of our peculiar condition.

Sweet-bitter

One of the characteristics of Eros is ambivalence, and this partly explains the widespread confusion in all matters of the erotic and the sexual. The ancient Greek poet Sappho was referring to the ambivalence of Eros, when she described it as *glukupikron*, meaning sweet-bitter. Not bittersweet, but sweet-bitter: the pleasure comes first, followed by pain. From its dawn, the western tradition has recognized the ambiguous, even wounding nature of eroticism. The very word *scandal* derives from the Greek *skandalon*, which indicates a *snare* for an enemy, a cause for moral stumbling, with its derivative *skandalitron*, the actual spring of a trap. To be at the centre of a scandal is thus to have walked into a trap and aroused the condemnation of the morally upright who are eager to hurl the first stone.

Such recognition of the ambivalent nature of sexual desire is gracious compared to the life-denigrating excesses of some Christian as well as Buddhist imagery. A twelfth-century Christian monk Odo of Cluny, in the attempt to disgust believers, declared that to embrace a woman is to embrace a sack of manure.

The existentialist tradition is instead concerned with the ways in which sexual desire can bind us. For Sartre (2003), erotic relations are a structure of endless reflections, a sort of unreliable game of mirrors with frustration built into its very fabric. There is, for Sartre, a kind of stickiness within the sexual dimension that is not conducive to freedom and clarity. He gives the example of a child sinking its fingers into a jar of honey, experiencing the gluey texture between liquid and solid, neither rigid nor flowing; it is soft but it clings.

If not handled skilfully, Sartre seems to suggest, sex becomes a trap. Rather than puritanical condemnation of sex per se, there is a recognition of how we can get stuck, hindered by our cravings just like the child who plunges its hands into a jar of honey. The Buddha's teachings on suffering and the causes of suffering are similarly motivated, not by ascetic condemnation of our inherently imperfect condition, but as encouragement towards greater freedom from hindrances and cravings.

Reality check

The chronicle of western sanghas has been punctuated by 'sex scandals' periodically involving the abuse of power and the misuse of sex from Buddhist teachers towards their students. In these cases too, the emphasis seemed to have been predominantly on the sexual rather than on the misuse of power. This is understandable, given the ethical and religious nature of Buddhist communal endeavour. I wonder, however, if this also has to do with two important factors: a) the hierarchical nature of most Buddhist sanghas, where the imbalance of power arguably prevents the possibility of a truly equal encounter and fosters instead the proliferation of fantasies directed at the teacher; and b) the absence of a support structure, of counsel and peer feedback available to both teacher and student. The latter are mostly available to therapists and therapy trainees and provide ways in which psychotherapy can contribute to the Dharma.

Psychotherapy has journeyed through many phases in response to societal changes over the course of the last 150 years, and the same needs to happen to Buddhism if the latter's contribution is to remain relevant to contemporary discourse. Changes, of course, are never pain-free; in the case of therapy, it meant giving up the claim that the analyst had the power to tell reality from distortions and projections, a process of change that went from the univocal appraisal of *transference*, to the gradual acknowledgement of *counter-transference* (i.e. the therapist's reactions to the client) and finally to a striving towards greater equality. The relationship in question is by definition *asymmetrical*: therapists and Dharma teachers alike are in a position of power with regard to clients and students. There are ways, however, to dent this inbuilt chain of command: via the open recognition that the therapist's perceptions are associations rather than interpretations; via the acknowledgement that a Dharma teacher's pronouncements represent the provisional insights of a more experienced spiritual fellow traveller rather than the ultimate truth. Both of these are possible if fostered by, and encircled within, a collective culture of common endeavour and practice.

If we consider for a moment a hypothetical Buddhist teacher with great charisma, one who has reached the highest rank and is regarded by their students as 'self-realized' or spiritually proficient: what are his/her chances of facing a reality check? In our avowedly secular and democratic societies in the west, a scientist, artist or mental health professional naturally and willingly submits their output to the encouragement and critique of their peers who will appraise, discuss, recognize or constructively criticize their contributions in the field. It is rather strange that in the domain of spiritual practice, and within Buddhist sanghas in particular, different criteria apply. These criteria might be the cultural residue of a feudal or pre-modern understanding of the organization of communities, where the spiritual head was also lord and proprietor requiring submission and obedience from his subjects. Moreover, the identification of spiritual, political and economic power is a problematic and even tyrannical notion going back, in the west, to the idea of the philosopher king expounded by Plato. A contemporary sangha would need to take into account how the world has changed and what there is to learn from modernity and post-modernity.

It would be naive to suggest that the incidents and scandals that took place in Buddhist sanghas as well as in therapeutic settings, can be avoided by simply paying greater attention to the workings of the unconscious. Despite the militant optimism of our neo-positivist era, the unconscious remains impervious to logical translations. Although there is no mention of the 'unconscious' as such in Zen (after all it was 'invented' in the early days of the twentieth century), some of the instances discussed below hint at the importance of areas of experience that are beyond our grasp.

Imperceptible mutual aid

Awareness of subtle and unknowable dimensions of experience are already present in Dharma teachings and have been since at least the thirteenth century – most notably in the writings of Dōgen (Dōgen, 2002), who speaks of *imperceptible mutual aid*, a phenomenon directly linked to the bodily practice of *zazen* and hinting at what is 'unknowable to human consciousness' (Waddell & Abe, in Dōgen, 2002 p. 12). The potential for transformation in sustained *zazen* practice entirely depends on processes that are beyond our conscious grasp.

Sitting in silent meditation together, we aid each other in ways that are neither traceable nor caused by our doing, as Dōgen writes in the fascicles of his *Shōbōgenzō* ('Treasury of the Dharma Eye'):

> Yet such things [phenomena related to imperceptible mutual aid] are not mingled in the perceptions of the person sitting in zazen because, occurring

in the stillness of samadhi beyond human agency or artifice, they are, directly and immediately, realization.

Dōgen, 2002, p. 12

We normally think of 'me' the meditator, perceiving phenomena. But who exactly perceives what? Dōgen invites us to think again past the artificial division between 'me' and the experience that 'I' am supposedly 'having' – beyond the demarcation of practice and realization:

If practice and realization were two different stages, as ordinary people consider them to be, they should perceive each other. Any such mingling with perceptions is not the mark of realization, for the mark of realization is to be altogether beyond such illusion.

Dōgen, 2002, p. 12

In the calm of meditative absorption, the artificial division between the person and the surroundings fall away. This is *jijuyū zammai* or samādhi of self-fulfilling activity – with samādhi understood as a state of consciousness that is beyond waking, dreaming, or deep sleep. Far from being something special, this state of affairs is one where things are allowed to be and emerge; where the practitioner, so to speak, gets out of the way: 'it does not disturb a single mote of dust, or obstruct a single phenomenon, but performs great and wide-ranging Buddha work' (Dōgen, 2002, p. 12). Waddell & Abe (2002) write:

Samadhi is not dead stillness without perception or consciousness; the mind (perception and consciousness) of the zazen practicer and its environment (the sphere of the mind) arise and subside, but do so within the realm of the *jijuyū samadhi*, in which the practicer is one with all things, so this does not result in any disturbance.

p. 13

This is *not* personal enlightenment. On the contrary, it is a leap from the boundaries of human agency and the human self into greater 'thusness' and 'suchness': not into *another* dimension but into the stream of the phenomenal world. It is from this *immanent* reality that the Buddhas of all ages expound 'the ultimate and profound *prajna* free from all human agency' (ibid). All one has to do is to get out of the way, throw oneself in *zazen* and cast off body and mind. The above may at first appear remote from the world of therapy and its concerns, yet when hearing colleagues emphasizing 'being' over 'doing', presence over intervention, or advocating the wearing of an 'invisible garment' over the embracing of an excessively professionalized therapist role, I see a clear parallel.

Notions such as these are increasingly difficult to convey because we are becoming, I believe, sadly unresponsive to the subtler aspects of Dharma teachings, choosing instead to focus on the ones that emphasize conscious effort. This *hypertrophy of consciousness* has reached new heights with the mindfulness movement and its applications to therapy, as well as with the near-disappearance of the notion of the unconscious in contemporary psychotherapy, including psychodynamic therapy. For Matte Blanco (1975) this tendency is already present more or less from the start: the unconscious, he writes, 'has been repressed in psychoanalytical thinking [and] replaced by neatly constructed rationalisations' (p. 10).

But there are still areas that actively resist this widespread tendency to over-emphasize the power of the conscious mind and its alleged ability to understand, measure and catalogue experience. It is to these exhilarating zones of resistance that we must turn if we are to bring about a more fruitful dialogue between psychotherapy and the Dharma. Zen teacher and psychotherapist Joseph Bobrow (2010) writes:

> In the psychotherapeutic register of connectedness, emotions are the cata-lyst, the glue, and simultaneously the transmitter, the receiver, and the 'stuff' that is being transmitted and received. The process is much faster and more seamless than this unwieldy language conveys. Buddhists do well to learn about how instantaneous this process is for it can help us make sense of what otherwise seem like disconnected events: eruptions of inter-personal anguish that tear asunder the *sangha*, out of apparently peaceful circumstances.
>
> *Ibid, p. 159*

Empathic attunement to all living beings, alongside a keen awareness of the co-created dimension of unconscious experience, is crucial to psychotherapy and instrumental in facilitating healing. Equally important is remembering how *paticca samuppada* (dependent co-arising) is a stark reminder of the absence of intrinsic existence. As we have seen in Chapter 6, without this realization the view of interdependence is inevitably starry-eyed. It is important to take into consideration that *sangha* (community) is not 'intrinsically connected or simultaneously inter-connected but is instead a kind of inter-random process' (Julie Webb, 2016, personal communication), the workings of which are both beyond our conscious radar *and* in need of greater attunement. Paradoxically, it is our conscious effort to *care* that alerts us to the double bind of human embeddedness and human separation. Awareness of 'interdependence' alone is insufficient, as we have seen in Chapter 7 with Binswanger's critique of Heidegger.

Symmetry and infinity

> Symmetrical being is the normal state of man. It is the colossal base from which consciousness or asymmetrical being emerges. Consciousness is a special attribute of man, which looks upon the (infinite) base and makes attempts at describing it.
>
> *Matte Blanco, 1975, p. 100*

One of the attributes of the absolute – a notion discussed in the Introduction – is *symmetry*. In the relative domain of everyday life we must distinguish and discriminate between this and that, self and other, inner and outer, past and future. The lenses we use in the relative domain of experience are *asymmetrical*: things, people and situations are *not* one and the same. This mode of perception is not 'wrong'; in fact, it is vital to our survival and is essentially governed by necessity and by the rules of logic and rationality. But in meditation 'symmetrical processes become more accessible' (Cooper, 2010, p. 141): one can momentarily glimpse that form is emptiness and emptiness is form; that samsara is nirvana and nirvana is samsara. On this absolute, symmetrical level, you and I are 'one'– islands joining hands beneath the sea. However, as my teacher used to say, you'd find it tricky if, motivated by this sense of oneness, I was to head off with your car and without your permission. In the asymmetrical, everyday mode of existence 'me' and 'mine' matter greatly.

Could symmetry also be a characteristic of the unconscious? Drawing partly on Bion (1980; 1984; 1990), for whom the idea of the unconscious did not go far enough in psychoanalysis, Ignacio Matte Blanco (1975) pioneered the notion of the *symmetrical logic of the unconscious*: for him, *symmetrical relations* portray the unknown and partly unknowable sphere of experience better than the term 'unconscious' (Cooper, 2010, p. 135). For Matte Blanco,

> psychoanalysis has neglected to a considerable extent its initial purpose of exploring the psychology of the unconscious, and of that mysterious world where everything is different from what we see in conscious life . . . psychoanalysis has lost its most distinctive characteristics.
>
> *Matte Blanco, 1975, p. 9*

In his view the unconscious mostly draws on symmetry: it detects sameness and disregards dissimilarity, whereas the conscious mind for the most part discriminates and notices differences. Whereas everyday life requires the discriminating awareness of *asymmetry*, the unconscious presents us with an altogether different logic, with what appears as a kind of orderly irrationality – orderly in the mathematical sense of one thing being interchangeable with another. I believe that being more acquainted with these modes of departure from logic can have creative applications as it is expedient in helping us suspend momentarily the stronghold logic has on psyche. It may also be useful in working more empathically with those clients who present us with a distinctly fragile processing of experience (Warner, 1991), and are conventionally diagnosed as suffering from psychotic, schizophrenic or borderline disorders.

In this context asymmetry relates to the everyday functional dimension ruled by logic and reasoning, whereas symmetry stands for the leaps found in poetry, dreams and the unconscious. Similarly 'relative' indicates our ordinary perception of a separate, self-existing 'I' relating to a world 'out there', whereas in the absolute dimension, as the word itself suggests, the self is dissolved and the experience of the world regains a natural fluidity. A clear-cut distinction between these two dimensions is of course arbitrary, at the most didactic. A central tenet in Zen teachings is that the two are inseparable and the practitioner's task is to learn how to move fluidly between the two without getting stuck anywhere but committing him/herself to ontological *ambiguity*, to a movement that, as the term suggests, moves in two directions at once.

> In light there is darkness, but don't take it as darkness; in the dark there is light, but don't see it as light.
>
> *Suzuki, 1999, p. 111*

One implication is that Zen practice is both 'spiritual' and 'material', forever shifting between these two imagined polarities. In that sense, Zen cannot be easily aligned with conventional religiosity or for that matter with therapeutic practices normally labelled as transpersonal. Similarly, it cannot be defined as 'materialist' because, although incarnate, it does not stoop to the explanations of the body as one *object* among others. By embracing both the relative and the absolute, a fluidity is created that injects a sense of mystery and poetry in the everyday while at the same time bringing down to earth any fleeting experience of the sublime.

Another attribute Matte Blanco ascribes to the unconscious alongside symmetry is that of *infinity*. Observing that in patients affected by acute distress conventionally labelled as 'psychotic' their emotion and feeling levels rose to a seemingly infinite point, he made a link, drawn from Whitehead (1978), with mathematics where infinity becomes the key problem as it disrupts the way numbers usually behave. Thus understood, what is conventionally called 'madness' can be seen as 'expressed, perhaps even rooted', in a mishandling of symmetry in the mathematical sense. The person in this case 'sees symmetry where the normal person does not'. In this scenario, 'emotion is inflated to an infinite extent' (Bomford, 1999, p. 26).

If we now join the two notions of *symmetry* and *infinity*, we may come to see the logic at play in psychosis. Someone perceived as hostile or frightening becomes 'interchangeable with any other person who has ever threatened them, or ever might threaten them or with any threat they may ever have dreamed of' (Bomford, 1999, ibid). What is operating here is a principle of generalization that does not relate to individuals but only to 'classes' of which they are a 'member' (ibid, p. 27). Another useful link here is that between *emotion and symmetry* particularly in people experiencing acute distress. The stronger the emotion, the more the chances of arbitrary symmetric deductions which may sound like this: 'John is a very caring friend' leaps into 'I'm the best friend he's ever had' and 'The two of us are best friends' (Bomford, 1999).

Making the conscious unconscious

> I don't think this idea of the unconscious – or even the idea of unconscious thoughts or ideas – extends far enough.
>
> *Bion, 1980, p. 20*

In the light of what has been discussed in Chapter 7, one could argue that symmetrization is at heart logocentric. Not only does it presuppose the existence of 'depth' and 'unity' below the surface of things, which is at variance with a thoroughgoing appreciation of phenomena. It also demarcates the line a little too neatly between conscious and unconscious. For Bion (1984) there is a *complementarity* between the two, which is in itself a criticism of the excessive 'value' that Freud tends to place on knowing (Cooper, 2010).

One thing that could be inferred from this is a reversal of the formula to which most therapists are acquainted, i.e. making the unconscious conscious. Making the conscious unconscious can have tremendous value as a way to valuing more as well as becoming aware of, not-knowing. It aligns with Bion's encouragement to clinicians to 'listen without memory, desire, or attachment' (Bobrow, 2010, p. 151). This therapeutic stance capitalizes on Freud's achievement and takes it further. Humanistic therapy trainees are often regaled with a caricature of Freud and Freudian psychoanalysis.

One day, as a trainee at a weekend residential training in person-centred psychotherapy, I asked during group process why there was no room in the building dedicated to Freud. Every room in the institute bore the name of a psychological pioneer – Rogers, Klein, Jung, Maslow, Perls, but no Freud; 'Sure we can do that'– the tutor promptly retorted to the general hilarity – 'we can give him the toilet'. I remember feeling mystified: in my naivety, I had thought an acknowledgement of Freud, the very first pioneer, would be obvious. What I didn't know at the time was that alongside valuable therapeutic theory and practice, I was also being schooled in the way of tribalism and parochialism. But it would be wrong to deny Freud's import and influence. If we owe to Copernicus the knowledge that neither the earth nor humanity is the centre of the universe, and to Darwin the awareness that we are bound to the very same laws as microorganisms, we surely owe to Freud the notion that we are not fully in control of our experience (Bobrow, 2010). Freud did not escape the positivist influence yet he was open to the limitations of consciousness (which he saw as the smaller sphere) and to the immensity of unconsciousness which he perceived as the larger sphere. My critique of his work is that he didn't take the notion of the unconscious far enough; that it was reified, i.e. made into a *thing* (as well as circumscribed by a narrow familial setting that has little place for the world and history) and later codified into a series of dogmatic assertions.

But the notion – albeit revisited, reconsidered and thrown again into the crucible of cultural and psychotherapeutic debate – remains valid, especially if we are to stand a chance in counteracting the neo-positivist consensus that dictates that the mystery of human experience can be duly measured. To this purpose Freud's central notion that the essence of the psychical cannot be *situated* in consciousness and that the latter is merely one of the attributes of the psychical is a formidable basis for offsetting the neo-positivist consensus.

Against neo-positivism

It would be fair to object that I am *using* the notion of the unconscious, particularly as conceived by Matte Blanco, as a way to counteract the dominant positivism of our times. Conventionally, positivism refers to a philosophical perspective that recognizes only that which can be scientifically verified or capable of logical or mathematical proof. We have seen a dramatic example of positivism at work in Chapter 1, with the McNamara fallacy. But the neo-positivist outlook is today so pervasive that it takes hold of practices whose origins and *modus operandi* are non-positivist. This has happened to Zen Buddhism, to existential phenomenology and humanistic psychology. In their prevalent manifestations, all of the above practices and theoretical orientations have developed versions of themselves which are at variance with their original ethos. They have effectively performed a 'historical compromise', adjusting worldviews and practices to dominant values. In the process, most of the key metaphors at variance with the positivist zeitgeist have been eclipsed. The notions of the *organism* and the *actualizing tendency* have taken a backseat in humanistic therapy. It is easy to see why. Even though they are essential in helping us describe experience, notions such as the organism and the actualizing tendency are not solid, quantifiable 'things' or 'facts' hence beyond the remit of conscious control.

Consequently, the 'truth-value' of a psychology compliant to neo-positivist (and neoliberal) ideology is no longer *organismic*, and it is no longer paying attention to the ebbs and flows of an organism seeking actualization or to the complex emotions and motivations intertwined with our actions. Instead, it is *factual,* relying on the quasi-scientific collection of quantifiable data. As a result, the unconscious is overlooked even in psychodynamic therapy or presented as an inert article of faith that reifies it and encourages the naive hope that it is possible to make it conscious, i.e. to be mediated, comprehended and hence taken over by human subjectivity.

Blindfold knowledge

What is most important is invisible.

de Saint-Exupéry, 1995, p. 90

Other versions of this overall 'dumbing down' of the unconscious include the compulsive search, pervasive in most therapeutic orientations, for the 'meaning behind'. This in itself overlooks the importance of sound phenomenological observation in the therapist; it also 'veil[s] obvious expressions of both *reversal* and *condensation*' (Cooper, 2010, p. 127, italics added). With the *reversal* (into the opposite) – originally described by Freud (1987) in relation to dream images – an idea, affect or representation turns into its opposite. Language itself (and root languages in particular) presents us with opposite notions: thus the Latin *sacer* means both 'sacred' and 'ruined' or destitute. With *condensation*, also originally described in relation to dreams, several themes are combined into one representation or ideation, thus condensing several wishes, ideas thoughts and feelings. Both cases require attunement and active listening in order to register not 'the meaning behind' but what is right there in front of our senses. The 'mysterious' is within the everyday if we remember with Bion that conscious and unconscious are complementary, and with Matte Blanco that symmetry and asymmetry are activated at various levels in everyday interactions.

Similarly, I believe that a contemporary prominence granted to the relational elements of therapy overlooks the wider, and 'neutral' sphere of *affect*. Recent research and theory (Massumi, 1995; Gregg & Seigworth, 2010) suggests that affect may denote a level of intensity that is not measurable until it gets summarily translated (and diluted) as subjective emotion. Affect is a realm of experience not readily accessible through facts and reason, but one that may be approached by means of a more diffuse awareness. There is in affect a different logic at play, one that does not rely on cause and effect.

For instance, the *relational* element, intrinsic in any encounter, is certainly *part* of affect. At the beginning, client and therapist co-create the therapy world (Spinelli, 2007) through mutual endeavour and cooperation. But affect also comprises another element, a more *impersonal* dimension that is then inhabited by the relationship. Gabriel Marcel (1965) similarly spoke of a given that *precedes* encounter, the mystery of being which for him is blind knowledge, a sort of blindfold knowledge of being, inferred in all particular knowledge.

One could say this has to do with the atmosphere, the tonality and texture permeating the therapeutic encounter. Gaining an insight, or at least an inkling of affect, however tentatively, may give us a sense of the general 'feeling' of our meeting with another. This in turn may provide us with a deeper understanding of process *beyond the relational*, which in turn can become useful to the therapeutic relationship. Openness to affect assists therapy because when attuned to affect we are not *enmeshed* in the relational – hence we can perceive the relationship more openly.

Dreams and the daimonic

It is not coincidental that Matte Blanco's formulation has been marshalled in support of mysticism and religiosity, with 'symmetry' becoming another facet, attribute, and in some cases even synonymous with God. From this perspective the unconscious itself, as the reified locus of symmetry, takes on numinous characteristics rather than being a descriptive pointer of the essential unknowability of the world. The more reified our notion of the unconscious becomes, the more separate it is from the conscious. And yet Matte Blanco's notion of symmetry provides us with an effective antidote to the tyranny of a reductively conceived logic. The task, both in Zen and in therapy, would then be how to render these two artificially separate 'realms' porous and coexisting. But this is a *two-way* process: not so much making the unconscious conscious, as the current consensus dictates, as making the conscious unconscious: not only bringing to the glimmering surface previously alien relics lying in the depths but also awakening to the mysterious, ambivalent nature of our conscious experience through a process of defamiliarization. The second manoeuvre is usually the province of art rather than Zen or therapy, but there are reasons to believe that both Zen and therapy can also operate as art forms. At its core, Zen can be described as affirmative art (Bazzano, 2006) and I like to believe that the same may be said of therapy, if the latter is understood in relation to an ever-actualizing appreciation of the world.

The conscious mind's forays into the unconscious are productive and at times very significant in the progress of psychotherapeutic theory and practice. These are not confined to psychoanalysis and psychodynamic therapy: one of the most neglected developments in contemporary existential therapy is Spinelli's (as well as my own) reformulation of the notion of the *daimonic* (Spinelli, 2007; Bazzano, 2010) both drawing on the writings of Rollo May (1969) who in turn fell back on Nietzsche's notion of the 'Dionysian'. The other is found in Spinelli's captivating attempt at sketching a way to work phenomenologically with dreams (Spinelli, 2007).

Equally important is our acknowledgement of the pervading presence of the unconscious in the conscious dimension. In Zen this is summed up neatly by the notion of the *identity* of the relative and the absolute, which is not entirely dissimilar from Bion's complementarity mentioned above. There is co-existence between symmetry and asymmetry. Acknowledging this may help bring about a fertile ambivalence that translates, for example, into what Hölderlin called dwelling poetically on this earth (Bazzano, 2012). The sublime becomes visible in the everyday and we find in ourselves the courage and humility of singing the world.

Via negativa

In light there is darkness, the Zen tradition teaches us, but do not search for that darkness. In darkness there is light, but do not search for that light. For Bion, darkness needs little less than an act of faith; it requires the stillness necessary to allow experience to unfold. What is emphasized in both cases is the unknowability and ineffable nature of experience. We venture into infinity and in our search we find neither something, nor nothing. What this quest asks of us, however, is 'an intensification of awareness and deep involvement with objects' (Cooper, 2010, p. 144). This is quite different from the conventional understanding of the mystical experience, for it does not resolve in merging, unity or logocentric absorption in God or infinity. It is instead *via negativa*, unbroken clarification of the inherent non-substantiality of all phenomena. As such, it bypasses Freud's originary uneasiness about the religious experience as regressive oceanic feeling. The Zen experience, as I understand it, does not lead to dissolution of the self but points towards a fluid relationship between the relative and the absolute, between symmetry and asymmetry, the conscious and the unconscious. Psychotherapy provides a useful adjunct to this project because of its emphasis on everyday experience and the difficulties and riches of interpersonal relationships.

Academia and the court therapist

I am aware of the fact that revisiting the notion of the unconscious, i.e. of a notion that is becoming positively archaic, is to go against the trends set by current academic discourse. I also realize that by suggesting a fluid movement between conscious and unconscious is hardly an orthodox position, neither do Zen practice nor the type of psychotherapy I'm interested in naturally belong to the world of academia. Nor do they belong to orthodoxy, whether within a humanistic or a psychodynamic frame. Although widely different in their history and methodology, they sprang out of experiences and sensibilities situated outside accepted, canonical wisdom. The practitioners who helped bring forth the key elements of these two traditions were close to what ancient Chinese culture would refer to as *wen-jen* (*bunjin* in Japanese) and similar to what in the west we signify by the word 'bohemian'. Many of the great eighteenth-century Japanese artists and writers, including Saikaku, Bashō, Monzaemon and Akinari are each a typical example of the bunjin, a 'non-conformist, independent artist' (Chambers, 2007, p. 5). What tells them apart is their belonging to a sort of in-between world. Unlike their predecessors, they are not members of the aristocracy or of the wealthier classes, yet are uncharacteristically dedicated to high culture as well as being royally disinterested in 'the vulgarity of contemporary society' (Chambers, 2007, ibid). Their disdain, however, is not snobbishly directed at what is popular among the wider public as well as the uneducated and the 'simple minded' but more pointedly at two things: a) commercial and political gain; and b) excessive rationalism.

We can draw inspiration from the above, reflecting on how the practice of psychotherapy may be tainted today by its unholy allegiance with market forces. In this scenario, the contemporary therapist/psychologist/psychology researcher is akin to a court poet or artist who happily adapts his/her Muse's valued intimations to his/her benefactor's twisted agenda, never daring to challenge the status quo. Besides, considering that the term 'commercial' is synonymous with 'below standard' (Wood, 2015, p. 37), the problem with any craft or scientific endeavour that strives too hard to become commercial is that it ends up becoming mediocre.

Similarly, the rationalist scientism that arguably permeates the world of therapy at present demands of the practitioners that they translate the subtlety and ambivalence of therapeutic work into classifiable, quantifiable data. I hasten to say that the rationalist mindset enforced in current psychological orthodoxy goes hand in hand with a superficially oppositional irrationalist agenda that is simply its complementary opposite. Simply put: both neuro-scientism and new-age transpersonalism rely on randomly applied, second-hand metaphysics; both help maintain the status quo.

A night sky

Educated at a Franciscan college as a boy, my father had also inherited the straightforward, simple piety of his uneducated, loving mother. Grandma Emilia taught me how to play cards, mainly *briscola* and *scopa*, and was fond of telling me *se nella vita vuoi aver fortuna amane cento ma non sposar nessuna*: 'if you want to be lucky in life, love many but don't marry any'. My father would frown at the unorthodox teaching but she would retort by saying 'leave him be; he's a poet', a term which meant to her more than versifying; studiousness, perhaps, and a certain lightness of character. But I'm not entirely sure; I may be flattering myself. In his own way, my father tried to instil in me a sense of the numinous, at first through the conventional means of religion. This had little or no effect on me. What I do remember fondly is that as a boy I would join him on the balcony after supper. We would both lean with our arm on the railing. From our fifth-floor apartment we could trace in the dark the winding road up the hill, thanks to the row of cars climbing up or driving down – one a necklace of rubies and the other of pearls, my father would say. He would then point at the sky full of stars. There was no light pollution in our small southern town. Look, he'd say. It's so vast, so incredible. It's a mystery. The awe he conveyed to me, the wonder of the Mediterranean night was real and greater than prayer. My spine tingled. This feeling stayed and was renewed each time I'd gaze at other night skies in my wayward pilgrimage around the world, whether alone or in love, anguished or enraptured. The vastness of the night sky, the sheer infinity that faces me. Or early in the morning, after dawn *zazen* on an intensive meditation retreat: the wind carries fast clouds across the heavens, a question smoulders in the living body: what is this? Feet on the crust of the revolving earth, eyes gazing in wonder at the inscrutable firmament; a sense of *bewilderment*, of going or being led off course – by the unforeseen and the immeasurable, by the sheer intensity of life – never fully comprehended by logical reason.

Human beings are finite – this is our curse and blessing. It is a curse only if one has difficulty accepting that there is so much one will never know – not so much because of the existence of a supposedly transcendent dimension but because one's own immanent experience is itself beyond reach. Our finitude is a blessing because only a finite being can conceive of infinity. Infinity is another name for God or, if you prefer, for the vast expanse left after God's demise – for what will remain forever unexplored because inexplorable. The least dishonest stance finite beings can afford is that of bewilderment.

The experience of bewilderment differs from not-knowing in a fundamental way. Historically, not-knowing belongs to a time-honoured tradition which begins with Socrates and finds contemporary equivalents in the stances of psychotherapists of various orientations – from Lacanians to existential phenomenologists – all convincingly advocating not-knowing at the same time as they implement their theories as 'highly effective tool[s] for dismissing the claims of others' (Goffey, 2016, p. 45), including their patients and clients.

Bewilderment is knowing without understanding, and as such linked to irony, at least in the sense meant by Robert Lowell in one of his letters to fellow poet and friend Elizabeth Bishop: 'as being witty . . . about what we can't understand' (Bevis, 2016, p. 10). The elevation of not-knowing conceals an equal elevation of knowing and knowledge; what is unfamiliar may one day become familiar; what is unknown may become known. More worryingly, not-knowing is linked to ignorance and ignoring, i.e. refusing to know, declining to acknowledge and take responsibility. It often hides our inability or disinclination to support a necessary course of action and as such this stance can become unethical. For example, a short-lived but rather interesting debate took place in the late autumn of 2015 in an existential psychotherapy social forum in the aftermath of the Paris attack at the Bataclan in November. At the time, I had lamented Labour MP Hilary Benn's rousing speech calling for the bombing of Syria as a piece of misplaced rhetoric and referred to him as the unwitting patron-saint of future jihadists. His rallying cry, I thought, had come unheeded and without the backing of the Syrian people who simply had not been consulted. One existential psychotherapist lamented what he saw as the onslaught of dogmatic pacifist statements in the media that took the place of real discussion which shut down those who had a different view or those like himself who simply did not know. Not knowing can be a disarmingly honest stance, provided it is not used to justify inaction and the safeguarding of a potentially dangerous status quo. The history of philosophy teaches us that the notion of 'not-knowing' originates with Socrates. Yet his stance is a dialectical trick, for Socrates knew all too well – if anything, he knew too much.

One thing perhaps he really did not know, or ignored: the potentially treacherous power of transference (Lear, 1993), or its equivalent in 300 BC Greece, the poisonous projection hurled at him from Athenian society. The challenge with not-understanding what one knows is how to navigate these ambiguous waters without abdicating to the siren calls of mysticism and scientism.

Holding on to my precious silence

Next to a silent meditation retreat in the Devonshire countryside there is a small cemetery. Parked just outside there is a jeep and from that corner I can often hear during the day someone whistling merrily. During the breaks from long meditation sessions, I'd go out for a walk from time to time and one day I saw a bearded old man giving me a thumbs up, laughing, shuffling from one foot to another in an awkward, happy dance. He must know we are in silence, I thought, and greeted him back with a smile. The scene happened time and time again during the retreat. I started to look forward to our daily speechless greetings. His cheerfulness and eccentricity were a nice contrast to the austere silence. For all I knew he might have been a little tipsy but the contrast made me see something I had missed, namely how contrived and overly precious my 'inner peace' was. The building of steady concentration is of course very valuable. A setting like a retreat or *sesshin* is supportive of and conducive to greater stillness. And in the early days I strived hard to hold this precious silence with me when going back to my everyday life. I remember puzzling over the Zen adagio that goes: 'forget what you have learned in the meditation hall'. At the time it didn't make sense. Surely, I thought, it's a very good idea to uphold, remember and maintain what I have learned while listening to a Dharma talk. Surely I need to hold fast to what I experienced while meditating. I can now see the naivety of my thinking. There is of course a time when valuing and treasuring what has been learned is all important. These are the days of the Zen romance and honeymoon. But a more expansive view would perhaps make little distinction between the trivial and the profound, between depth and surface. In phenomenology this is often referred to as 'horizontalization' and it is used by phenomenological therapists to foster equanimity when listening to their clients' content, i.e. by giving equal attention to what is presented. The interpretation of the term is controversial. I for one understand this to be a mistranslation of Husserl's 'horizon-making'. But the basic insight definitely strikes a chord.

If what I learn in the meditation hall has any value, it will be absorbed; my body will, whether I am a beginner or an 'experienced' practitioner. Holding on for dear life to my hard-earned inner peace strikes me as ineffectual. Encountering the hustle and bustle of the world at rush hour in a busy station after a week-long silent retreat in the country can be enlightening. Perhaps this is the moment where practice really begins – in the transition between stillness and speed, nirvana and samsara, awakening and delusion.

Supermoon, hazy moon

I scribble the last words to this book on the afternoon of the 'supermoon' day, 14 November 2016, announced in the media as the most spectacular moon since 1948, appearing 14 per cent bigger and 30 per cent brighter than usual. The London sky being predictably overcast, we won't get to see it. A glimmer of the moon hidden by clouds haunts Zen paintings and writings as if to say: the moon is there. You can't see it, but know that it's there. No matter how troubled, confused, and despairing a client may be, my task is to *be with* that. I renew my faith in their intrinsic ability to heal by being in touch with their core. The confusion and despair is momentarily clouding their innate wisdom. But the wisdom is there from the start.

Another recurring image in Zen that of the 'hazy moon' of awakening: it is said that a hazy moon is more beautiful than a full moon in plain sight, and more subtle than a brilliant sun. Through dedicated practice we may stumble into an insight or a breakthrough. The excitement will lead some of us to embarrass ourselves by declaring to the world our self-appointed wisdom. The other option, warmly endorsed by some great teachers within the tradition, is to do our best to hide the crumbs of wisdom that might have dropped from the Gods' banquet at Mount Olympus. Sure, it is valuable, and it feels great; but really, in the greater scheme of things it doesn't amount to much anyway. I have written this book in this spirit.

My thoughts, imperfect grasp and shreds of experience laid out here are, in a way, more exposé than expounding. I would be overjoyed if readers were to get something from my scribblings. Bowing three times in gratitude to my teachers and fellow practitioners across space and time, I submit this little effort for the benefit of all.

References

Aitken, R. (1997). *The Practice of Perfection*. Washington DC: Counterpoint.

Bazzano, M. (2006). *Buddha is Dead: Nietzsche and the Dawn of European Zen*. Eastbourne: Sussex Academic Press.

Bazzano, M. (2010). Empathy for the Devil: a tribute to Jean Genet on the centenary of his birth. *Existential Analysis*, 22(1): 150–159.

Bazzano, M. (2012). *Spectre of the Stranger: Towards a Phenomenology of Hospitality*. Eastbourne: Sussex Academic Press.

Bevis, M. (2016). The lighthouse strikes back. *London Review of Books*, 38(1), January: 9–10.

Bion, W. (1980). *Bion in New York and São Paulo*. Perthshire: Clunie Press.

Bion, W. (1984). *Elements of Psychoanalysis*. London: Karnac.

Bion, W. (1990). *A Memoir of the Future, Volume 1*. London: Karnac.

Bobrow, J. (2010). *Zen and Psychotherapy: Partners in Liberation*. London: W.W. Norton & Co.

Bomford, R. (1999). *The Symmetry of God: If God Exists, Only He Knows It*. London: Free Association Books.

Chambers, A. H. (2007). Introduction. In U. Akinari (Ed.), *Tales of moonlight and rain* (pp. 1–35). New York: Columbia University Press.

Cooper, P. (2010). *The Zen Impulse and the Psychoanalytic Encounter*. Abingdon: Routledge.

de Saint-Exupéry, A. (1995). *The Little Prince*. Ware: Wordsworth.

Dōgen, E. (2002). *The Heart of Dōgen's Shōbōgenzō*. Translated and annotated by N. Waddell & M. Abe. Albany, NY: State University of New York.

Dorje, R. (2001). *Dangerous Friend: The Teacher-Student Relationship in Vajrayana Buddhism*. Boston, MA: Shambala.

Freud, S. (1997). *The Interpretation of Dreams*. Knoxville, TN: Wordsworth.

Gallop, J. (2002). *Anecdotal Theory*. Durham, NC: Duke University Press.

Goffey, A. (2016). Guattari and transversality: Institutions, analysis and experimentation. *Radical Philosophy 195*, January–February: 38–47.

Gregg, M. & Seigworth, J. (Eds.) (2010). *The Affect Theory Reader*. Durham, NC: Duke University Press.

Lear, J. (1993). An interpretation of transference. *The International Journal of Psycho-Analysis*, 74(4): 734.

Marcel, G. (1965). *Being and Having*. New York: Harper & Row.

Massumi, B. (1995). *The Autonomy of Affect*. http://brianmassumi.com/textes/Autonomy %20of%20Affect.PDF Retrieved 2 December 2015.

Matte Blanco, I. (1975). *The Unconscious as Infinite Sets: An Essay in Bi-Logic*. London: Duckworth.

May, R. (1969). *Love and Will*. New York: W.W. Norton & Co.

Nussbaum, M. (2003). *Upheavals of Thought: The Intelligence of Emotions*. Chicago, IL: Chicago University Press.

Sartre, J. P. (2003). *Being and Nothingness: An Essay on Phenomenological Ontology*. Abingdon: Routledge.

Spinelli, E. (2007). *Practising Existential Psychotherapy: The Relational World*. London: Sage.

Stone, H. & Winkelman, S. (1989). *Embracing Our Selves: The Voice Dialogue Manual*. Novato, CA: Nataraj.

Suzuki, S. (1999). *Branching Streams Flow in the Darkness: Zen Talks on the Sandokai*. Los Angeles, CA: University of California Press.

Waddell, N. & Abe, M. (2002). Translators introduction. In E. Dōgen (Ed.), *The Hart of Dōgen's Shōbōgenzō* (pp. ix–xiii). Albany, NY: State University of New York.

Warner, M. S. (1991). Fragile process. In L. Fusek (Ed.), *New directions in client-centered therapy: Practice with difficult client populations* (Monograph Series 1) (pp. 41–58). Chicago, IL: Chicago Counselling and Psychotherapy Center.

Whitehead, A. N. (1978). *Process and Reality*. New York: The Free Press.

Wilber, K. (1983). *Up from Eden: A Transpersonal View of Human Evolution*. London: Routledge.

Wood, M. (2015). At the movies. *London Review of Books*, 30, July: 37.

INDEX

Abe, M. 144, 145
Abhidharmic tradition 123
absolute and relative 1–2; Arjuna 2–3;
    dialogue between Zen teacher and monk
    4–5, 6–7; differing perspectives on 2–8;
    fluid connections between 132–133,
    147–148; the sick mother 3–4; as two
    truths 127
Acampora, C. D. 103
Acampora, R. R. 103
active and reactive forces 54
actualizing tendency 51, 71, 150
'adaptive killing' 22
Adorno, Theodor 23, 52, 117, 131
affect: management 67, 69, 100; relational
    elements of therapy and 151
Aitken, Robert 141
aloneness 111
Ancient Greeks: *ataraxía* 26; care of self 60;
    hospitality 44; life and death 32–33, 34
animals: in Buddhist texts 102; cockroaches
    clinical vignette 106–107; human–animal
    continuum 103–105, 107–108; learning
    from 105–107; New Materialisms
    108–109; and tangled web of life 108
Ansell Pearson 109
apophatic language 130
archetypal psychology 91–93
Arendt, Hannah 49
Arjuna 2–3
askesis 60
aspiration 102
asymmetry 143, 147, 152

ataraxía 26–27, 37
authorship of client 87; creating space for
    87–89

Bacon, Francis 23, 24
Batchelor, Stephen 54, 62–63, 102, 121,
    122, 129, 133
Beat poets 137–138
Beginner's mind 5–6
being-towards-death 35–36, 37
Benjamin, Walter 25, 131
Benn, Hilary 155
Bennett, J. 109
bereavement 39, 40
Bergson, H. 109
bewilderment 154–155
Bion, W. 147, 148, 149, 152
birth: and death 23–24; re-enactment in
    therapy 40
Bishop, S. R. 67, 69
Blofeld, J. 128
Blyth, R. H. 4–5
Bobrow, Joseph 12, 146, 149
Bodhidharma's Skin, Flesh, Bone and Marrow
    116
bodhisattva 44, 51; acting in response 56–57;
    citizens of world 56; second vow 54;
    third vow 97
body: and notion of self 98–99; and sexual
    imagery in Christianity 96–97, 143; shift
    towards 99–100; similarities between
    Dōgen and Nietzsche in views on
    99; -subject 99, 125; in Zen practice 97

bourgeois understanding of therapy 48–49
Bowie, David 28–29
brothel, tale of redemption 95–96
Browning, Robert 131
Buddha-nature: deconstruction 131;
    embodiment 76; Huineng's story 68–71;
    meditation 74–75; realization 75–76
bunjin 153

capture, avoiding 105–106
care of self 60–61; therapist's 59–60, 61
Chan Buddhism 25–26, 128, 129, 131;
    teachings of Linji Yixuan 129–130
Christianity: body and sexual imagery in
    96–97, 143; Christ as God incarnate 67,
    96; reincarnation 21
citizens 48, 49, 56
citizenship 49, 56
civilization, as distinct from culture 103
cocaine 83
commercial forces in psychotherapy 153
communal practice in Zen meditation and
    therapy 14–15
concentration (samādhi) 110, 145
condensation 150–151
conscious: complementarity between
    unconscious and 149; fluid movement
    between unconscious and 151–152, 153;
    making unconscious 148–149, 151–152
consciousness, hypertrophy of 146
contemporary and modern 10
control 65–67; affect-regulation and 67
Coole, D. H. 109
culture 8, 103–105; as distinct from
    civilization 103

daimonic, notion of 152
dāna (generosity) 35, 52, 53
Davids, R. 40, 121
Davis, Miles 8
de Saint-Exupéry, A. 150
death: ending of therapy and parallels
    with 40; life and 23–24; presence
    and reflecting on possibility of 63
    see also living-and-dying (*shoji*)
Debord, Guy 53
decoding of Zen 11
deconstructive Zen 128–129, 131
Deleuze, G. 21, 72, 108, 109
dependent co-arising (*paticca samuppada*)
    111, 146
dependent origination 111, 127–128
Derrida, Jacques 24, 103, 105, 122; on
    Heidegger 124, 125; 'metaphysical
    determinations of truth' 119–120

Dharma 91, 97, 100; accessibility 16; early
    days of transmission to the west 137,
    139; embodying 76–77; gate 26–27;
    logocentrism and 120–122; mindfulness
    and 65; in our time 25; practice
    transmission 140; psychotherapy
    and 11–12, 16, 50–51, 143, 146;
    secularization and 'privatization' of 74;
    transmitting 71, 116; unique nature of
    teachings 122
Dick, Philip K. 48
difference, philosophy of 8–9
differentialism 7–8; /logocentrism
    distinction in therapy 124–125; and
    'dried shit-stick' 129–130; and
    eccentricity 130–131; meeting of
    phenomenology and Zen 127–128;
    Nāgārjuna's position of 123–124; and no
    focus 130; a path of radical scepticism
    131–132; reality itself as deconstructive
    128–129; Zen path of 125–127
Dillard, A. 64
Dōgen, E. 23, 24, 99, 116; imperceptible
    mutual aid 144–145
doing the next thing 25–26
doubt 116–118
dreams: and the daimonic 151–152;
    differing interpretations 89–90;
    reversal and condensation to describe
    150–151
'dried shit-stick' 129–130
drug use: a client's experiences with LSD
    86–87; experience in transpersonal
    psychotherapy 83–86; use of
    psychotropic substances 85–86
dukkha 65

eccentricity 130–131
ecological self 111
ecology 110–111, 112
ecopsychology 110–111
embodiment 76–77, 96
emptiness (*śūnyatā*) 9, 63, 70, 111,
    121–122; and impermanence 25,
    132–133; meditation and 133;
    openness of therapist to 130;
    unfocused 130
ending of therapy 40
enlightenment 1, 12, 128
environmentalism 112–113
Epicurus 37
epoché 62–63, 101
erasure 128–129
eroticism 142–143
ethical therapeutic practice 47–49

ethics 4, 20, 137; and care of self 60–61; and morality 47–49; shipwrecks to illustrate changing 55–57
everyday sublime 82–83, 148, 152
exaltation 27–28
experience, Buddha's description of 123

Faraway, So Close! 82
formative tendency 71
Foucault, Michel 60, 61, 119
four noble tasks 122–123
Freud, Sigmund 15, 36, 62, 83, 130, 149, 150
Frost, S. 109
fully living person 112

Gaddis, William 88
Gallop, Jane 142
Gateless Gate 127
Geller, S. M. 59, 60, 68
generosity (*dāna*) 35, 52, 53
Giacometti, Alberto 64
gift of therapy 53–54
Greek myths, 'mortal immortality' and 32–33
Greenberg, L. S. 60, 68
The Guardian 107–108
Guattari, F. 21, 108

Hakuin Zenji 38, 76, 96, 118
Hare, David 1
'heaps' 123
Hegel, G. F. W. 9, 26, 48
Heidegger, Martin 23, 35, 36, 37, 124–125; *Dasein* 133; Derrida on 124, 125
Heraclitus 9, 93
heresy 7
heretical cosmology 137–138
Hillman, James 34, 38, 91–93
Hokusai 54–55
homelessness: ethics and morality 47–49; existential 44; existential migration 47; and indigenousness 46–47; *Kikujiro* and subject of 43, 44; leaving homeland 44–45; and nationalism 47; and patriotism 44–45; sense of place 45–46; Zen teachings on 43–44
Hongzhou School 128, 131
hospitality 44; act of generosity 52; active and reactive forces 54; conditional 44; ethics and shipwrecks 54–57; good hosts 50; judicial 44; linking psychotherapy and Zen practice 50–51; potlatch 53–54; right-brain and left-brain responses 51–52; of tea

ceremony 50; of therapist to client 50–51, 52, 53–54; unconditional 44, 52
Huang Po 128
Hughes, Ted 88
Huineng 68–71, 72, 128, 131
human: being a 81–82; meaning of 93–94; naturalizing the 99–100; spark of 'divine mind' 94
human–animal continuum 103–105, 107–108
human nature: Confucian and western notions of 71; and transformative tendency 71–72
humanistic therapy 15, 25, 47, 71, 149, 150
Hume, David 9, 34
humility 28, 93, 94

identity 9, 25, 120–121, 123, 125, 126, 128
idiocy 87
idiotic stance of therapist 87–89, 119
imperceptible mutual aid 144–146
impermanence 3, 6, 13, 25, 40, 112
incarnate subjectivity 99
indigenousness 46–47
infinity 154; and symmetry 148; and unconscious 148, 154
interdependence 111–112, 146
intersubjectivity in Zen practice and therapy 14–15, 130
Isan, dialogue between monk and 4–5, 6–7, 126–127

Kant, Immanuel 99, 116
Kanzeon and samurai 19–20; parallel with practice of therapy 20
kataphatic language 130
Keats, John 52
kenshō (realization) 75–76, 97; as deconstructive 128–129; paradox of unity of practice and 115–116; practice and 145
Kierkegaard, Søren 51
Kikujiro 43, 44
Kitano, Takeshi 43
knowledge–wisdom (*prajna*) 6, 132
Kramer, R. 40
Krishna: dialogue with Arjuna 2, 3; and story of sick mother 3–4
Kübler-Ross, Elizabeth 39, 40

left-brain and right-brain responses 51–52
left-to-die boat 55–56
Levi, Primo 33
Levinas, Emmanuel 23, 49, 62–63, 118
Lieberg, C. 33

Linji Yixuan 129–130
living-and-dying (*shoji*) 31–41, 64;
    being-towards-death 35–36, 37;
    bereavement 39, 40; canonical Buddhist
    reflections on 41; connections with
    Zen Buddhism before death 38–39;
    contemplation of death 36–38;
    expectations for a serene death 40;
    five stages of emotions 39; freedom to
    choose death 33–34; generosity (*dāna*)
    in will to die 35; last words of a Zen
    teacher 38; 'mortal immortality' 31–33;
    naturalist view of death 36; poems 38;
    staring at death 35–37; and thanatologists
    35–38
Locke, John 120
logocentrism 118; /differentialism
    distinction in therapy 124–125;
    interpretations of Zen and Buddhism
    121–122; and metaphysics of presence
    119–120; middle path 120–121,
    122–123; multiplicities of language and
    speech 118–119; power and ubiquity
    of 130–131; 'speaking speech' 119;
    'spoken speech' 119; of western and
    eastern religions 122
loss, five-stages model of 39
Loy, David 68
loyalty to the Earth 112–113

McNamara fallacy 22
Magliola, Robert 5, 24, 120, 122, 123, 124,
    125, 127
Mahabharata 2–3
Mahler, Margaret 15
managerialism 22
Mara 102
Margins of Philosophy 122
Mars-Jones, Adam 39
masculinity, exploring 104–105
Massumi, Brian 67, 103, 105, 107, 108,
    151
Matilal, Bimal Krishna 127, 128
Matte Blanco, Ignacio 146, 147, 148
May, Rollo 91, 104, 152
May, Theresa 56
Mazu Daoyi 129
MDMA 83, 84, 85
medicalization of psychology and
    psychotherapy 92
meditation (*zazen*) 9, 74–75, 91, 99–100,
    133; aims of 64; imperceptible mutual
    aid 144–145; presence and absence 63;
    scientific claims for 68; for self-care of

therapist 60; solitary and communal
    practice of 14–15; and symmetry 147
Merleau-Ponty, M. 14, 62, 87–88, 99, 119,
    125, 127–128
Merton, Thomas 36
metaphysics 13–14; of presence 119–120
Middle Way 127
military, psychology applied to 22
mindfulness 16, 64–65, 81; affect
    management 67, 69, 100; apps 64;
    critiquing 67–68; and mind control
    65–67; parallels with Huineng's
    story 69, 70
Minima Moralia 52
mirrors: gazing exercise 20–21; reflections
    in 24
modernity 10; engaged recognition 10;
    impact of 16; and modernism 11; refusal
    of 10; unengaged acceptance 10
monetary transactions 53
morality and ethics 47–49
mortification 27, 28
multiplicity 21
mutual aid, imperceptible 144–146
mysticism 117, 124–125, 151

Nāgārjuna 9, 120–121, 126, 127–128, 131,
    132; four-cornered logic of *tetralemma*
    123–124
Nan-in 101
Nansen 127
narcissism 28
nationalism 47, 56
naturalism 109–110
nature: loyalty to the Earth 112; Zen and
    100–101
negative capability 52
neo-positivism 14, 149, 150; alternative to
    14–15
neoliberal influence on therapy
    103–104
New Materialisms 108–109; rethinking
    matter as materiality 109
Nietzsche, Friedrich 26, 27, 47, 92, 99,
    104, 105, 110, 131
nirvana 26–27; samsara and 76, 96, 147
no-birth 24
'no-self' 26–27
'no-thought' (*wunian*) 70, 128
no-view 101–102
non-directivity 89, 130
not-knowing 38, 153–155
now of knowability 25
Nussbaum, Martha 99, 138

Olendski, A. 66
ordinariness 28

Parks, Tim 33
Pasolini, P. P. 33–34
paticca samuppada (dependent co-arising) 111, 146
patriotism 44–45
person-centred psychotherapy 15, 25, 71, 89, 130, 149
phenomena, learning from 96–97
phenomenology 96–97, 124–125, 127–128, 156
Pippin, Robert 26
poetic intuition 12–14
poets, strong 132
poisoned arrow, parable of 71
positive psychology 22
positivism 150
post-modernity 10, 11
post-secularism 72
potlatch 53–54
power: asymmetrical relations of 143–144; as strength and vitality 104–105
prajna (knowledge–wisdom) 6, 132
Prajnaparamita tradition 123
pre-criminal space, therapy work in 48–49
presence: and absence 63; defining therapeutic 59–60; *epoché* and cultivating 62–63; logocentrism and metaphysics of 119–120; neutral 61–62; as a way of being 64–65
presentism 11
'Prevent' training 47, 48
The Prose of the World 87–88, 125
psyche 12; plurality of 21, 92, 131; soul a rendition of 93
psychopharmacology 83–86
psychosis 148
psychotherapy and Dharma 11–12, 16, 50–51, 143, 146
Purser, Ron 68
Pyrrho 62

The Question of Being 125

radical scepticism 131–132
Rajneesh, Osho 117
Rank, Otto 15, 36, 40
Raqs Media Collective 55, 56
reactivity 54
realization (*kenshō*) 75–76, 97; as

deconstructive 128–129; paradox of unity of practice and 115–116; practice and 145
'rebirthing' 117
refugees, ethical response to 55–56
reification 111, 131, 132
reincarnation 20–21
relational psychology, move to 14–15
relative and absolute 1–2; Arjuna 2–3; dialogue between Zen teacher and monk 4–5, 6–7; differing perspectives on 2–8; fluid connections between 132–133, 147–148; the sick mother 3–4; as two truths 127
religion 72–73; body and sexual imagery in 96–97, 143; logocentrism of 122; private and community practice of 14–15, 74; return to 72; sexual misconduct in name of 141; symmetry in 151
religious experience in therapeutic work 97–98
resilience 22
reversal 150
right-brain and left-brain responses 51–52
ritual 77
Rizq, Rosemary 47, 48
Rogers, Carl 15, 25, 27, 51, 52, 54, 59, 61, 112
Rud, Claudio 61–62, 71, 108

Salzberg. Sharon 66
samādhi (concentration) 110, 145
samsara and nirvana 76, 96, 147
samurai, Kanzeon and 19–20
Samyutta-Nikaya 121
Sappho 142
Sartre, Jean-Paul 143
scandals, sex 141, 143, 144
Schore, Allan 52, 67
scientism 11, 13, 153
secularism 72; post- 72; unsettling the certainties of 72–73
self: aspiration to play a different role 19–20; Bowie's chameleonic re-inventions 28–29; 'configurations of self' 21; doing the next thing 25–26; ecological 111; emergence of *dividual* 27; -erasure 129; exaltation 27–28; fluid/multiple and/or insubstantial 23–24; humanistic perspective 25; -identity 25, 120, 125, 128; mortification 27, 28; multiplicity of 21; and 'no-self' 26–27; notion of body and 98–99; and notion of emptiness (*śūnyatā*) 25, 70, 111,

121–122; psychology and substantiating of 22–23; -realization 111; reflection and reflected 24; relativization of 111; *Samyutta-Nikaya* teaching on 121; separate thinking 100
self-care 60–61; of therapist 59–60, 61
Seng-ts'an 126
sense of place 45–46
sex scandals 141, 143, 144
sexual: desire 142–143; harassment 141–142; imagery in Christianity 96–97, 143; misconduct 140–141
Shatz, A. 8
The Shipwreck 56
shipwrecks 54–57
shōji (living-and-dying) 31–41, 64; being-towards-death 35–36, 37; bereavement 39, 40; canonical Buddhist reflections on 41; connections with Zen Buddhism before death 38–39; contemplation of death 36–38; expectations for a serene death 40; five stages of emotions 39; freedom to choose death 33–34; generosity (*dāna*) in will to die 35; last words of a Zen teacher 38; 'mortal immortality' 31–33; naturalist view of death 36; poems 38; staring at death 35–37; and thanatologists 35–38
the sick mother 3–4
signifiers 24
silence 90–91
Sittlichkeit 4, 48
soul 92, 93, 100
The Soul Code 91–92
'speaking speech' 119
Spinelli, Ernesto 87, 119, 151, 152
'spoken speech' 119
Stern, Daniel 59
Stevens, Wallace 39
Still Life: Broken Statue and Shadow 24
strong poets 132
student–teacher relationship in Buddhism 138–140
stupidity 88
suicide 33–34, 35
śūnyatā (emptiness) 9, 63, 70, 111, 121–122; and impermanence 25, 132–133; meditation and 133; openness of therapist to 130; unfocused 130
Suzuki, D. T. 15
Suzuki, S. 5, 148
Swift, Jonathan 32

symmetry 146–148; coexistence with asymmetry 152; and emotion 148; and infinity 148; mysticism, religiosity and 151

Taizan Maezumi 12, 26, 73, 136
teacher–student relationship in Buddhism 138–140
Thacker, E. 110
thanatologists 35–38
therapist–client relationship 140
Thomas, R. S. 132
Three Studies for Self-Portrait 23
three treasures of Buddhism 12
Tóibín, Colm 23, 24
tradition 77
training: to *be* with a client 59; experiences of Zen 27–28, 82, 136, 139, 140; psychotherapy 6, 11, 20, 47, 48, 59, 136, 137, 149; threefold schema of Zen 74–77
transaction between therapist and client 53
transformation 5, 6
transformative tendency and human nature 71–72
transpersonal psychotherapy: and archetypal psychology 91–93; assumed 'spiritual authority' of therapist/trainer 84–85, 89; imposition of interpretation in 89–90; problem with 'self-actualization' claims of 100; and psychopharmacology 83–86; silence 90–91; teaching 80–81
tree of life 108
'true person of no status' (*wuyi zhenren*) 129
Trungpa, Chögyam 102
truth: metaphysical determinations of 119–120; Nansen's concept of 127; relative and absolute 127; as unconcealedness 97
Turner, J. M. W. 55

uncertainty 6, 38, 65
unconditional hospitality 44, 52
unconditional positive regard 15, 48, 51, 61
unconscious 144; complementarity between conscious and 149; in contemporary psychotherapy 146; dumbed down in search for 'meaning behind' 150; fluid movement between conscious and 151–152, 153; imperceptible mutual aid 144–146; and infinity 148, 154; making conscious 148–149, 151–152; and neo-positivism 150; and notion of daimonic 152; and

sense of bewilderment and not-knowing 153–155; symmetrical logic of 147; taking an unorthodox, non-conformist position on 153; *via negativa* 152

Vattimo, G. 27
via negativa 152
vitalism 109
voice dialogue 136

Waddell, N. 96, 118, 144, 145
Watts, Alan 126
Under the Wave off Kanagawa 54–55
web of life 108
Webb, Julie 9, 140, 146
Weiwei 56–57
wen-jen 153
Wenders, Wim 81, 82
Wings of Desire 81

Winnicott, Donald 60, 91
wisdom 132
wunian ('no-thought') 70, 128
wuyi zhenren ('true person of no status') 129

Xinxin Ming ('Trust in Mind') 126

Yalom, Irvin 35, 37
Yampolsky, P. B. 68, 69, 71, 72
Yeshe, Lama 6, 13, 45
yoga 65, 66
Yogācāra 126

zazen (meditation) 9, 74–75, 91, 99–100, 133; aims of 64; imperceptible mutual aid 144–145; presence and absence 63; scientific claims for 68; for self-care of therapist 60; solitary and communal practice of 14–15; and symmetry 147

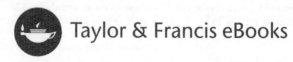 Taylor & Francis eBooks

Helping you to choose the right eBooks for your Library

Add Routledge titles to your library's digital collection today. Taylor and Francis ebooks contains over 50,000 titles in the Humanities, Social Sciences, Behavioural Sciences, Built Environment and Law.

Choose from a range of subject packages or create your own!

Benefits for you

>> Free MARC records
>> COUNTER-compliant usage statistics
>> Flexible purchase and pricing options
>> All titles DRM-free.

REQUEST YOUR **FREE** INSTITUTIONAL TRIAL TODAY

Free Trials Available
We offer free trials to qualifying academic, corporate and government customers.

Benefits for your user

>> Off-site, anytime access via Athens or referring URL
>> Print or copy pages or chapters
>> Full content search
>> Bookmark, highlight and annotate text
>> Access to thousands of pages of quality research at the click of a button.

eCollections – Choose from over 30 subject eCollections, including:

Archaeology	Language Learning
Architecture	Law
Asian Studies	Literature
Business & Management	Media & Communication
Classical Studies	Middle East Studies
Construction	Music
Creative & Media Arts	Philosophy
Criminology & Criminal Justice	Planning
Economics	Politics
Education	Psychology & Mental Health
Energy	Religion
Engineering	Security
English Language & Linguistics	Social Work
Environment & Sustainability	Sociology
Geography	Sport
Health Studies	Theatre & Performance
History	Tourism, Hospitality & Events

For more information, pricing enquiries or to order a free trial, please contact your local sales team:
www.tandfebooks.com/page/sales

 Routledge
Taylor & Francis Group

The home of
Routledge books

www.tandfebooks.com